Advance Praise for *Once a Marine*

"If you want an honest answer, ask a Marine. If you want an honest view of a war, ask a Marine gunnery sergeant. Nick Popaditch's transcendent memoir of military service and its personal consequences should be read by every one of our nation's political leaders—to help them understand the incomparable quality of those who fight on the front lines. Read this inspiring story, recommend it to friends—and send a copy to your member of Congress!"

> — Ralph Peters (Lt. Col., ret.), *New York Post* columnist and author
> of *Looking For Trouble* and *Wars Of Blood and Faith*

"America has always been blessed by wonderful, patriotic, and often anonymous men and women who have sacrificed so much in defense of liberty and freedom. *Once a Marine*, Gunny Sergeant Nick Popaditch's heart-wrenching and inspiring memoir, puts a name and a face on this sacrifice. Every American should read this book to remind them of what these brave warriors of freedom endure on our behalf."

> — Congressman Bob Filner, Chairman of the
> House Committee on Veterans' Affairs

"Gunny Popaditch's story is as inspiring as it is dramatic. This wounded warrior suffered grievous injuries — an RPG to the head! — but refused to give up on life, even when his wounds forced him out of the Corps. *Once a Marine* is a 'must read' story of one of today's real heroes."

> — Jerry D. Morelock, PhD, Colonel, U. S. Army (Ret.),
> Editor in Chief, *Armchair General* magazine

"Author Gunny Sergeant Nick Popaditch, a Silver Star recipient and the subject of the world-famous AP photo, has penned what must surely be classed as among the best personal memoirs of any combat soldier in recent memory. *Once a Marine* is an in-your-face blast of raw emotion and realism that will strike a raw nerve and keep you up at night. This autobiography of combat, courage, and recovery should be required reading for every American, young and old, who yearns to grasp the true cost of freedom."

— Caspar Weinberger Jr., Military and Current Affairs Columnist

"A riveting and inspirational story of the consummate professional warrior. It is impossible to read *Once a Marine* without being proud of our military and grateful that our Nation produces men like Gunnery Sergeant Nick Popaditch."

— Michael F. Nugent, Major, US Army (Ret.), co-author of
*One Continuous Fight: The Retreat From Gettysburg and
the Pursuit of Lee's Army of Northern Virginia, July 4-14, 1863*

"Gunny Popaditch's story makes me incredibly proud to have worn the same uniform. Without intending to, *Once a Marine* articulates life in the modern Marine Corps more clearly than anything I've read. No blindly loyal fanatic, Popaditch candidly acknowledges the bullshit, yet artfully captures the inimitable spirit of camaraderie and commitment that makes the Marine Corps unique. Extraordinarily motivating and compellingly honest book, it made me pine for my own long-finished Marine Corps career."

— Jay A. Stout, Lt.Col. USMC (Ret.), author of *Hornet's Over Kuwait*

"'Gunny Pop' Popaditch's courageous memoir of his life in and out of the Marine Corps is intelligently written and imbued with a brazen honesty rarely found elsewhere. His personal courage—and that of his wife, April—gives the term "home of the brave" an entirely new meaning."

— Sgt. Michael Volkin, author of *The Ultimate Basic
Training Guidebook: Tips, Tricks, and Tactics for Surviving Boot Camp*

ONCE A MARINE

*An Iraq War Tank Commander's
Inspirational Memoir of Combat,
Courage, and Recovery*

Gunny Sergeant Nick Popaditch
with Mike Steere

SB

Savas Beatie

New York and California

Once a Marine: An Iraq War Tank Commander's Inspirational Memoir of Combat, Courage, and Recovery

Cataloging-in-Publication Data is available from the Library of Congress.

ISBN 13: 978-1-932714-47-0
10 9 8 7 6 5 4 3 2 1 / First edition, first printing

SB

Published by
Savas Beatie LLC
521 Fifth Avenue, Suite 3400
New York, NY 10175
Phone: 610-853-9131

WEIDER
HISTORY
GROUP

In cooperation with Weider History Group

Photos courtesy of Nick and April Popaditch unless otherwise noted.

Savas Beatie titles are available at special discounts for bulk purchases in the United States by corporations, institutions, and other organizations. For more details, please contact Special Sales, P.O. Box 4527, El Dorado Hills, CA 95762. You may also e-mail us at sales@savasbeatie.com, or click over for an informative visit to our website at www.savasbeatie.com for additional information.

Dedicated to

My wife April,

my boys, Richard and Nicholas,

and all my brothers in The Corps.

Gunny Sergeant Nick Popaditch with wife April enjoying a night out prior to his deployment in 2004 (Operation Iraqi Freedom 2). "We both knew I was going, but only I knew I had volunteered to go back."

Popaditch Family

Contents

Maps

Operation Desert Storm

236

Operation Iraqi Freedom

255

The Battle of Fallujah

285

Photos

Frontis

Gunny Sergeant Nick Popaditch and his wife April

A gallery of photos can be found
following page 142

— Foreword —
Colonel Bryan McCoy

"The worth and value of a man is in his heart and his will; there lies his real honor. Valor is the strength, not of legs and arms, but of heart and soul; it consists not in the worth of our horse or our weapons, but in our own. He who falls obstinate in his courage, if he has fallen, he fights on his knees. He who relaxes none of his assurance, no matter how great the danger of imminent death; who, giving up his soul, still looks firmly and scornfully at his enemy—he is beaten not by us, but by fortune; he is killed, not conquered."

— Michel de Montaigne

Morale is often defined as an emotional or mental condition with respect to cheerfulness, confidence, zeal, etc., especially in the face of opposition and hardship, i.e., *the morale of the troops.* In his new book *Once a Marine*, Gunnery Sergeant Nick Popaditch, USMC, or simply "Pop" as he is known, through his actions advances a new definition of morale, and perhaps one more meaningful: Morale as the <u>utter</u> <u>absence</u> <u>of</u> <u>self-pity</u>. This book, and the extended definition of morale, comes amid today's popular cultural movement in our country that not only seems indifferent to, if not ignorant of, stoicism, but goes so far as to celebrate victimhood and the elevation of self-promoting histrionics to nothing short of a cottage industry.

Popaditch has written a must-read work for anyone who is a warrior, leads warriors, cares for wounded warriors, loves a warrior, or is interested in our warriors. *Once a Marine* provides spectacular insight into the mind and spirit of a Marine struck down in battle and who, in that instant, is taken from his men. He endures life-threatening and life-altering wounds—injuries so severe and so permanent that he loses not only his vocation as a Marine tanker, but threatens to lose his identity as a Gunny, a Marine, a father, and a husband.

Pop also provides a priceless look into the sacred fraternity of fallen warriors. His experiences guide readers on a tour through the process of the wounded's re-entry into the world—a world at once filled with loved ones, those who hate, and the bureaucratic tyranny of clerks that runs counter to the core values we as Marines hold dear. Pop describes in blunt detail the very real struggle to overcome the red-tape apathy and morbid complacency of a broken system intended to administratively care for our wounded. What makes this injustice sting is that it is delivered not by faceless bureaucrats, but by the hands of fellow service members, active and retired, content to admire a problem rather than solve it. On the positive side, Pop highlights the long-standing principle in the Marine Corps that concerned leadership mitigates apathetic administration. In the end, right-minded leadership and the dogged determination that has served Pop so well in life and in combat prevail. Pop 1, Clerks 0.

Once a Marine is not just about Pop's struggle to recover, or to put himself out there in the spotlight, grandstanding. That is not his style. This book is less about him (for when he does speak of himself it is self-effacing) and more about a tribute to his crews on both "Carnivore" and "Bonecrusher," the Marine Corps, the doctors and nurses who saved his life and helped him recover, and certainly about his family that endured it all with him.

This is a story of success and failure, of hope and endurance, and of faith and shame. It is also a story of habit. Pop is a Marine through and through. He embodies the Corps' values of honor, courage, and commitment. What prevents that statement from being a cliché is that Pop is a man who turns esoteric values into concrete action, on and off the battlefield. In short, he is obedient to the habits of an uncompromising Marine, and holds himself to that same high unbending standard. In doing so, he imposed his will on the enemy, his crew, and the faceless administrative monolith known as the Physical Evaluation Board.

This is also an emotional book. Pop's wife April is deserving of Sainthood. If ever there was a cause to define love and loyalty by action, April's actions would achieve it. Those suffering loss of control of their lives and the lives of their loved ones can look to her example of devotion born of love and character. Providence conceals from us the ways in which we will be tested. We may either submit to victimhood and capitulate our honor, or we may do as April does, everyday: commit to the cause and create belief in those around us. In doing so she exemplifies faith as novelist and poet Josiah Gilbert Holland defines it: "Faith draws the poison from every grief, takes the sting from every loss and quenches the fire of every pain; and only faith can do it." Pop knows he is lucky beyond reason to have her; in fact, we ALL know it!

I can personally vouch for Pop's fighting prowess. He was always up front and leading by example. When things were at their worst, he was seen the most. In combat, there are things you can control and things you cannot control. Pop controlled his men, their emotions, their actions, and their performance and that of their equipment. What he could not control was the enemy. But what he could not control he simply overwhelmed with will and determination, and so broke the enemy.

Then, in his words, for the first time in his life he lost a gunfight in 2004 during the First Battle of Fallujah. His loss threw him into another struggle to reclaim his life, and a fight against an administrative Maginot Line—a battle that on the surface he seemed wholly unprepared to wage. Truth be known, Pop was purpose-built for this fight. Obedient to habit he behaved as he always had, as a Marine, and knocked circumstance on its ass.

— Collaborator's Note —
Working with "Gunny Pop"

O*nce a Marine* reads a mite loud and in-your-face because that's the Marine Gunnery Sergeant manner of communication, and it is true to the spirit and voice of Gunny Pop. It's also the way we put this book together.

Most of the time we really were in each other's faces, Nick reliving and retelling his tale, and me running it through my mental story processors and writing, and then reading it back to Nick. After our back-and-forth sessions we had our finished copy. Literary live fire, you might call it, because the words flying around hit the page right then and there. Now they're hitting you, with very little change.

This is one weird way to produce a book. And it is not necessarily recommendable because very few collaborators could stand being stuck in a room for six or eight or even ten hours at a shot. But in our case—for me, anyway—prolonged proximity never got old. Nick's a good guy to hang out with. To our sessions he always brought his A-game and moto-Marine discipline and energy. No time went to waste and, unless non-book life got in the way, we didn't quit until our IQs tanked and we started putting out drivel we both knew we would throw out and write again.

Even if we had gotten on each other's nerves, it wouldn't have mattered, because we took our orders from this big, demanding, merciless SOB that didn't care about anything but the mission. By that I mean Nick's great story. Very early in our collaboration it started yelling to be told, and anything less than max effort, as Nick would say, was not acceptable. It's strange and wonderful how creative projects take on lives of their own and put themselves in charge. This one you did not want to disappoint.

Our work consumed seven months, starting with just one or two sessions a week and building up to four- and five-day brain burners at the end. As the final days of work approached we pulled a few marathon phoners, putting out whole chapters before we hung up. By then, though, we were so hardwired into the project that physical presence no longer mattered. If we were working, we were there. And mostly we really were, in San Diego where Nick lives or at my place in Los Angeles.

Some days we made huge, easy gains; some were like MS Word root canal. But we always ended up with something worthwhile. Throughout we carried on in Nick's Marine way—straight toward the objective. One session that probably should have been interrupted shows the sort of roll we were on, and just how dialed in we really were. Not long after Nick arrived on the Amtrak Pacific Surfliner from SD, I got a call from my four-year-old daughter's preschool. Ellie, they told me, was sick and needed to be picked up. On the way home she was so weak she could barely lift her little head. Anyone in such shape needs watching, but the mission was calling—hard. Pages needed writing, deadlines loomed, and Gunny Pop was there with his A-game. I made Ellie a little warm blanket nest on the floor by Nick and me, and we went back to work as if she wasn't there. Somehow she slept comfortably through all the back and forth and give and take. Thank God neither of our wives witnessed this. The next day Ellie bounced back, as four-year-olds do, and we turned out all the pages we would have if the preschool had not called.

And then we were there. Nick was (and still is) surprised with how good his story is, but he will never say that out loud. It is simply not his way. For my part, I am astonished at how well we were able to tell it. *Once a Marine* is so true to Nick himself and the incredible events in his life that mark him as a father, a husband, a Marine, and a damn good man.

Human truth is always bigger and better than the mortals privileged to work in its service.

Mike Steere
Los Angeles, California

— Introduction —

by Nick "Gunny Pop" Popaditch

I don't mind that you can sit down next to somebody and shoot the breeze for a while and not know much of anything about who that person really is and where he or she comes from. And I am perfectly content if people don't know my story, which I feel no great need to tell.

If somebody asks, though, I'm proud to say I'm a retired United States Marine. Though many people act like it's rude or insensitive to ask, I don't mind telling how I lost my right eye and practically all the vision in my left, as well as the hearing in one ear, a good deal of my sense of balance and equilibrium, and all of my sense of smell. I was wounded in battle, leading Marines, fighting for a cause that I believed in my heart and soul to be right. If you turned back the clock, I'd do it all again, even if I got wounded again—even if this time the enemy fighter made a better shot and killed me. I can't think of a better way to die. I also can't think of a better way to live, than as a fighting Marine.

But I wouldn't say anything unless you asked. Proud as I am of my service in the Marine Corps, my pride is a private matter. And I am very reluctant to tell war stories in public because when other guys do it, it often comes off like bragging, which I do not like.

So why do this book? For one thing, my story is about all the people who helped me get going after I was wounded. I'm here, in the shape I'm in, because I have had heroes at my side every step of the way. I want, too, to honor all my fellow wounded warriors. There are thousands of us who fought with pride in Iraq and Afghanistan and now have to get on with our lives, facing challenges we never expected. Compared to many, I got off very, very light.

Americans should know more about us and be proud that we receive such wonderful care and support. We are the best-treated combat casualties in history. On the other hand, there are legitimate gripes. Not everybody gets a fair shake. This story lays out my own long and complicated fight to get complete recognition of my disabilities and all the benefits I rate. Sad to say, vets fight such battles to this day.

Finally, I especially want to honor the great branch of the military in which I spent fifteen years of my life and would, if I could, have spent more. I am what I am because I served as a United States Marine, and I want to tell of the great gifts the Corps gave to me and the important lessons it taught me, only a few of which came in combat. Most of a military career is spent far from the battlefield. Service is a professional, community, and family life that my wife and two boys and I loved. The Corps was our home, and I want people to appreciate what a wonderful home it was.

And this story of mine isn't just for and about the military. Millions of people come to a point where all their plans and dreams and expectations go right out the window. Everything changes and they can't be what they were, so they've got to be something else, and their past helps them go forward and succeed. In my own case, I can't be a Marine tank commander and Gunnery Sergeant any more, and that's all I ever wanted to be. Now I'm out of uniform and in college with kids half my age, looking forward to a future I didn't dream of until very recently. Though I'll always be a Marine, I can't live looking back. And I believe, with all my heart, that life's greatest challenges and accomplishments lie ahead. I sincerely hope this book helps you realize the same about your life.

Consider yourself warned: The G-rated writing ends here. I tell the story the way many of us Marines speak, using some rough, tough, and *extremely* salty language. The point is not to shock or offend, but to put you there with me and my brothers.

— Acknowledgments —

There are many people who made this book possible. If anyone does not find his or her name here, please know that its absence was an oversight, and your contribution is deeply appreciated.

First, we owe deep gratitude and appreciation to Eric Weider, who conceived of this book, put us together as a collaborative team, and provided generous support. Without Eric, *Once a Marine* would never have come to be.

More of the same goes to our publisher, Savas Beatie LLC, and its managing director, Theodore P. "Ted" Savas. Ted shared our vision, flew to Los Angeles to meet with Nick and Eric, and accepted this book for publication with whole-hearted enthusiasm and respect for the integrity of the story.

Word surgeon Dan Ferrara performed an exceptional line edit that made the book leaner, meaner, and harder hitting.

From the beginning of our work, April Popaditch provided moral support and opened her heart so the family side of our story could be told more fully and frankly. April also keeps the Popaditch archives, to which we often referred for facts. Mike's wife Sue Cross recognized before he did the great potential of Nick's story and encouraged him to get on board. Both our families lost serious husband- and dad-time, but with no complaints.

Jen Haskamp, Sgt. Haskamp in the book and now out of uniform but still a Marine through-and-through, was—and remains—our first, best reader. She provided crucial early encouragement and reassurance that the story does the Marine Corps proud.

Marketing Director Sarah Keeney has been our indispensable logistics chief at Savas Beatie LLC. Lee Merideth produced the index and Ed Coleman drafted three maps; both did so on a very tight schedule. Eric Weider's Executive Assistant Sari Kahn provided able assistance and backup. Transcriptionist Barb Krultz put hours and hours of digitally recorded blah-blah down on paper, making it look clearer than it sounded. We got smiles, along with incredibly fast turnaround of sundry printed versions of the manuscript, from Jennifer and Michael at FedEx Kinko's on Napa Street in San Diego.

Everyone who touched this book, at any stage of its progress, helped us, and we are mindful and thankful.

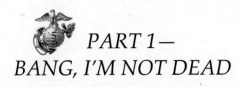

PART 1—
BANG, I'M NOT DEAD

1

Bang

Wednesday, April 7, 2004
1300 Local
Jolan District, Fallujah, Iraq

The last human being I see with perfect clarity—the last I will ever fully see—does his damndest to kill me.

Though my right eyeball is now glass and the left mostly unserviceable, the mind's eye sees 20/20. There the man stands at my 3 o'clock, no more than 50 feet away from Bonecrusher, the M1A1 Main Battle Tank I command. He's skylined on the roof of a mud-colored building on a little cul-de-sac off the street the tank follows, its machine guns chewing up walls while a half-dozen enemy fighters zigzag out in front. They're the cattle, trying like crazy to get away from this 68-ton cattle dog, which is rabid and roaring and spitting death. An M1A1 in a fighting mood makes a hell of an impression, and I always do what I can to amp up the enemy's terror and cause uncontrollable panic.

For the four United States Marines crewing Bonecrusher—commander, gunner, loader, driver—this action is much more calm and quiet than you'd think. The rear-mounted turbine engine makes only a low electric-sounding whine. My helmet has built-in ear protection that knocks back our machine gun fire to a dull fast hammering that's not even loud enough to be distracting. Visuals—looking for targets and watching our hits and misses—make a much bigger impression than sounds.

What little talking we do is over the earphones and mikes built into our helmets. Some tankers yell all this Hollywood nonsense—"Smoke check the motherfuckers!" "I got him in my sights!" "Grease him!"—but my guys would never dare. We communicate like doctors doing major surgery, and the crew's reactions better be as efficient as the words. I will absolutely wear a man out if he doesn't pull the trigger before I get to the r-sound in "Fire."

On this street so far, Bonecrusher does all the shooting, but coming into this intersection, with the cul-de-sac right and a cross-street running left, seems like a good place to get popped. I push my loader, Lance Corporal Alex Hernandez, down below the armor line and keep my own head up just high enough to see. You can't kill 'em if you can't find 'em, and I do that better with my own optics than with the tank commander's periscopes. I see my guy on the roof making a big beautiful target. Of course I return the favor, showing him the whole flank of the tank and a piece of my own personal armored turret, which is to say my head. And he's got the drop on me, no question, his weapon already shouldered and in firing position. I'm square in his sights, looking straight at the tip of a rocket-propelled grenade, an RPG, the bad guys' weapon of choice in Fallujah. I know he won't miss Bonecrusher, not at this range and especially not with the trigger discipline he shows. He sets up to shoot the Marine way. Sight alignment. Sight picture. Slow steady trigger squeeze.

The fact that he's the last person I see with two fully functional eyes must explain the extraordinary clarity and vividness of the picture in my head. Even now I can look it over, so to speak, and realize new things. The shooter is pretty much your typical Iraqi on the street, middle height and trim in a long dark shirt and dark pants, not old enough to show gray in his black hair or his beard but not so young, either. I have a strong impression he's about my age, more than 35 and less than 40, and an equally strong impression he has a military background. Since we're deep in the Saddam loyalist Sunni triangle, I would guess a former Republican Guard. Experience and professionalism show in the way he stands and aims, putting himself at risk in order to make the shot count. No enemy I have seen in Fallujah has done such a thing. They either shoot completely wild and run like rabbits or make fanatical attacks that accomplish nothing except give us some easy targets to shoot. Here, though, I square off with one of my own kind, a pro with some miles on him, too old to be doing what he's doing but also too old to get scared or excited and fuck it up.

All this stuff comes to mind long after the fact. At the time I perceive a target and think, if you can call an instant brain flash thinking, "Kill him before he gets away." I give the command "Driver stop." The bad guy's shot concerns me not one bit. He has one of the world's shittiest anti-tank weapons, witness the dozen RPG hits taken in Fallujah by Bonecrusher, a model that happens to be the world's best tank. In terms of combat effectiveness against an M1A1, the RPG is a great big paintball gun. It leaves a black splatter on the hull that we can wipe off with a rag. I've been wiping and laughing for days. As I duck down to put my eye to the sight and traverse the commander's caliber-50 machine gun toward the shooter, his RPG makes a short sharp sssst in the air and explodes against the right front of the turret. The hit makes a sort of ringing thunk like banging one of the cardboard tubes that come inside rolls of gift-wrapping paper. I know from seeing a captured diagram that the enemy believes there's a vulnerable spot about where the grenade strikes. This information is erroneous, but the guy obviously believes it, and going for the caliber-50 I feel better and better about my own shot. The guy has nowhere to go where my machine gun can't get him. The walls of that building might as well be made out of paper.

Another one bites the dust.

Wrong.

Surprise, surprise, the shooter I am about to shoot has a buddy I never see, also with an RPG. As I reconstruct he has a position in the same cul-de-sac but in a different building, so he's slightly behind my hatch and also above it. A great position—this I know because he makes a great shot.

Remember these are words put down on paper three years after the fact, and reading the rest of this sentence takes longer than the entire chain of events. While I duck and reach for the caliber-50 and the first hit still reverberates, here comes another ssst, which happens to be the last thing I will ever hear with two ears receiving the full range of frequencies. After the ssst, the whole world goes blinding white like I'm inside a camera flash. Then comes total darkness and a horrible electric-sounding hum in my ears. Though I'm off the air in terms of visual and auditory input, I know what happened. The RPG—a 4-pound missile going 300 miles an hour, more or less—hit and blew up on my helmet. There's a feeling of impact like somebody just brained me with a sledgehammer and knocked everything up there loose, but nothing really hurts.

Get up! Get up! Get up! I yelled it at recruits who got knocked off their feet, and now I'm yelling it at myself. Once I'm standing I act like I'm still in charge, telling my crewmen to get the tank moving and trying to call in a contact report to Red Three, my wingman's tank about a half-block back. Moving is right, because if the enemy hits you and you don't move he will sure as hell do it again, but the urgent need to report to Red Three is pretty goofy. No way could he not know we have contact with the enemy, unless he somehow missed two grenades exploding on my turret. And nobody hears a thing I say because the grenade blast tore the talking parts off my helmet, which is no longer on my head, anyway.

Gunny still is Gunny, even blinded and deaf and pumping blood out of numerous new holes in my head. I wonder what the hell is wrong with Corporal Ryan Chambers, my gunner and second-in-command, because he fails to respond to my commands. I stop being annoyed when the tank gets going, after which I relax and assess the damage to myself. My hand touches nothing but goo on the right-hand upper quandrant of my forehead and face, and the blood gushes fast enough that I know I'll bleed out pretty soon without expert medical attention. Dying is not authorized, though. I won't even consider it. Two overwhelming urges come on: I want, in the worst way, to go to sleep. A soothing voice in my head says that if I do, everything will be fine when I wake up. But the Gunny voice says Forget that, Marine. Losing consciousness after a shot to the head is a good way to die. I also desperately want to puke, but I refuse to do so because I'm a wimp about throwing up. Besides the focus on not sleeping and not puking, a sense of surprise keeps coming up.

I can't believe one of those bozos actually hit me.

In different circumstances—if I were out in the open or in unfamiliar surroundings—sudden blindness and deafness might throw me into a panic, but there's nowhere on Planet Earth more familiar to me than the inside of an M1A1's turret. Once we're moving I give no thought to where we're going. Who cares? Wherever it is, somebody there will help me.

After ten or fifteen minutes the tank pitches back, climbs, and then slams down hard. This tells me we just went over a berm under a railroad overpass up on the northwest edge of Fallujah, which marks the cityside perimeter of the Marines' defensive position. A day-and-a-half ago I crossed the berm going the other way, toward the fight. Back on the safe side I know help will come running.

There's no place like home.

2

The Animal Hospital

I climb up on the loader's seat and stand with head and shoulders above the armor line. Nothing happens, and I wonder, What the hell? Who knows how many times I have drilled my crew to get a casualty off the tank as fast as humanly possible, so what is taking them so long?

In memory I wait and wait for somebody to get me, but I'm really there for less than a minute. And the problem isn't the crew but the fact that I am blind and deaf and clueless about the pandemonium on Bonecrusher. Both my gunner and loader, Chambers and Hernandez, caught some of the RPG. Chambers isn't hit bad, but Hernandez bleeds like a stuck pig from arm wounds. On top of that, the back of the turret is in flames. The tank's fine, but the personal gear we keep up there is toast. Goodbye extra skivvies and socks, letter writing gear, and my book of pictures from home.

A TV crew records Bonecrusher's return to safety, which viewers all around the world watch while I'm still on the table at our forward trauma center. April and I have it on DVD. The footage shows the tank pull up and stop, gear on the turret still on fire. Hernandez bails to get immediate treatment to stop his bleeding. I come up dazed and confused and looking like I just pulled my head out of a bucket of blood. Then Chambers stands on the turret favoring his injured arm and yelling at people to come up and help because Gunny is all ████████ up. He also squirts water from a personal drinking bottle onto the fire, a gesture so useless it's funny. I get the need to take action, though. We Marines like to joke that it's better to do the wrong thing than nothing at all. Chambers yells some more before guys finally come up and get me. They hang back before climbing aboard because they've been taught to be very cautious around a tank, a dangerous machine even when there's no hostile intent. As the tankers' saying goes, it's designed to kill and it don't care who.

Bonecrusher's crew earns my highest possible praise—they are real Marines. Were they anything less, the four of us would have been the lead story on Al Jazeera, not CNN, and the bad guys would have defiled our bodies just like they did to the four American contractors they burned and dismembered and strung up on a bridge a week before. That happened only a couple blocks from where I got hit. A wrong turn, taking us farther into Fallujah instead of out, would have been the end of the exercise, as would have throwing a track or smashing into a building and getting stuck. That must have been some kind of chaos on Bonecrusher. With me out of action and out of my mind and the seconds ticking away before I die from blood loss, Chambers takes command. Though bleeding like crazy, Hernandez stays up top and helps guide us through a maze of streets not much wider than Bonecrusher, all swarming with bad guys.

Our driver and boot, Lance Corporal Christopher Frias, really comes through. Barely a year out of high school and in his very first fight he expertly maneuvers a flaming tank carrying three wounded who are the same older Marines he depends on for experience and guidance. When there's confusion about which way to turn, Frias picks out landmarks and finds the way. I can't say enough about this kid's courage and presence of mind. I can't say enough about any of my guys who by the time we get hit have fought almost continuously for thirty-six hours, putting down more enemy fighters than entire companies did elsewhere. As I tell them to this day, if everybody did what you did, this war would have ended long ago. I've spoken my gratitude to them many times, and now I'll write it.

Thanks, Marines.

On the stretcher I want to go limp and rest, just rest, but the voices of medical corpsmen come through the buzzing in my ears. Over and over they ask my blood type. The good news is I can hear, sort of, but they don't need to annoy me like this because they can read my blood type on dog tags around my neck and on one of my boots and written in Magic

Marker on my body armor. The medics know that, of course. They're really checking alertness to see how badly I'm concussed and whether I might be brain-damaged. One conducts an interview.

Where are you from?

Are you married?

Got kids?

"Look, man, I know what you're trying to do," I tell him, "but I am not going to go into shock. The only thing that really hurts is talking to you."

What talking really does is make me feel like throwing up, which I've been fighting since I got hit. Keeping hands on me for reassurance, the corpsman stays quiet, which I deeply appreciate, but then his chief comes over and lights him up, yelling at him to keep talking like he's supposed to. Come on, Chief, go easy on the poor guy. He's just doing what I asked. By the same token I'd light up one of my guys if he deviated from procedure. For their trouble the chief and the nice-guy corpsman get to wear my last MRE, chicken with salsa, which happens to be my favorite. They might not like it, but it feels good to lighten the load.

Suddenly people pile on stuff like they're trying to bury me. "What the hell are you doing?" I ask, and they say, "We're being mortar attacked, Gunny. This is body armor." The armor comes off the corpsmen's own bodies. To me they're faceless, and I don't even pick up a name, but to this day I would be proud and honored to shake their hands and say thanks. From the moment I'm wounded I rack up debts to people that I can't repay. While it happens I feel helpless, and afterward there's lingering guilt. Nothing to keep me up at night, but still I wish I could do something to pay back what was given so freely and selflessly.

The corpsmen cut off my uniform so I'm pretty much bare-ass by the time they're ready to evac me to the Animal Hospital, a forward treatment center in a much bigger firm base east of Fallujah. Modesty is not an issue for me or any other Marine, but I beg for somebody to cover me up for warmth. I'm freezing, especially when they strap my stretcher to the outside of a Humvee and drive me to the hospital.

Right as the docs at the Animal Hospital start working on me everybody suddenly goes quiet.

"How are you doing, Marine?" The voice belongs to an older man.

"Who's asking?" I say.

"General Hagee."

"But you're the fucking Commandant of the Marine Corps!"

"Yes I am," he says in a perfectly matter-of-fact manner, not minding that A, I don't recognize him, and B, I swear and fail to show proper courtesies to the Corps' highest officer. Plenty of Marines reach retirement age without getting close to the Commandant, much less having a personal visit. This is like the Pope dropping in on a Roman Catholic. Stateside, if General Michael Hagee, 33rd Commandant of the United States Marine Corps, was coming, my unit would be field-daying for a week until every little thing shined like a diamond in a goat's ass. Of course General Hagee makes a different type of visit. He came to observe firsthand the First Battle of Fallujah, which the whole world watches.

Out of respect I give the Commandant a big "Oorah!" and assume the position of attention while lying down.

Now meet Major Agony. I have no idea, but my right eye is gone—parts of it are probably still on the tank. The docs go to work on the left eye, which is swollen shut so they have to pry the lids apart and clamp them open. All around the eye they clean, probe, put in stitches, pull out debris. The shrapnel that went in painlessly damn sure hurts coming out, and I feel like somebody's stabbing me over and over in a part of the body that instinct screams to protect. Anybody who has suffered eye damage knows what I mean. It goes against nature to allow contact near the organs of sight, especially with things like stainless steel probes and scalpels. What the docs do creeps me out and hurts like a bastard, and all at once everything that happened in Fallujah—the fighting and the wounding and the shock to the psyche—catches up.

Leave me the fuck alone.

Whoever you are, whatever you're doing, stop it.

Stop fighting.

Stop running around in front of Bonecrusher's guns and making me kill you.

Stop shooting at me.

Stop blowing up grenades on my head.

Stop asking stupid questions and making me throw up.

Stop driving me around and freezing my ass.

Stop stabbing me in the eye.

Stop fucking with me.

Right here and right now.

Or I will make you stop.

On top of doing their job, the docs have to physically subdue 200 pounds of fed-up Marine. One of them leans down and speaks. "Listen to me, Gunny," he says. "You have got to help me. I need you to work with me."

The words possess incredible power. He doesn't talk doctor to patient, or officer to enlisted man or yell or plead for attention. He talks like my oldest and best friend with something very serious to say, which is that the fight's not over and I have to man up and be Gunny.

The doc does something that hurts the eye worse than ever, but I don't let the pain in.

He asks, "Can you see any light?" then inflicts more agony and asks again.

I feel more than see. Along with the worst pain of my life I get a flash of brightness like when the RPG exploded.

"Yes, I can see it!" I say, dying for him to stop because the pain penetrates the emotional armor.

Thank God he stops, and I get medication that knocks me out. Looking back, I see that the docs kept me awake and in agony so I could respond to the most important question of my entire life. They have serious doubts about my left eye, which sits down in my sinus cavity—the technical term is orbital blowout—punctured and leaking fluid. It is full of blood from retina damage, and the docs are concerned about possible serious harm to the optic nerve from all the metal that came ripping into the front of my head. They are about an inch from popping the eyeball like a balloon and pulling it—the technical term is enucleation—and mostly what stops them is me saying "Yes, I see light." "No," and I'd probably have two glass eyes instead of one.

Dark now, dark forever.

Hearing "Yes," though, the docs commence a major salvage operation on the left eye and clean up the mess on the right. They do such a good job that surgeons stateside have very little to do. They're downright amazed at the quality of work done in the field. Since the two lead surgeons later communicate, I can thank them by name. Doctors Sullivan and Grove, you have my lifelong gratitude and admiration. Words are inadequate, but they're all I've got. I'm not the only one saying thanks, either. Many casualties coming out of Fallujah owe the world to medical professionals at the Animal Hospital, who work around the clock within sound of the gunfire, sometimes under rocket and mortar attack. One doctor I know of was killed. Rumor has it, he was rotating home the next day.

One last memory from Iraq. I wake up after surgery and have a spectacular puke. For maybe a half second I wonder whether this is a bunk-type rack and somebody underneath me catches it, but I'm too dopey and tired to ask or really care.

Next time I wake up, straps hold me in place.

"I need some help here," I yell.

"What is it?" somebody asks.

"I need to get up."

"Why?"

"Head call."

Somebody hands me a urine bottle, which I'm supposed to use lying down, but I insist on standing up because I don't want to piss on myself.

Whoa, why does the deck move like this?

"Where am I?"

The guy helping me says, "You're on a plane to Germany, dude."

I have no sense of elapsed time and no memory of being moved. The news surprises the hell out of me.

For all I know we're still over Iraq, but Fallujah fades to history, a million miles away.

The war's over. Lights out. Sleep without dreams.

3

Not in My Book

Stuff you might be looking for but will not find here:

1) TWO THINGS JOHN WAYNE WOULD HAVE DONE

Frankly this first one bothers me because I consider myself a Marine's Marine and want to live up to the tradition and image in every possible way.

I would like to report that after I issue orders to get Bonecrusher moving, the next words are, "Is anybody else hit?"

It wouldn't have made a damn bit of difference, and I wouldn't have heard the answer, but concern about my guys should have been on my mind.

It wasn't, at least not in memory.

Was I knocked stupid?

Didn't I care?

Because I don't know the answer, I still think about it from time to time.

Also, why don't I yell and struggle to get up and get back into the fight? The Duke would do this for sure. He'd rip off the pressure bandages, grab a rifle, and crawl to the front if he couldn't walk. If he couldn't see to shoot, he'd fight by feel, using his K-bar on the bad guys, and die a glorious death.

Once I'm hit, however, I am perfectly content to be medevaced out of the combat zone. Of course, reality is on my side here. If I made a commotion and refused to leave, I'd be a nuisance if not a danger to my own side. And a glorious death at this point would be stupid. The prospect of dying in the fight doesn't bother me a bit. Once giving up my life serves no purpose, no thanks. I fully intend to live. Fuck Death.

Looking back, I believe there might be more here than meets the eye. Maybe way down deep in some secret still operational part of my mind, I already know something that I will not admit to myself or anybody else for months to come. I am out of the fight for good. I am not and never will be what I was, a trigger puller in the U.S. Marine Corps, which is all I ever wanted to be. Since I'm not, I quit acting like I am. Just a theory.

2) "TELL APRIL I LOVE HER"

My thirteenth wedding anniversary happens to fall on April 8, eleven hours after I get hit, Iraqi time. At no time, though, do I speak the famous Hollywood wounded warrior line. It never even occurs to me. For the first day or so my thoughts don't reach as far as home and loved ones, whom I really do love with all my heart. This will change in Germany, where I re-boot and have time to think. Also, "Tell April I love her," sounds much too much like goodbye, like giving up and signing off. I never doubt that I will speak my love to April, our 10-year-old son Nick Jr., and 20-year-old Rich, my stepson.

3) FEAR

There's plenty to be scared of, but fear does not come into the picture in the spring, 2004 Battle of Fallujah. Maybe I had to deal with this issue a bit more in my first two combat tours, Desert Storm, the 1990-91 war to liberate Kuwait, and Operation Iraqi Freedom in 2003. Even then, though, fear for my life and limb was a drop in the bucket compared to the much, much bigger fear that I'd screw up and let down my fellow Marines. Credit goes to the Corps' training here. Most guys, even boots facing enemy fire for the first time, feel the same way, and in my experience out-and-out cowards are much rarer than you'd think. Even if I were a fearful sort of guy, my job comes with all sorts of fear-killers. As a platoon sergeant I'm one hundred percent mentally engaged making sure all my Marines do the right thing, and inflicting damage matters more than damage coming my way. And a 68-ton tank works wonders for self-confidence.

4) CONCERN ABOUT MY MEDICAL CONDITION

The thought that I might be blind for the rest of my life crosses my mind, but it doesn't bother me, at least for the first few days, because I'm so unbelievably glad to be alive. I'm glad, too, to be a hundred percent myself—I always worried about brain injury turning me into a vegetable or knocking me slow. And I never accept complete blindness as part of reality, even though it's entirely possible or maybe even likely. I always have the idea that some if not all of the vision in my left eye will come back. Don't ask me why.

5) PERMANENT PYSCHOLOGICAL EFFECTS

In combat I do not discover my true self or find God or have any sort of transforming experience. And sorry, mental health professionals, I do not currently suffer flashbacks or flinch at loud noises or otherwise have the past screw up the here and now.

Things might be very different for young guys, but I come to the fight fully cooked, in my late thirties, 15 years in the Corps, most of them in leadership positions, and I leave pretty much as I arrived except for the permanent disabilities. These will change things, naturally, but nothing I see or hear or do in Fallujah alters my inner being or my outlook. Although I take great pride in my performance and achievements in combat, my biggest, proudest, most formative and defining events— which made me the Marine I am and the man I am—came in peacetime. The fights verify what I already know about myself. I'm a Marine.

6) GUILT, REGRET

In three combat deployments I have killed, by my best estimate, something like 200 enemy combatants. Such is the nature of tank warfare, where a single main-gun hit on a vehicle can kill a dozen men, and the machine guns do to dismounted infantry what weed whackers do to crab grass. A tank kills ugly, guys cooked alive in armored vehicles and bunkers, vaporized by main gun rounds, chopped to pieces by machine gun fire, smashed under the tracks. Such things are not good to look upon, and nobody in his right mind would derive any enjoyment. I never feel bad, though, not when it happens and not now.

Putting down enemies feels pretty much like shooting up plywood targets. Now and again things have seemed ridiculously unfair—Marines versus the enemy in our Iraq wars, especially the Iraqi Army, is like the Chicago Bears versus Shitville High School—but that's too bad for them because they're on the wrong side. I know, in my head, that they're somebody's sons and brothers and maybe husbands and fathers just like me. What I know in my heart, however, is nothing. Nada. Zilch. Zip. Not in a fight. I never connect in a human way to the enemy in my gun sights—no hatred, no passion, no bloodlust, no pity, no recognition that these are, in fact, human beings.

Based on my experiences and what other guys say, it seems that I am above average at depersonalizing combat and going about my job, destroying the enemy, in a level-headed and professional fashion and with a complete absence of feelings that might interfere. Generally I keep this particular personal attribute to myself, but when I needed it, my ability served me very well—the Corps and the country, too, if I do say so. I guess I'll never need it again, here in the civilian world.

Away from war, things are entirely different. When all the killing stops and we are finally at peace, God willing, there will be absolutely no hard feelings for the people I fought. If somehow I ran into the man who fired the RPG round that hit me in the head, I'd be perfectly willing to sit down and buy beers—which would not, by the way, necessarily be an affront to the man's beliefs. Iraqis, in my experience, don't mind a drink when the occasion calls for it.

Do you know what I would say?

"Hey man, nice shot."

We might even find something to laugh about. Maybe this seems crazy, but it makes sense to me. Other trigger pullers probably get it, too.

Of course people not in the fight die, too. Surely, inevitably, a few of the thousands upon thousands of rounds shot by my tanks' weapons have hit uninvolved, innocent individuals, the same people I fought for, doing all in my power to free them from oppression and fear. More than other weapons systems, a tank can engage the enemy up-close and cleanly and spare the innocent. But you'd be stupid or delusional to think there were no accidents. Do I wish they didn't happen? With all my heart. But do I blame myself or feel guilt? Never. Not crying in my beer with other Marines, not waking up at two in the morning, not sitting in church and thinking about my immortal soul. Warriors make war, in which both bad and good people die, and I am a warrior. This is the life path I chose and followed until I could follow it no more.

4

Reconnecting

Give this wheelchair to some poor guy who needs it and let me walk. Just guide me, I'm fine.

As a matter of fact I'm fine only because my ass is firmly planted in the chair. Shortly I will attempt to stand, and I'll keel over. At the moment, though, I derive immense enjoyment from feeling okay, which after what I've been through feels great.

Could be midnight, could be noon. Waking up here, in the wheelchair, I have no idea how they got me off the plane. Just as "Where am I?" comes into my head somebody speaks.

"I am Gunny So-and-So. I am your Marine liaison here. You are in the military hospital at Landstuhl, Germany."

No slight to the man that I miss the last name. "Gunny" is the part that counts. His words come out Gunny, in a clear and forceful manner that says he has needed information to impart. I trust him. I could be listening to myself.

"How are you doing, Gunny?"

"I'm fine." This happens to be true, but I would say exactly the same thing with blood shooting across the room from a hole in my carotid artery or dying of some horrible illness. "I'm fine," is the only acceptable Marine Corps answer.

"You need anything, Gunny?"

"No, Gunny, I'm good."

Once again, the Marine answer.

"Actually, you need a lot. You need hygiene items. You need a rack assignment. You need clothes because you don't have shit."

The Gunny hands me a backpack containing sweats, socks, skivvies, t-shirts, hygiene items, and a CD player. Every $99 in donations to the non-profit Wounded Warrior Project buys such a pack. Whoever paid for mine, thanks.

The Gunny says to count on him for further assistance as needed, leaving no doubt whatsoever that he can be counted on.

A more soft-spoken individual introduces himself as a chaplain and asks, "Is there anything I can do for you spiritually?"

"Yes sir, there is. There's a Bible verse, Romans 1:11. My wife and I read it back and forth when I'm away. Sometimes we put it in letters."

He finds the passage and reads aloud:

> For I long to see you that I may impart unto you some spiritual grace, to strengthen you: That is to say, that I may be comforted together in you by that which is common to us both, your faith and mine.

The words get to the chaplain, too. "Wow," he says, "That's a good one."

For April and me, Romans 1:11 functions as a secret commlink, and even across the world and completely out of contact it puts us in touch because one can turn to it and know the other one did the same not long ago or maybe is reading it right now. And the words speak of something we share besides man-woman, husband-wife love. We share a deep religious faith and make a gift of it to each other. With God comes April and vice versa. And as the words say, this gives us comfort and strength when we need it. Like now.

Like now.

"Would you like to call home?"

The chaplain, God bless him, asks for the number, punches it into his satellite phone and hands it to me.

And April, thank God, picks up.

"Hey, Beautiful," I say, "Beautiful" being one of my pet names for her, as is "Pretty Woman." Husbands say such things to women as cute as Bonecrusher, but the name fits my wife, who is recognized far and wide as a babe. More on this subject later.

After "Hey, Beautiful," I say, "You'll never guess where I am."

April, obviously, already knows, and she talks right past me; "Sweetheart! Are you all right? Are you okay?"

"I'm fine," I say. In truth, talking with April, I feel fantastic, even after she says, "Sweetheart, I heard they took your right eye."

I reach up and feel the sewn-up eyelids over an empty socket.

"Yeah, I guess they did," I say. In another time and place this could bring a man down. Not now, though. I'm mainly surprised that April knows so much more than I do about what's going on.

We have a conversation not a lot different from hundreds we have had before. Listening in, you would have no idea we're Nick and April because everything is Beautiful this and Sweetheart that. And you wouldn't pick up much information, because we mostly make lovey-dovey small talk. We just want to hear each other's voices.

At the time it goes right over my head, but there is something odd about this particular conversation. April and I have two completely different missions. I make a morale call. April, on the other hand, needs to ascertain whether her husband has lost his memory or some significant portion of his marbles. Thinking a little more clearly, I would find some of my wife's chitchat pretty strange, like her bringing up certain family activities before my deployment. The point, she later tells me, is to see if I know, among other things, that I have a 10-year-old son named Nicholas Jr., and parents back in Indiana named Duke and Dolores. I remember just fine, but April stays serious and concerned and will for days.

When I blurt out, "Hey, Beautiful, Happy Anniversary," April gives me some sort of half-hearted, same-to-you-honey reply. Clearly she does not feel like celebrating. I do because I am not dead and I hear my beautiful wife's beautiful voice and we still love each other like crazy.

Much as I want to go home to April, we don't say a lot about missing each other and how we're dying to be back together right now. In our world that kind of talk just makes you crazy. The United States Marine Corps will send me home in its own good time, and judging by previous experiences that might not be soon. I sat in Kuwait for six weeks after Desert Storm, and after the 2003 Iraq deployment went home on a Navy ship that took two months to reach California. And that was without medical problems. My conditions now could tie me up for who knows how long. So I have no thoughts about being home with April and Nick Jr. in the immediate future. I am just happy, more than words can tell, to hear April's voice. And just talking, we come together in a place all our own, far from our current physical locations.

Too soon I must say to April, "I think the man wants his phone back. And they've got a rack ready for me."

She says she'll call back soon and puts Little Nick on the line.

One last "I love you," the line goes dead, and I fly back from our private heaven to this wheelchair in a hallway in a hospital in Landstuhl, wherever the hell that is, Germany. I can't see and don't hear very well and continue to experience nausea to the point that just thinking about food makes me want to puke. And here comes this giant wave of exhaustion, so I'm dying to rack out and sleep.

But all of the above beats the hell out of being dead, doesn't it?

5

April's Epic

I don't find this out until much later, but April had a bad day of epic proportions before my call from Germany.

Since I catch her at home, I assume she's been there all along, in our house on-base in Twentynine Palms, California. In fact, she and Nicholas, along with another base wife and her daughter, who is Nick's age, are at a Marine resort high in the San Bernardino Mountains at Big Bear. From the deep desert we live in, this is like an instant trip to Colorado, with pine trees and snow. The women and kids stay in a cozy little cabin, with a sledding hill nearby.

April went to the mountains to get away from the constant bombardment of information from Iraq. She knows I'm in the fight at Fallujah, and the news networks show nothing but. Theoretically, she could watch old movies or just keep the TV at home off, but she, like all the other Marine wives, is a news junky. If you want to know all the latest breaking stories, talk to the spouse of somebody who's deployed in the war zone. They don't want to see it, but they can't look away—that's how it is with military wives and husbands and CNN and the Fox News Network. Walk into any home at Two Nine, click on the TV, and I guarantee one news net or the other is the last thing the people in the house watched. Go anywhere on base with a TV, like a restaurant or the staff NCO club, and the news is on. You just can't escape it.

April has a particular anxiety about seeing footage of me all shot-up. Of course, she would see just that if she hadn't gone to the mountains because the video of me coming off Bonecrusher is the flavor of the day, streaming pretty much constantly on television. I'm glad we've got a copy of it now, because it gives me such a vivid picture of what went on at the medevac site when I was blind and still pretty punchy. I like seeing how the guys and I kept our professional cool. But I thank God April doesn't see it real-time, especially before she knows how things will come out. From the clips, she could think I'm at death's door.

She does, in fact, assume that I'm dead when her cell phone rings at 1:35 am. She keeps hearing death when our battalion Executive Officer speaks the words no spouse or loved-one wants to hear, "I regret to inform you . . . " It takes her a minute to get that he says "was wounded in action in Al Anbar Province." Further words add to her confusion because the XO says I'm VSI, very seriously injured, in the head, and it is not yet known if I'll survive.

April naturally wants to get back home fast, but she knows it's foolish to drive off the mountain on a bad road in the dark in a state of upset. She lets Nicholas sleep because there's no point to upsetting him prematurely. No prayer of sleeping herself, my poor wife goes out to a convenience store, for coffee, crying so hard the clerks want to know if she's okay. She tells them she's fine. April is not the type for dramatics. My son isn't either. At dawn, when April wakes him and tells him what's up, tears come to his eyes, but he keeps his composure, showing a lot of backbone for a ten-year-old.

On the way to Two Nine, April gets a call from Bravo Company's tank leader and a very close family friend, Master Sergeant Johnson— Top J to me and Alan to April. "Don't turn on your TV when you get home," he says, "Don't look at the news. There's footage of Pop that you don't need to see."

At home, others call and tell her the same thing. Officers from the battalion come by, as they would have to notify April of my wounding if she had been home. She also gets more complete information on my medical condition, based on a report from the field sent to battalion.

Think of what my wife gets hit with in less than a day, on almost no sleep. First, a report pronouncing me VSI after a grenade hit to the head. Then video images too awful for her to see. What can she think, except maybe she's now married to a vegetable, or that I'll die before she can get to me overseas and say goodbye?

Then, out of the blue, I call her sounding coherent and pretty much normal, telling her Happy Anniversary, Beautiful.

Talk about whiplash. No question who had the more upsetting 24 hours here. I mean, I spend most of the same period unconscious.

April, who thinks a lot more about Fate than I do, sees significance in how things occurred. Before the trip, she went out of her way to make sure others had her cell phone number, just in case. This bothered her because even saying "just in case" seemed like inviting trouble. The right people had the number, anyway, but she still felt the need to make sure. And the idea that she tried to escape the news strikes her as significant, too, because this is the one weekend the news featured her husband soaked in his own blood.

If you really want to get all Twilight Zone, think about which wedding anniversary of ours this is.

Number 13.

6

Landstuhl Laughs

So long as I lie still in the rack, I'm reading a one on the ten-point pain scale the medical people use. But all I have to do to get bigger numbers is stand up, which I do as often as possible because it creeps me out to lie here like a living corpse, no outside stimulus, nobody to talk to, no nothing. I need some company, man, some commotion, some life. More often than not, I also need to take a leak. But then moving lights up my whole damn body like I was in a car wreck. My left foot, the farthest part of me from my actual wounds, hurts worst. Weird.

Considering what happened up there, a phobia about contact with my head is less weird. I don't even put my own hands anywhere near Ground Zero. Letting the docs monkey with it feels wrong, wrong, wrong. The human skull is constructed to ensure privacy, but somebody knocked a new entrance into mine and everybody and his brother pokes inside and pulls stuff in and out. I hate it. This is not to mention the pain, like hornets stinging deep inside the head. But I don't squirm because it's all for the good, and I won't even say I hurt because I'm Gunny.

What the docs do, though, is nothing compared to bumping into a foreign object at head level—IV stand, heart monitor, somebody's hand reaching up, who knows what. It never actually happens, but just thinking about it freaks me out. When I finally get around to hygiening, I won't even splash water up there. This crazy obsession, this fear, rules. Getting out of bed and walking down the hall causes, honest to God, more anxiety than getting off the tank and walking down the street in Fallujah.

It must be pretty funny to see me in motion. Even standing still, I hang onto something with one hand and use the other to make target acquisition sweeps in case something tries to sneak up. Always I'm waving my arm around like the place is full of cobwebs.

April, bracing for permanent total blindness, gets on the phone and says it won't be so much of a problem. As long as she's talking, it sounds doable and not so bad. It also seems the same way lying in the hospital bed. But then I step out into the real world, where blindness kicks my ass. As soon as I bust the room hatch, I fly on instruments that I have no idea how to use. Worst of all is passing an alcove between the room and the head. There I must give up contact with the wall. I will not follow it around the corner, because who knows what they parked in there. Wheelchairs, crash carts, IV stands, they change it all the time. So I solo for ten whole feet, swinging one arm high, one arm low, until Thank God here's the wall.

All this to piss on my own. I will spare you the details, like determining if a given stall is occupied and urine marksmanship. I used to put less thought and planning into protecting resupply convoys. But, hey, I'm moving independently. It's a start. I have no doubt that eventually I'll be as good as the best hotshot blind guys in the world.

Nobody has said how blind I'm really going to be, for how long. Since I lost one eye and I can't see out of the other, I'm thinking this might be the future. In truth, though, I don't think that much. Discomfort and challenges and concern don't even put a dent in my personal morale. Looking back, feeling this good seems borderline weird, but every waking minute I know how lucky I am that the RPG didn't take my head clean off. And unless somebody hits me with another grenade, the worst is over. There's no way to go but up.

Even if I were dying on the inside, I wouldn't show it, because I have to set an example for the younger Marines. A Gunnery Sergeant displays leadership traits and Marine Corps values like courage, honor, commitment. I have to be Semper Fi walking and talking so the guys say, "Look at Gunny, man. He's got holes in his head and he can't see shit, but he's still in the fight." Maybe this helps them stay in the fight and feel better about their own current circumstances. Just by being a shot-up Gunny, I motivate the junior Marines by showing that we in the Corps really do lead from the front where the bad shit happens.

When I think jarheads are looking I keep my Gunny face on, trying to walk to the pisser the way I would walk from Bonecrusher back to infantry positions. Darting doorway to doorway would have been saner, but I strutted like I just wrote a check and bought Fallujah. Sometimes I could feel the sniper's crosshairs on the back of my neck, but I took my time anyway so the Marines would say to themselves, "Look at Gunny, he ain't scared of nuthin'. Why should I be?" The flip side was telling the bad guys to be afraid.

Truth be told, the busted-up Marines do me more good than I do them. My favorite part of the day is getting together and shooting the shit. This puts us right back in our platoons doing what we always did, telling sea stories, giving each other a hard time, having laughs. The number-one topic is, "How did you get fucked up?" Whatever a guy says, he gets rude and sarcastic comments about how this never would have happened to a good Marine. If a sniper hit him, he's an idiot with no tactical discipline because he presented a target, a disgrace because he got outshot, probably so lazy he took out his sappy plates, which would have made him bulletproof. Guys go over the top, play-acting like superior officers reprimanding some poor, hopeless turd. Not only do you suck, you're a burden to the quality Marines. How many guys did it take to carry your big ass? How many valuable military assets were wasted on the medevac? Did they have to call a humvee? A helo?

The routine always ends with the ultimate insult, "Aw, your unit's better off without you, anyway."

By this time everybody, even the victim, busts a gut. I can see how this might seem brutal, but we do it with love, and it does us good, certainly more so than some kind of pity party. We're telling ourselves and the world we're still Marines, the same guys we were before, with the same strengths, the same camaraderie. You can't harass anybody like this but your brothers, brothers who are there for you, who will never let you down.

We treat loss of life as sacrosanct, however. Nobody makes jokes when a Marine died in the same action. The guy in the hospital sends up a flag, letting us know right off that his wounding involved somebody else's death. Then we get in step. We will not add to the misery of a guy like one of my roommates, a Recon Marine in deep mourning about two guys killed in the same IED explosion that hit him. He's especially torn up by the loss of a lieutenant he idolized.

"Come on, Corporal," I say, "He wouldn't want you feeling bad about him. He was doing what he believed in."

"I know, Gunny, I know," the Corporal says. He does know, but he needs to hear it from others.

I go on, "What would you expect the Lieutenant to do if you got killed? He'd carry on, keeping kicking ass, wouldn't he?"

On top of the grief, this poor guy is hurting physically. If he takes home souvenirs he'll have a coffee can full of shrapnel and debris the bomb blew into him, which the docs remove from his lower body. Every time they go to work, I hear him choke back screams. I have no doubt that a kid this strong will beat the thing about his lieutenant.

The Corporal assists me by describing the layout and contents of our quarters. When he feels up to it he acts as my seeing eye Marine, and I'm his legs, pushing his wheelchair on trips around the hospital.

Coming up to a window, he says, "Porthole on the left, Gunny."

"Gimme a Sitrep, Recon."

"Looks like it just rained. No leaves on the trees. Cloudy."

We don't actually go outside or even to a different floor, but this is fun, better than a Ninety-Six, a four-day liberty.

Since he's my roommate, I talk with him more than anybody else. I never make a picture of the Corporal in my head, though. All I can see is generic, hair cut high and tight, jock build because he's Recon, but with no distinguishing detail. Looking back, I'm struck and sort of mystified by my inability to picture him or any of the other seriously wounded Marines. Maybe I just don't want to envision the damage they carry, the bandages, the empty space where arms and legs used to be. Or maybe it's too weird to ask, "Hey, what do you look like? What are you missing?" Whatever the reason, our bull sessions are like talking over radios. Voices without faces and bodies.

Meantime, I can "see" everybody else. The chaplain has gray hair, a gut pushing on his cammies, a wrinkled, fatherly face full of wisdom and compassion. For all I know, he's a mean-looking marathon runner, but I see him my way, just like I see a certain young female soldier who brings around chow and does things the nurses tell her. What she does most of all is complain and spew negativity. Her I see as a Generation X she-dude with the standard-issue barbed wire tattoo and undoubtedly a piercing somewhere I don't want to think about, with dark hair and a face that might be cute except her disposition shows.

But here's somebody good to look upon—Captain Miller, the boss Army nurse. Her face shows forty-odd years of kindness, with the good kind of wrinkles from her long career of doing right and smiling while she does it. A woman, the real deal, but I do not eyeball the chest and chassis because that would disrespect a fellow military professional. Even before hearing the voice I know when she steps on deck because the ward starts hopping. Then come nonstop verbal corrections—"What's this doing out here? Let's get this swept and mopped. Who's watching that soldier's IV?"—all delivered in a voice she doesn't have to raise because there's true leadership behind it. No wasted motion with this lady. If she's asking about my pain level and the specifics of any discomfort, she's also fluffing the pillow and policing the room. In my dependent position, such competence and devotion to duty provides comfort. She tries to make me more comfortable by telling me to use her first name, but Captain expresses my high regard, and I refuse to call her anything but, even with that smiling face looking down on me in my mind's eye.

I don't get much of a mental image of myself. People on the phone keep asking about my face, undoubtedly picturing some kind of horrific, disfigured mess. I can tell they're surprised to hear clear speech from me. When my son Nicholas asks me what I look like, I tell him to think back to that scene in The Terminator, one of his favorite movies, where the robot guy cuts his own eye out. "I look like that," I say, in a no-big-deal sort of way.

My face is a big deal, though, to one poor little boy at the Sunday service at the base church. This happens to be Easter. I hear the kid in the next pew monkeying around and his Mom telling him to sit still. Then the airman who walked me to church says, "Gunny, that kid's looking at you." I smile at him, trying to telegraph "It's okay, son, I'm a daddy, too," and he screams and keeps screaming while Mom carts him away.

A few days later, after almost a week in Landstuhl, I'm lying in the rack while one of the hospital people squares away the bedding and makes me more comfortable. I turn and get the shock of my life.

Here stands a woman. Her arms move, pushing her hands out to the side to smooth the linen.

It isn't a woman, actually, but a really shitty picture like some kid who can't draw made an outline in dots, black pencil lead on a dark gray-brown background. But I am thrilled out of my mind.

"I can see you!"

"I am sorry that the first you see is me," she says. A very odd remark, in retrospect.

"No, no, you look great!"

By the time I say it, the picture is gone. But I do not mourn its passing because I'm so unbelievably ecstatic and elated and suddenly hopeful that black blindness might not be forever. Listen to what the lady says. She's the first thing I see, not the last. I will see, this I now know.

Who cares how long it takes?

If a Marine knows anything, he knows how to wait.

And this is not a bad thing to wait for.

7

Heroes, Whiners

Checked luggage must feel like this, but what good would it do me to know when and how I'm finally going to get back home? The thing is to trust that somebody somewhere has his shit together. I've been trusting for fifteen years, and the Corps has yet to lose me.

I'm pretty well resigned to a long stay in Landstuhl. But suddenly, on Day Seven, Captain Miller comes through the hatch and says, "Gunny, you're on tomorrow's flight stateside."

"No way."

"Get down to the PX and draw some civilian clothes," she says.

Good thing it's the Captain, because I wouldn't believe this coming from anybody else, especially not the Lance Corporal Underground, where I do pick up one solid fact. The planes from Landstuhl fly to DC, where the Marines and sailors go to Bethesda Naval Hospital and the soldiers go to Walter Reed Army Hospital. Even though we're all dying to get back home, we Marines don't admit to it. With our units still in the fight, it feels dishonorable to be headed away from the action, and even more dishonorable to want it that way. God knows a Gunny could not pine for home out loud. Any talk here about shipping out means going back to Iraq. Even really busted up guys say they'll be back in the fight. In most cases they're dreaming out loud, but "Yeah, I'm going back to my platoon. Got some ass-kickin' to do," sounds a hundred percent Marine, and it feels good to say it and hear it.

I go to the PX expecting to receive acceptable liberty attire—tuck-in shirt, belted trousers. What I want, more than anything else, is a pair of shoes. Any shoes will do. I've been barefoot since Fallujah, and this is starting to wear on me. Since I joined the Corps, I have had some kind of foot gear on every minute, even in the shower. Even at the beach, I wear sandals damn near to the water. No luck, though. Shoes are not part of the deal. Real clothes aren't, either. The PX guy offers small, medium, or large sweats. I tell him I'll stick with what I've got, green USMC sweats with the eagle, globe, and anchor. No way am I putting on some kind of Army shit. I don't say this, but I think it.

On the other hand, I want to pay proper respects to my favorite Army officer, Captain Miller. When it's time to move out, I ask her to guide me to the formation. Somebody has to do it, and I want it to be her.

When we get to where the Marines are mustering, I tell her, "We've got a special way of saying goodbye in the Corps."

She probably thinks I'm going to slug her in the shoulder or call for the guys to dog pile on her.

Instead, I tell her this: "I wish you fair winds and following seas." And I explain that this is our way of wishing a person the best of luck and a long, good journey through life. I mean it, too, genuinely. And my respect and gratitude aren't just personal. They're for everybody before me and those coming after me. I know that as long as she's on duty, the guys on that ward will be taken care of.

Somebody bellows like a Sergeant Major, "Cover down and align!" The command means to form up into straight ranks for marching. Given that the few guys who are physically capable of marching carry stretchers and everybody else is in a wheelchair or on crutches, it's just smartass Marine talk. Once we start moving guys chime in with "Get in step!" and "Column right!" Before the joke gets old we're on a bus, rolling toward the plane.

Nobody acts like it's odd that we sit on the bus, right next to the plane, for two hours before somebody barks, "File off. Follow the man in front of you. Don't leave anything on my bus."

Since I'm able-bodied, I carry another Marine's stuff onto a C-141 set up for casualty flights with a rig for stretchers running down the middle. Most of us sit on benches along the plane's sides. At wheels-up I couldn't feel better. Alive. Moving closer to home. But then the pain goes up with the altitude. My head is a wreck, both inside and out, and it feels like it's going to explode. No kidding, any minute now the thing's going to pop. Since I figure that the problem is cabin pressure, and nothing threatening, I lowball the pain score when the flight surgeon makes her rounds.

"Two," I say, when it feels more like twenty-two. My face must tell the truth, because the doc keeps coming back and asking, but what's the point of bellyaching? It sucks. Deal with it.

Meanwhile, I've got a couple of world champion whiners on my right.

"This is bullshit, man."

"The National Guard's bullshit."

"Why were we in Iraq?"

"The Captain, why'd he push us up there anyway?

"That was real bullshit."

"Kissin' the Major's ass."

Blah, blah, blah. No complaint is too small. I should shut these assholes down, but why bother? Every unit has its ten percent, and theirs is lucky enough to lose these two clowns. They're not Marines, anyway.

I pick up the fact that the whiner on my immediate right has shrapnel wounds in his forearm, which makes him one of the most abled-bodied men on the plane. So far as I can tell, he's looking at a full recovery, probably pretty soon. And he must feel pretty strong now, because he puts a lot of energy into his bitching, moving around on the bench and gesturing. I can't see it, but I can feel it. Nevertheless, he's a complete drama queen about his wound. When the doc comes around and asks his pain level, he says "Seven," in a shaky little voice that's nothing like his bitching with his buddy.

That tears it.

As soon as the doc's gone, I click off safe. "Shut the fuck up! What are you, special? You feeling something different from anybody else on here?"

Not a peep out of him for the rest of the flight.

In the flow of things, the few days I spend in Bethesda are pretty much a long layover between flights. If I lost a leg or arm instead of an eye, DC would be home for a long time. This is where amputees get treatment, followed by prosthetics and rehabilitation at a specialized clinic at Walter Reed. The entire process sounds grueling but with a big payoff. Guys I know came out of it fired-up, ready to take on anything and kick major ass. The attitude therapy is as good as the physical. Since my case involves the eyes I'll be sent somewhere else. No idea where, until somebody tells me I'm headed for Balboa Naval Hospital in San Diego, which has the ophthalmological clinic closest to where I'm based.

The young Marine corporal I room with is a big fan of the Jerry Springer Show, which he watches with the volume cranked. Another case of hearing loss from an explosion, is my guess. Until this moment, I had no use for Jerry Springer, but now I love hearing it. The disgusting weirdo guests speak my language and come from home towns like mine. Even the commercials are music to my ears. Burger King. Home Depot. I know those places. I've been to them. I'm home.

Compared to Landstuhl, Bethesda is a happening place. Lots of coming and going, people looking in. One of the drop-ins happens to be the Assistant Commandant of the Corps. When he asks my roomie how he got hit, I am flat blown away by the answer. The corporal caught a load of shrapnel from an enemy grenade while shielding a wounded buddy with his own body. He left a position of safety to save the other man, who couldn't move. And my roommate was smart as well as courageous, positioning his body armor for maximum protection. Otherwise he and the other man would probably be dead. He describes all this as if it was a routine event. If the General hadn't asked, I'd have no idea that I'm bunking next to a no-shit hero.

At Bethesda, I rack up another debt to a selfless individual. A TV doesn't do much good to a blind guy, so I ask a nurse if I can get a radio. "Sure," she says and brings me a portable. "What kind of music do you like?" she asks. I tell her everything, and she tunes in a jazz station. Normally this isn't my favorite, but it sounds just great.

Before I leave, I ask at the nurses' station where to return the radio, and one of the women says, "It goes right here."

So I could have music; the nurses went without.

8

Love with a Capital L

Hallelujah, I can tell light from dark. And I pick up actual images, blurry and in black and white. They come and go, like the connections are corroded, but coming from total blackness, seriously degraded sight scores outstanding.

The next biggest thrill comes after a guy busts the hatch carrying a garbage bag and says, "Is there a Popaditch in here?"

"Yeah, that's me," I say, and he hands me the bag and walks out. No idea what I'm getting, I feel around inside and find stuff that was in my pockets when I got hit. And my boots! Two weeks later, six thousand miles away, who the hell knows how, they're here, and I've got something solid and respectable to put on my feet. It took hitting me in the head with a grenade to get me to give them up. If you want them now, you'll have to do it again.

I break the Marine rule against lying in the rack with boots on. I know I look like crap, with a two-week beard, shaved head grown out, stitched up like Frankenstein, in sweats and combat boots that I find out later are all bloody. But with the footwear I've got Marine feet, at least, and more confidence about walking because this is the way it ought to feel.

On the way to the medevac transport to California, I set off an alarm and tell the security guard it's these boots of mine, which have a lot of metal on them, but the guy laughs and guides me through.

"It's not your boots, buddy," he says, patting me on the shoulder in a way that expresses both sympathy and the idea that I'm sadly out of the loop.

I still laugh about this guy who thinks he has to tell me that I have a head full of shrapnel. And now I know for sure I look like hell.

Prepared for the worst, April leaves Nick Jr. home when she meets me on arrival at Balboa Hospital. In a way, I'm already home on the bus coming down from the Marine Corps Air Station at Miramar to San Diego, with two Marines from Two Nine riding along. They drove 165 miles just to make me welcome. One of them thinks my bloody boots are a riot. Then I come down the steps into the open arms of April. Somehow I know it's her before I hit the deck and we hug for the longest time. Commotion all around—other reunions, guys BSing and lighting up cigarettes—we cling as if we're the only ones there. In memory I'm the only wounded man coming off the bus. And what could be greater than having April in my arms? I don't have one problem in the world. Everything that happened before was meant to get me right here, right now.

"I missed you, Beautiful," I say.

"Nick. I can't believe it. You're finally in my arms. You're here. You're home!" She says it like she really does have a hard time believing, after all the months apart.

This experience is a little more complicated for April than it is for me. Hugging me, she later says, she gets a snoot full of unpleasant smells, like rot deep in my head, burned flesh, and antiseptics. On top of that, she's looking into holes packed with rolls of gauze and blood and pus coming out. Also the lids over my missing eye are sewn shut and stuck together with a peg, like a toothpick through a club sandwich. She's scared to touch my face for fear of breaking something or spreading germs. She can't even bring herself to ask what all is wrong.

God bless her, though, she makes me feel like a movie star. All four nights at Balboa, she'll sleep with me in my hospital rack, a bed so small she has to wrap herself around me and hang on to keep from falling out. Not so hot for her, but it's not bad for me at all. I feel taken care of. The docs and staffers get a kick out of April's devotion to her busted-up Marine. No doubt it's against regulations for her to bunk in here, but nobody says a word. One corpsman giggles when he pulls back the curtain and sees Beauty and The Beast, this gorgeous woman and her banged-up beau.

Get your mind out of the gutter. This is Love with a capital L. What you're thinking of is not part of the plan of the day.

9

Doc-A-Thon

Monday, April 19, 2004
0600 Pacific Time
Four East Ward,
Naval Medical Center,
Balboa Park, San Diego

Whehen a tank gets hit and can't be fixed in the field, the M88 retriever tows it back to the boneyard, where a mob of mechanics jumps aboard with an unbelievable amount of tools and plugin diagnostic machines they call octopuses. The mechs take down the tank like army ants devouring a dead animal, and in less than an hour the thing sits stripped of armor with all the guts and bones showing. Even the engine lies out on the deck, and the whole apparatus looks like anything but the iron monster killing machine that it is. But there comes a moment when the guys start to put it all back together, and before you know, it's rollin'.

Shock. Firepower. Mobility.

Balboa is my boneyard. Time to turn some wrenches, figure out what's busted, and fix it. Whatever you want to do, I'm cool with it. If a doc walks up and says he needs to stick a bayonet in my throat to make things better, I'll turn my head to make it easier. Let's get to work.

No time to screw around walking, which takes me forever, so I accept the offer of a wheelchair and let the corpsman push me to the Ear, Nose and Throat clinic.

First words out of Dr. Healy's mouth: "What happened, Gunny?"

"Got hit in the head with an RPG," I say and crack up because it seems like a laugh line, the military version of saying I got run over by a Mack truck.

The doc laughs, too, and I say, "But you should see what we did to the bad guys before they got me. One of them made a lucky shot, that's all. We're kicking their asses, and doing great things over there."

Later I hear this particular doctor knows what I'm talking about. He just got back from Iraq where he earned a commendation for conspicuous gallantry for some serious lifesaving heroism. When I ask him, he changes the subject. First time around, though, all I know is that he's a good guy, yucking it up while he does his work like we're back in the squad bay. He pokes and prods, getting the big picture about what's wrong, what might be fixable and what isn't. April later tells me he uses some kind of big white machine to look into my head. Caught up in BSing, I don't even notice. From my perspective this is a social visit. And for no particular reason, I feel very encouraged.

Next comes Audiology, where they check my hearing every which way. Not much happening in my right ear, which took the blast, so the doc vibrates my skull to see what's screwed up. Nerve damage is the verdict. With connections between the ear and the brain mostly severed, there's no fix. Surprising, because my hearing's so much better than after I got hit. I am, in truth, a little more than surprised. This is the first time I hear the word "permanent" in connection with my injuries, and it makes an impression. Never before has a part of me broken that couldn't be fixed. What the hell, though, it's only one ear. Most old tankers can't hear shit, so I always figured I'd end up partially deaf, anyway. April, who stays by my side every minute, is fine with this, too.

After lunch I'm really fired up. Hell no, I don't need a wheelchair to get to the CT scan unit. Guide me, corpsman, and I can walk faster than you can push me. No problem, either, standing in the waiting room, which is packed. Seats go to women and kids, and a man stays on his feet. That's how it ought to be and that's how it is for me for maybe an hour. But then, out of nowhere, weakness ambushes me. If I can't sit down I'll pass out, but I am not about to ask somebody to give up a seat. As a grown man, a Marine, a Gunny, there's just no way.

"April," I whisper, "We need to get out of here."

But April is now a pissed-off lioness. Anything involving me or the little guy can set off her protective instincts, whether we want it or not. She goes to the check-in desk and asks the clerk, "Can't you see my husband's been hit in the head with a grenade? Why is he waiting so long? He doesn't even have a place to sit down!"

The poor clerk, who apologizes every which way, says combat casualties normally have priority, but today a military dependent demanded to get her scan immediately, and this bumped me back.

April comes back to me, fuming, and tells the whole story in a voice loud enough to let everyone present know about the crime that has just been committed. Justice awaits the woman who barged in ahead of me. She's going to face a roomful of indignation.

Could I feel less of a man? It's bad enough that I look like a bum instead of a Marine and I can't stand on my own two feet, but now my wife's fighting my battles in front of God and everyone. Now I'd rather pass out than face such an embarrassment, but then, thank God, somebody calls my name, and we go back to prep for the scan.

Last stop on Day One is the office of an older doc who looks over my remaining eye and says, "The globe has been ruptured. You've got fragments in it, and it's full of blood. You've got sutures on the front of it." This is all news to me.

He winds up telling me that the eye very well could die, cease functioning and collapse so it has to be removed, like hauling away a body.

At this point, April and I start down two different roads. She picks up on the doc's real message: brace yourself for the worst. For me, what he says barely registers. I pick the upside of every "could," "might," "potentially." I mean, if he says the eye might die, it also might not. Indefinites mean little, because I know I see a little bit better every day. What is this, my eye's having a deathbed rally? I don't think so, Doc.

That night I get a lot of company, docs and staffers dropping in mostly to shoot the breeze. People seem to get a big charge out of this shot-up Marine who talks up what we're doing in Iraq and laughs off his own wounds. Maybe they see too much of the price we're paying without hearing about the payoff. And they don't see the ultimate payoff of their own hard work. Every day more wounded warriors come in, and the patched-up guys are gone. For the length of my stay one corpsman will keep bringing friends around, saying, "Hey, I wanted them to meet the Gunny." I seem to be good for morale. A staff sergeant I know who works at the Medical Center actually enlists me as his morale officer, taking me to motivate other wounded Marines and sailors. I have big laughs with a grunt who got hit in the arm with a dud RPG, telling him, "Hey, we're the unluckiest motherfuckers in here because we're the only two they managed to hit with those things." We turn the joke around, too, saying we're the luckiest ones because we're still alive.

Day Two

Instead of one doc at a time, I get a whole gaggle in the ENT exam room. It can't be a good sign that they keep leaving to talk things over. On the other hand, this isn't a funeral. After a probe goes in too far—I think the thing scratches my brain—I climb half-way up the back of the exam chair and curl up like a monkey hanging onto a branch. The room goes quiet, and after a long pause, one of the docs says, "Are you comfortable like that?" And everybody, including me, cracks up.

Everybody but April. For her not one thing about this is funny. She excuses herself frequently for various reasons, to hit the head, call and check on Nicholas, get a soda, and so on. Obviously she's making up reasons to go out, but I think to myself, so what, she's bored. This must be like watching paint dry.

Negative, Gunny. My wife goes off to cry. She doesn't want me to worry about her, so she does it on her own. That's April for you. What burdens she has, she does not ask others to share.

And the docs keep giving her new reasons to cry. They drop the first bomb of the day in ENT, when the crew goes out and doesn't come back. At first it seems like another sidebar, except longer, but then a new doctor comes in, introducing himself as Captain Michael Keefe, head of the department.

Right from Jump Street I like this guy, who's now a close family friend, even though the words he speaks, coming out of somebody else's mouth, would sound a lot like I'm fucked.

"Here's what's going on, Gunny," he says, "You're pretty well peppered with shrapnel, but one big piece penetrated your skull and traveled laterally across your head. I have a concern about the drainage coming out of your nose. We need to run a test to see if it's brain fluid."

I haven't mentioned it, but my nose has been running continuously since I woke up in Germany. Blood and guck and probably pieces of my sinuses coming out, but mostly just snot. Since I was freezing most of the time, I thought maybe I caught cold and never gave it a thought. Even now I don't, partly because of Dr. Keefe's manner. He talks like he's just keeping me in the loop and leaves no doubt that he could handle brain fluid leakage, however serious that might be. Always with this guy, the fix runs out ahead of the problem. The clincher for me, though, is common sense. After two weeks, wouldn't my brain run dry and seize up, or whatever happens?

April secretly goes up a wall. Then, while we wait for the test results, we report to a retinologist who tells us that the eyeball is so full of blood he can't tell for sure, but he strongly suspects serious damage to the retina. He also talks about a good possibility of damage to the optic nerve. Either way, he says, he won't be able to do a thing for me because the retina and the nerve are unfixable. Bottom line: What I see now could be what I see for life. I get the idea he's betting on the worst-case scenario and wants me to get used to the idea of permanent near-total blindness. To hell with that. I just don't buy it. I know things are better than they were, and I hate this glass-half-empty bullshit. Besides that, this guy is no fun to be around. Not a joke, not a laugh, not even a smile the whole time we're with him. Come on, man, cheer up. I'm the guy who took an RPG hit and left his eyeball in Fallujah—you don't think I know it's serious?

Now look what Dr. Death did to poor April. Outside the office, she stops at a quiet spot for a private moment.

"This won't be so bad, sweetheart," she says.

"Of course not," I say, "We'll be fine." I mean it, too, and looking back, I think she's really talking to herself. What's brand new to her has been my reality for two weeks. Though I don't need consolation myself, I like what she's doing, because I think it helps her to help me.

"We can move to the beach," she says, "We'll go for walks. When the sun goes down, I'll describe everything for you, so you see it in your mind. And you can smell the ocean air. You know how much you love that, Sweetheart."

Damn, you paint a beautiful picture. You know what I like. The beach is my place. When I was a drill instructor, I used to come home so wound up, and I'd ride my motorcycle down to the oceanfront and breathe, just breathe. Even at midnight the air was like medicine, and I went home feeling like a human being.

I know how desperate April is to help when she says, "You can have one of my eyes. They can take it and implant it, so we both see the same." If it were possible, I believe she really would do it, and even though I know it's impossible, I love hearing it. It's the thought, the feeling. She fights right beside me.

10

Super Docs

Here's another reason to think highly of Dr. Michael Keefe. He's married to another Navy doctor, Captain Kelly Keefe. Not only is she competent, she's a riot. If you're with her, you're laughing. Around this lady, everything is good.

Mrs. Dr. Keefe happens to be the next eye specialist we meet. Night and day after the last guy. Looking at exactly the same set of facts, she says this: "Gunny, this is where we are. Because of the blood, there's no way to tell until the fluid in the eye clears up. But based on what I can see, there's no reason to assume this eye can't come back a hundred percent."

Damn right. This is a woman of my own heart. Why borrow trouble from tomorrow? She tells me that after I get a new prosthetic, people will think the right eye is real. It'll feel natural, too. Best case scenario, I'll end up losing less than 15 percent of my peripheral vision on the right. She tells me, too, that I'll still have effective depth perception even with no binocular vision because the brain adapts and all sorts of things show where objects really are.

Keep talking, Doc. I'm already back in the turret, putting rounds down range, picking up where I left off in Iraq.

"In three months' time, people might not be able to tell you were ever wounded," says Mrs. Dr. Keefe. If I had the pick of every M.D. in the world, she would be the one. For sure the combination of her and Mr. Dr.

Keefe is better than I could have hoped for. I get them as a team, too, because my injury involves both their areas of specialty.

"You'll be seeing my husband again next," Mrs. Dr. Keefe says. "He's going to tell you about a special procedure that you need. He's one of the few people in the world who can do it."

In truth, I think he actually helped develop a new way to get deep into the front of people's heads without leaving a mark on their faces. In my case, he can go after a piece of shrapnel sitting on my optic nerve behind the left eyeball and, as a bonus, not make me any uglier than I already am.

Mr. Dr. Keefe's operation on me will rate mention in a medical journal article he co-authors called "Use of Image Guided Systems in the Reconstruction of the Periorbital Region."

Putting it in jarhead terms in our pre-op briefing, Mr. Dr. Keefe tells April and me that the shrapnel is serrated like a saw blade, and, since it pushes against the nerve bundle that carries all visual information from eyeball to brain, we've got a bad thing waiting to happen.

The doc outlines his plan: The target—the shrapnel—has already been located and marked with the cat scan. Tomorrow, using sort of a high tech micro-drain snake with a camera on it, he'll go in through my upper jaw, grab the shrapnel and pull it out, then fill in the hole the shrapnel made with some sort of skull bondo.

"Without this, you will certainly go blind. Sooner or later, it's going to happen. But it's also possible the operation will blind you," Mr. Dr. Keefe tells me. But he makes it all sound easy, like he does this every morning before breakfast.

What are we waiting for? That thing has to come out so I can get my life back, get on a tank. That night April and I talk about everything but the operation. What's the point of bringing it up? The deal is done. If you think about it, this isn't any different from every one of my nights going back to the moment I went into the Sunni Triangle two months ago, or the earlier deployments. All the time, bad guys were racking their brains trying to figure out how to kill me. Every second of every day, I could die. Tomorrow I could go blind. If I let downside what-ifs eat at me, I would have gone nuts a long time ago. Second-guessing would have driven me nuts, too. Use sound judgment to make timely decisions and live with the results.

If I couldn't do that, I'd be a substandard Marine.

Day Three at Balboa

No chow in the morning. No water either. To make things more entertaining I tell a few jokes before the anesthesiologist knocks me out. Since females are present I use my best non-dirty material, like this: Did you hear about the snail who got mugged by a gang of four turtles? When the cop takes a report, the snail says, "I don't know what happened, Officer. It was all so fast."

Okay, it's stupid. At the time, though, I wonder why nobody in the room laughs. Since my other jokes are worse, they probably can't wait until I go under.

Next thing, I gag on a breathing tube coming out of my throat and look at the medical people crowded around the bed I lie in, everybody leaning in and staring, holding their breath. I have no idea why. Give me a clue, people. Are life's great questions about to be answered? Are you watching a mystery movie on my forehead, and the killer is about to be unveiled? Whatever it is, I want in.

"Can you see me?" Mr. Dr. Keefe asks.

"Sure."

He puts his hand up close to my face and asks, "How many fingers am I holding up?"

"Three."

What an odd question.

He immediately runs out of the room, while other people relax and go about their business, like some unheard voice said, "Carry on." Whatever they were waiting for, they got it.

And now I get it. Holy shit, I still can see. Not only that, I can see better than before, with colors and no fading in and out. The room's dark as night, and if my TV had a picture this bad I'd scrap it, but every dim smear and blur is beautiful because I can make things out. The white blotch there is a doctor in a lab coat, I see a rectangular cutout I know is a door and the curtains by my bed.

If I look, I see. Give this a ten on the thrill scale.

When Mr. Dr. Keefe charges back into the room, it's hard to tell who's more fired-up, him or me.

"I can see the clock on the wall!" I tell him, and he beams like a human Christmas tree, then gets down to business, telling me to look up, look down, follow a flashlight beam with my eye.

Two nights ago, as I write this, April and Nicholas and I ate dinner at the Keefe's home and we relived all this together. Mr. Dr. Keefe tells me something I never would have guessed at the time. All I got from him then was confidence, but he felt the crushing burden placed on his shoulders, taking on the responsibility for another man's eyesight, which is really the man's future.

Before the operation, he prayed to God to guide his hands.

11

Two Nine

April 25, 2004
0100 Local
Marine Corps Air-Ground Combat Center, Twentynine Palms, California

If day looks like night, night throws a black bag over my head, but coming up to the First Tank Battalion grinder—parade ground to you civilians—I make out floodlights and hear the diesel generators roar. A setup like this after midnight means a unit's getting ready to deploy, working into the wee hours packing fly-in echelon gear to take to the fight.

"Who's leaving?" I ask the sergeant bringing April and me home from San Diego.

No response. He pulls into the lit-up area, where I see silhouettes, at least a hundred bodies out there. Now I know for sure they're shipping out soon. If not tonight, tomorrow.

The driver slides the van hatch open.

"This is for you, Gunny," he says.

What the hell's he talking about? What's for me?

As my foot hits the deck, one of the silhouettes comes up close. "Welcome home, Gunny," he says. Wait, I know that voice. The guys on the grinder must be going right now, because this man is the Battalion Six, Colonel Chartier, CO of First Tanks. As the colonel shakes my hand, the night fills with sound that drowns out the generators. Horns blare and drums bang out the most thrilling six seconds of music that I know of. Thunder-claps of sound with trumpet fanfares in between, everything getting louder and gaining power. Even if you never wore a uniform or heard our song before, you'd know these notes are the prelude of something very important. Something huge is about to happen, and you want to get on your feet and be part of it.

After the intro, the band launches into The Marines' Hymn. Thirty-some of our base musicians, who would otherwise be in the rack, stand out in the desert night and play the living hell out of the most stirring song in the world.

This really is for me. The band plays for Marines coming back, not going away.

If ever I hear our Hymn and fail to come to the position of attention with the words to the song ringing in my head, box me up and ship me home. No, come to think of it, it'll still do the same great things for me when I'm dead. Like the lines from the final verse say, "The streets of heaven are guarded by United States Marines."

And every time the song plays, those Marines stand among us. Leathernecks. Devil Dogs. Warriors who never knew defeat going back 230 years. Kicking the shit out of the Barbary pirates. Running toward German machine guns in Belleau Wood. Landing on the beach at Tarawa. Names of men, battles, hallowed places sound in the head and heart. Chesty Puller at Chosin Reservoir. The grunts dug-in at Khe Sahn. Guys, sung and unsung, putting their asses on the line right now. The big things Marines have done and do to this day make each of us bigger. The strength of the Marine is the Corps, and the strength of the Corps is the Marine. These aren't just words. Men fight and die because they refuse to be anything less than Marines and do all that our great tradition requires. This is why I've got to get fixed so I can go back where I belong.

Any jarhead worth a damn, past or present, knows that my feelings are just as I express them and that he or she would feel the same way at such a moment.

The instant the band finishes, I call over, "Hey, that's my favorite song. Can you play it again?" To my everlasting gratitude, they give us an encore while I receive another gift I will never forget. The battalion commander guides me forward to where, in formation, stand the four platoons that make up Bravo Company, First Tank Battalion. Most of them I know because I deployed and fought with them a year ago. Bravo Company spearheaded the First Marine Division's advance to Baghdad during Operation Iraqi Freedom. In a week the unit will go back. Not a man here doesn't have someplace better to be—at home with the wife and kids, on the town with buddies on a last night of liberty, getting some rack time because these pre-deployment days of theirs are long and will get longer. What nobody has to spare is time, and that's just what the tankers of Bravo Company give to me. This is one of the most moving moments of my life.

And I'm not the only one who gets something out of the experience. The next morning one of the musicians will compose a letter. About me she writes:

> As we play, he stands tall. At this point he makes his way past the four platoons of Marines waiting to welcome him home. He slowly feels his way along each 1st squad, stopping to shake hands and receive hugs from some of the Marines. He comes back toward the band and we can see his sore and swollen face. With an incredible air of thanks and pride, this GySgt . . . again gives us gratitude. Love for the Corps, our country, and life itself radiated through every movement he made, every word he spoke.

She goes on to write that three Marines from our base will die in combat on this same night, and concludes that seeing me, in my condition, makes the ultimate sacrifice those guys made seem more real.

I worry about making risk and loss a little too real for one small group that turns out to welcome me. After I shake the band-members' hands I come to maybe ten wives, some holding babies, whose husbands belong to Charley Company, the unit I just left behind in Iraq. Probably they're here as much for April's sake as they are for mine. They've been at her side since I first got wounded. Much as I appreciate that they're here, I'd really rather they didn't see my combat injuries up close. I don't want to add to their burdens. I don't want somebody's wife thinking of her Marine getting shot up or killed.

However, I never give a thought to demoralizing Team Bravo, the company that greets me on the grinder. At least half these men have seen combat, and I don't worry about the others because Marines prepare for the grim realities from minute one of Boot Camp. Recruits call their clothing bags body bags, and if the drill instructor calls the name of a guy who's out of the platoon for any reason, everybody yells out "Dead, Sir!" I used to make an outline on the deck when we dropped a recruit, like that's where the body was found. Constant First Aid training, which continues after Boot Camp, hammers into us the correct field fixes for sucking chest wounds, arterial bleeding, and guts hanging out of an open abdominal wound. If you don't get that you could be maimed or killed in our line of work, you're just unbelievably stupid. I get so pissed off when some Marine telling war stories whines about the realities, like they're a big traumatic surprise. What do they think goes on out there?

If somebody in Bravo Company gets scared by seeing me, there's no sign of it in the bull session that follows dismissal of the formation. For another couple hours we yack in the company offices with a lot of laughing and no more dramatics than as if I'm telling guys about a particularly successful hunting or fishing trip, except the deer and the walleyes are enemy fighters. The idea that there's a lot of them and that they shoot back thrills the hell out of everyone present.

To a Marine, the scary scenario would be flying that far and finding out nobody wants to fight.

12

Home

Damn near dawn and a mile and a half from the grinder, I pass through a door and cease to be a Gunnery Sergeant. The property and I belong to the Corps, but different rules apply in the Popaditch family base house, 3202-D Ludwig Court. Things go on here that I would not tolerate anywhere else. Second-guessing, challenging authority, personal dramatics, keeping me out of the loop. And I love it. I wouldn't have it any other way because the people who live here are not Marines, they're April and Nicholas, and with them I am husband and father and Nick.

Home, home, home. Sleeping next to April and down the hall from my boy's room. The one place on earth I walk barefoot. My own shower. Faucets where I can get a drink without calling for a nurse. And the good vibes, the things that happened here—say "Club Pop" to staff NCOs at Two Nine, and they'll know you mean my garage, all-rank Jarhead heaven, scene of countless hours of shooting pool and shooting the breeze. Most important, though, here is a place where there are no hidden mysteries, where I can't get lost. Here, memories will serve as my eyes.

We decide not to pull our 10-year-old out of the rack at this hour, so we let Nicholas keep sleeping at the home of friends on the base who took care of him while we were at Balboa hospital. April and I come in and turn on every lamp and overhead fixture in the house. It's still dim, which disappoints me but doesn't put a dent in my morale. The docs told me to expect this. My wife and I go through our home room by room. Wherever I expect something to be, there it is, and sameness gives me comfort and reassurance that I, too, will be the same. In fact, I feel more the same already.

But this is not the old Nick Popaditch lying down on the king bed next to his gorgeous wife April. Much as I want to roll over and throw an arm around her, dizziness says to stay absolutely still. And I'm not so cool with her touching me because she might get hurt. Slivers of shrapnel poking out of my forehead snag the pillowcase, like I'm a werewolf growing steel hairs. This, on top of the three-week beard and scratchy stitches and blood and whatever else is coming out of the empty eye socket and shrapnel holes and sometimes my nose and mouth. I didn't sweat the leakage before, because hospital linens are supposed to get messy. Here, though, I don't want to stain April's good stuff.

All the little things add up. I can't see the clock to tell what time it is. Quiet and darkness, which used to be a good thing, creep me out. I don't much like how I feel, but nothing in the world will keep me from falling asleep.

13

Get Up, Get Out

Doped-up and tired as I am, I'd sleep through somebody banging on a bass drum in the bedroom. But then a sound I've been waiting to hear—my son's voice—wakes me in a flash.

"Hi, Dad. How are you feeling? Are you okay?"

"Yeah," I say. "I feel great."

A small part of the "great" is me being Dad. A 10-year-old takes his cues from his father; if I'm cool with this, he will be, too. The bigger deal, though, is how great it is to be with him.

"Hey, I hear you're playing Little League," I say.

"Yeah."

"What position?"

"Centerfield."

"How are you hitting?"

"Okay."

From the way he says it, I know he needs some instruction and practice. I do a little catch-up fathering, asking if he has been helping his Mom around the house, keeping up with his schoolwork, and cleaning his room. Except for the fact that I'm sitting on the bed and see only a dim silhouette, our talk goes down familiar paths. A little father-son reconnecting, that's all—it wouldn't be any different if I were coming home after a couple weeks of gunnery. This is what we do, going away and getting back together, and we're good at it, the boy as much as his parents. In his world, kids whose Dads don't leave home for extended periods are odd. Today he acts same-old, same-old, making me so happy that I'm still Dad even this screwed-up. Later I find out he's happy that I still look like Dad to him. He prepared himself for a horror show. Thanks to Hollywood and video games, a kid this age has no trouble visualizing gore and human monstrosities.

A few hours later, my older boy, Rich, arrives from San Diego. April has asked him to stay for a few days to provide brotherly support to Nick. Surprisingly, the 20-year-old takes my condition way harder. He tries to keep it to himself, but I can tell he's crying. This makes sense, because an older individual sees the reality of the situation and understands we may be looking at serious lifelong impacts on us all, whereas Nicholas will be more guided by me. But damn, it is good to have Rich home, too. Four of us under one roof, all present and accounted for. We are complete.

Once we're done talking, I go back to sleep and sleep almost round-the-clock for the next few days, with interruptions mostly to eat and relocate from my primary sleeping position, the bed, to alternates like the couch and the recliner chair. The household runs smoothly and on schedule without me, as it has for the past three months. April and Nicholas would have gone on just fine if I had stayed away for the rest of my eight-month deployment. As I said, this is what we do. So nobody especially misses my active participation. In truth, the Marine husband and father disrupts the daily routine when he first comes back home from a deployment, so maybe having me in hibernation actually makes things easier.

A few visitors bring on my most extended periods of wakefulness. One impression in particular cuts through the mental fog. Damn, Eva Chartier, the battalion commander's wife, can cook. She comes by with another Marine's wife, bringing a pot of absolutely outstanding spaghetti with red sauce, thus establishing a pattern: Females like to feed wounded Marines. I love it.

What I'm not so crazy about is the universal male response, which is to hug me. Where this comes from, I have no idea. The guys really feel the need, though. They think they're communicating something important, but what it is I have no clue.

Nobody in his right mind would have hugged Gunny Pop a month ago, guaranteed. If anybody would ask first now, I'd say, "Can't we just shake hands?" They don't ask though; they just do it. When I later start to brief wounded guys, I warn them about this.

As soon as the visitors leave, I conk out again. At first I think being Rip Van Winkle promotes the healing process. It doesn't take long, though, before I get concerned. By day three I do what I did back on Bonecrusher when I wanted more than anything in the world to go to sleep. The Gunny in my head yells, Get up, Marine, Get on your feet and get out of this house. This shit won't do you a bit of good. But this raises the question, Get up and do what? Take the Suzuki out for a ride? Go shoot hoops? Take in a movie? If I stay within my capabilities I might be able to find my way to the park and sit on a bench, but that's just a hard kind of couch, and sure as hell I would fall asleep again. There's one place, and one place only, where I have to go, which is right back into a billet, a job. Time to rejoin the team.

April, probably against her better judgement, helps get me cleaned up to go back to work. She has to bypass sutures and open wounds like my face and neck are minefields. Running clippers over my head is pretty much a monkey screwing a football. I'm so freaked out about clippings falling onto my wounds that I lean way back, which brings on uncontrollable dizziness. Meanwhile, we both try to take command of the operation. One of the interesting things about my marriage is that April is every bit as alpha as I am. It works for us, in spite of the occasional clash of wills.

I doubt she recognizes this, but love for my wife and Nicholas and our beautiful home makes me more impatient to get out of the house. I love these people too much to be a fifth wheel and pain in the ass who starts to wear on them. And I love home too much to let it become my prison.

14

Marine Thing

"What are you doing here, Gunny?"

"Reporting for duty. I'm here to work."

"Weren't you authorized convalescence leave?"

"Yeah, but I'm waiting 'til I see better so I can really enjoy it."

Whatever surprise Sergeant Major Reed might feel, looking at my busted-up mug in his office at Zero-Nine four days after I get back to the base, doesn't show. I say this from knowing, not actual visual confirmation. Shut one eye and squint the other to the last possible fraction of a millimeter before it's actually closed, and you get an idea of what I see. To capture the sight picture even more accurately, you should also shut off the lights and pull down the blinds. The only reason I'm confident about the ID, is who the hell else would dare to be in the office of the Senior Enlisted Advisor to our Battalion Commander? I get further confirmation from the height and bulk of the blur in front of me. Sgt Maj Reed is built like the proverbial brick shit house, in this case a two-story unit. Throw in a Brooklyn street-fighter manner of speaking, and you've got a man designed by nature to scare the hell out of lesser ranks.

On the other hand he stands by his Marines and does right by them— witness how he goes out of his way to accommodate my obvious need to make myself useful.

"Let me call over to the BAS and make sure they didn't screw this up and run you as being on leave now," he says. This doesn't register at the time, but the Battalion Aid Station probably has nothing to do with my current status.

"Get the chief over here ASAP," the Sergeant Major says into the phone. Given who called you, know the Chief, the Naval equivalent to a Gunny who's in charge of our unit's medical corpsmen, comes running.

At this point April peeks in. She drove me to the office and then stuck around in case I got sent right back home. Seeing her, the Sergeant Major stands and greets April like the gentlemanly family friend that he is to her and other Marine wives. When our company deployed, the battalion big shots became the go-to people for spouses and children.

"Is there anything we can do for you?" he asks April.

He means it, too. If she said we haven't had time to get to the commissary he'd write down items we need. If the washer went bust he'd find a Marine who used to be a Maytag man and send him over. The brotherhood thing is for real. Believe it.

The Sergeant Major excuses himself to step out with the chief, like April and I don't need to be bothered with their trivial business. Then they both come back in.

"How you doing, Gunny?" the Chief asks.

"Outstanding. Good to go."

"How's that eye?"

"Getting better every day."

After a little more conversation the Chief takes off, and the Sergeant Major reaches for the phone, saying, "Let me get the Master Gunns down here."

Now we're getting somewhere. He means Master Gunnery Sergeant Dangerfield, Top Dangerfield for short, the Operations Chief for the First Tank Battalion. If I were able-bodied and checking in for duty, this would be the man I would see because he assigns our billets. Since he works down the hall, Top Dangerfield arrives quickly, and we pretty much replay the previous conversations.

"What are you going to do with Gunny Pop?" the Sergeant Major asks.

After maybe half a minute Top says, "I'll put him to work with me in the Three Shop."

Hey, it's a start. In other circumstances I'd be pissed about being a Pogue riding a desk and pushing paper in S-3, designation for the battalion operations section, which organizes and coordinates all the steps necessary to accomplish any given mission, anything from attacking Baghdad to putting together a battalion PT, Physical Training, run. Below the S-3 operations officer and Top, who are mission-critical fighting Marines, this means banging out a bazillion LOIs, or Letters Of Instruction. Out in the field the enlisted men provide security to the Ops-O and Operation Chief and monitor communications when the bosses are asleep. Basically you're a secretary in the rear and an armed receptionist in the field. It's important, and somebody's got to do it, and I don't mind if it's me until such time as I'm fit to get back on a tank.

I kiss April goodbye and go with Top to the 3-Shop where his desk sits out in the open marked with a sign that reads, "Military Historical Exhibit," a smartass way to proclaim that Top's pushing fifty, ancient for an active-duty Marine. On the other hand, he could run most young, in-shape guys into the ground and teach them a trick or two about unarmed combat. In the Corps, old means tough, salty, and wise, not over the hill.

It's traditional, at this point, for a boss to explain the responsibilities of a newly assigned billet and arrange for any necessary training, but we're of one mind about what I'm really doing here. Top, who speaks in a courtly Southern accent says, "Gunny, I'm not going to bother teaching you any clerical stuff. Your number-one mission is to get yourself fixed so I can put you back on a tank."

"But what am I supposed to do until then?"

"You're a Gunny. Do what Gunnys do. Supervise Marines."

"But there are no Marines in here for me to supervise."

"Exactly."

I get it. He wants me to rove and improve performance. Obviously I can't work on the tanks, but I can work on Marines. For years my units have used me as a hammer, and a hammer doesn't need eyes to come down hard and make a lot of noise. Top doesn't assign me a desk. Instead I get an inbox and my name on the signout board in case anybody wants to know where to find me.

Friday flies by, and I'm back at home for the weekend. But this time I'm wide awake. The job does me more good than my daily truckload of pharmaceuticals. With a purpose in life and somewhere to go come Monday, down time with April and Nick and Rich is a reward, not a sentence.

We see here the Marine mind-set in action. Mind over matter. Whenever we encounter a physical limit, we push through it and come out the other side, thus discovering capabilities we never knew we had. Positive mental attitude rules in our world. If you cramp up on a PT run, you push through it, telling yourself, "It's no big deal. I'm not hurt. Keep running."

You do the same in combat, saying, "I'm not tired. I can go another six hours. I'm not scared. Move out. Rush, rush!" If somebody asks how you're doing, you say "Good to go" no matter what. We don't even have expressions for "So so," or "Could be better," or any other downside comebacks.

So when I say to my two leaders that my vision's better than it really is, and that it's getting better even though I have yet to see meaningful improvement, they know exactly what I'm doing. They get it.

They also get that they are in a position to do me a huge favor by providing me with a billet, even if it's a little too early and it involves some risk for them. Looking back, I can imagine what goes through the Sergeant Major's mind when this one-eyed unserviceable Gunny reports for duty. Obviously he uses the nonsense about leave status to buy time to figure things out. And he calls in the Chief from BAS to get better situational awareness about my medical condition. Without showing any cards, he asks himself what's at stake here.

Will Gunny Pop set back his recovery if we let him stay?

Is he a danger to himself?

Will he get run over in the parking lot or brained with a traversing main gun on the tank ramp?

Every year we break a lot of fully sighted Marines down there, so what will happen to a blind man possibly addled by medication?

These aren't small questions. If something does go wrong, the Sergeant Major will be accountable. I know, though, that he does not make that part of the equation. What he does, he does for my sake and the sake of the Corps, as does Top Dangerfield.

Sooner or later the Top's Major could conceivably say, "Why did you bring this guy in, instead of an able-bodied Marine?

Is this a good precedent?

Are you showing this Gunny preferential treatment?"

With the wrong kind of officer, I could be trouble to this man who goes out on a limb to help. But both of my leaders see what I need and provide it, even though the most expedient and trouble-free move would be to send me home and let me drive April crazy. But they take the high road and hard road, and they'd do the same thing for a private.

It's not a Gunny Pop thing, it's a Marine thing, which makes it all the more right. Oorah, for sure. Semper Fi.

And thanks.

15

Home Front

Negative about memory and eyesight. One does not sub in for the other. April removes breakables from all surfaces within arm's reach. Thank God we don't have little ones or I'd be picking pieces of toys out of my feet if not stepping on the kids themselves.

I chase and dodge shadows because all dark blurs look solid. Interesting thing about doorways: Though I know where they are, the door itself blends in, and partly opened it becomes a booby trap. Reaching out and feeling nothing, I charge ahead and smash into the door's edge. This isn't so bad with room doors, because the whole body takes the impact. Cabinet doors at head level hurt like a bastard, though, just like an open drawer down by my shins.

But, like we say on the drill field, pain retains. Stimulus response and muscle memory worked for Pavlov's dog, and they work for me. Good thing I'm a Marine, because I understand the power of developing a system and following unvarying procedures and routines. And extreme anal retentiveness becomes a blessing. If something goes here, that's where it goes. Within about 72 hours, I have a detailed load plan for the entire house and I have mentally written a TM—Technical Manual—for pretty much everything.

Operate The Kitchen Stove Under Usual Conditions.

Step A: Approach the stove moving hand in sweeping motion below waist level to make contact with oven door rather than stove top.

Step B: Upon contact, orient yourself centered on the stove, which is at 12 o'clock position and approximately one foot distant from the operator.

Step C: Check all control knobs to ensure that they are at the 12 o'clock (off) position.

Step D: Sweep hand at neck level above stove top to detect presence of heat and possible burning hazard.

Step E: If heat is not felt, the stove is clear and prepared for operation. If heat is felt, proceed to following section.

Meanwhile indigenous friendlies cause problems without meaning to. When April sees me bump into something she immediately puts it somewhere else. Her heart's in the right place here, but she guarantees a future collision with the same object because now I don't know where it is. Meanwhile I deny myself the safe path she clears because I mark it off limits. So I fight in a constantly changing battlefield. As usual, communications would clear it all up. If I said out loud, "Now I know where this thing is. And I'm not going to forget because my knee hurts like hell," April undoubtedly would let it sit.

I'm lucky in our climactic environment, the Mojave Desert, because the sun beats down on Twentynine Palms pretty much constantly at a wattage so high it cuts through some of the darkness in my vision. At first full daylight April and I throw up the blinds on every window. I love going outside where I enjoy better eyesight than anywhere else. I can see just well enough to get around on my own. Independent mobility! And my world grows a little bit every day.

I start walking the mile-and-a-half to work, turning down lifts from pretty much everybody who passes by me in a car. Even those with no idea about my sight make the offer because that's the thing to do when you see a Marine walking here in the desert. I'd do it, too, and I understand and appreciate such helpfulness. But I wish the Marines I know, seeing me for the first time since I got back, didn't feel the need to jump out and hug me. If a car pulls to the shoulder, I know it's just a ride offer. But if it pulls clean off the road, I prepare for the manly embrace.

Really, brother, it's okay. Stay in the car and we'll just talk.

Ten days home, I start to run.

Two weeks home, I hit the weight room. Mr. Dr. Keefe tells me to take it easy for a while so I don't blow the eye out of the socket that he bondoed in for me at Balboa or otherwise undo his good work.

I could get a driver from the base for the weekly trips to see the docs at Balboa, but I figure, hey, let's get some fun out of this. Why not make it a mini-vacation? So once a week April drives the 350-mile round trip, and we usually overnight in order to play tourist and visit with my stepson Rich, who lives on his own in San Diego. I especially like staying at the transient quarters available to us for $25 a night at the Marine Corps Recruit Depot, San Diego, aka Boot Camp, where I spent three happy years yelling in young guys' faces and transforming raw material into Marines. I loved being a hat, a Drill Instructor, almost as much as I loved combat. They both either bring out the best in you or break you.

I know the Depot so well that I can take off on my own. How great it is to walk around early in the morning, thousands of human voices echoing from the squad bays and training areas. Drill Instructors shout out commands, like cracking whips with their voices, and the recruits shout back what we call isms, verbal responses that permanently program in the proper reactions to commands. It all begins here, the inner sanctum, center of our world. Here I first came into the world as a Marine, doing my own Boot Camp twelve years before I earned the campaign cover and saw it all from the other side. I'm much more at home here than in East Chicago, Indiana, where I was born.

Back at Two Nine, the escalating conflict in Iraq makes my fresh information a very valuable commodity, and I work the Guru side of the Gunnery Sergeant role, briefing hundreds of guys on the evolving tactical situation. In and out of classrooms and formal training sessions I give anybody who asks the benefit of my recent experience, which Marines preparing for second deployments need every bit as much as boots.

A sample of the World According to Pop:

1) Go after the enemy at night, which truly does belong to us. The bad guys have lousy night vision, and they have no idea how good ours is. They lack the discipline, command, and communication for night operations. They also really enjoy their sleep. Between 2200 and 0400 they're mostly racked out with no sentries.

2) The enemy gets brave when you're leaving. If you want to draw them out of cover, back up as if you're retrograding and they'll come out of the woodwork to take shots, thereby giving you somebody to attack.

3) Don't let the bad guys bait you into firing at innocents. Engaging you from crowds is one of the enemy's go-to plays. If you lose discipline and shoot, you become the enemy's recruiter. If you hold fire and control the area, citizens will become allies and point out the shooter in their midst.

4) Perception is critical to victory. See yourself through Iraqi eyes. Would you get behind the force that acts belligerent and scared, or the guys who appear powerful and in control?

5) Face-to-face with an Iraqi, always act like a friend, but have a plan to kill him before he can kill you.

6) Leaders should dumb down the rules of engagement, which are ridiculously complex, so the Marines under their command don't get confused and become afraid to act. The idea of making a mistake scares guys a hell of a lot more than the enemy.

Funny that nobody says, "Why should we listen to you, Gunny? You're a living example of what not to do. You got popped." But the Marines treat my wounds as badges of honor and authority. I've got a hundred pointers, and I love giving them in the simplest, most direct possible language, relating everything to something even the lowest-rank boot already knows. I've got a golden opportunity here to let some light into the swamp, making sense of the overload of complicated info that we get before we cross the border into Iraq.

The other truths that need to be told involve how well we're doing over there. The Marines love hearing about the great deeds I saw their brothers in arms perform on the battlefield. The skill, the courage, all their training paying off, just like it will pay off for the guys about to deploy. I tell them about the fight before I got hit, then my crew coming through for me, the medical corpsmen risking their lives, shot-up guys in the hospital who can't wait to get back to the Sunni Triangle. The Marines at Two Nine really love to hear how we're kicking the shit out of the bad guys, and doing a lot of good as well. Even deep in the heart of Fallujah, the everyday Iraqi Moe doesn't hate us a bit, I say. I could still get off Bonecrusher and shake hands. However, people can't be so openly pro-American any more because the bad guys might find out and retaliate. Piss off the wrong people, and the wolves come after wives and kids and parents and even grandparents. All this stuff is huge for the Two Nine Marines, because protecting the innocent against predators is a one hundred percent Marine mission, and something that does us all honor.

Guys seem surprised to hear all this good news. Just like members of the public, they get most of what they know from the mainstream media, which dishes up a steady diet of bad news and political blah, blah, blah, with no hint of the successes I saw every day.

I love motivating Marines. I love being a fog-cutter. For the time being I can't kill bad guys, but helping the guys who will is the next best thing.

16

Going Public

A Marine comes walking into S-3. At close range hair and stature show this to be a female. Undoubtedly she's here on some sort of S-3-related business and comes to me assuming I have a supervisory role in actual office matters.

"What do you need, Marine?" I say.

"I need to talk to you, Gunny."

"State your business," I say, trying to seem Gunny-like even though there's no way in hell I can competently respond concerning 3-Shop matters. I'll get her what she needs, though, because every Marine deserves an answer.

"I'm Sgt. Haskamp from the base public affairs office," she says.

"And?"

"We want to interview you for a story."

"Why me?"

"Because you've got a story to tell."

"A lot of guys have a story to tell."

"We want to tell yours."

If public affairs had sent anybody else, you wouldn't be reading about what happened next, because it wouldn't have happened. But Sgt. Jennie Haskamp knows exactly how to reason with a trigger-pulling male Marine without pretending to be one of us as she-dudes in the Corps sometimes do. She is simply a no-fooling female who speaks our language and conducts herself in a thoroughly professional and forceful manner. Once she starts talking, I realize we've crossed paths before.

Sgt. Haskamp conducted a pre-deployment media brief for Charlie Company before my last pump to Iraq. She stood in front of a room full of tankers, most of whom went in thinking media training is bullshit, and at least some of whom would be disinclined to take a female seriously, and established right off the bat that she was the duty expert and a for-real sergeant. Every single man present went away knowing that media relations is an important tactical consideration. Say or do something stupid in front of a reporter, and you do as much damage to the Corps and the cause as if you fell asleep on post. They're both the same sort of mistake, brought on by lack of discipline. And they have the same end result, which is to fuck over everybody else.

As I'm about to find out, Sgt. Haskamp takes the fight to one Marine as well as a roomful.

Concerning the interview, I say, "I don't think so."

"Every bad story gets told, Gunny," she says.

Have to agree with her there.

"You've got a good story, and you don't want to tell it," she says.

"Talk to somebody else. I don't want that kind of attention."

And I don't, either. To my mind she's asking me to be this asshole I don't want to be. Every media interview that I've seen from this war spotlights some guy six terrain features back from the action talking stuff like, "Yeah, we're really taking the fight to them!" They never get the guy who's in the fight. I was that guy, for sure, but this is ten thousand miles away and a month later. I don't want the attention this far from Iraq. I can't stand prima donnas. Sorry, sergeant, you're talking to the wrong guy.

"It's not about you, Gunny," she says. "It's about your crew, the Marines you fought with, the Corpsmen who saved your life, the doctors, the hospital personnel, the other wounded Marines. If you don't want to tell your story, tell theirs."

Having overrun my defenses, she has nothing to do but hoist the flag. Definitely not the outcome I expected, but instead of appealing to any sense of ego or need for attention, she speaks directly to my sense of right and wrong and our core values. In her I recognize another true believer. Refusal to do what she asks would let down my fellow Marines every bit as much as refusing some other unpleasant duty. Suck it up, Gunny. She doesn't say it in so many words, but she doesn't need to.

"What do you need me to do?" I ask.

Sgt. Haskamp knows I would never refuse an opportunity to help my fellow Marines and The Corps. What's a little more personal discomfort and embarrassment, anyway? For us, that starts in Boot Camp and never stops.

My first media exposure involves talking to Sgt. Haskamp, who reports for the base newspaper as part of her duties. Shortly thereafter the PAO office gets contacted by the boxing promoter Don King, who wants to make some of the Marines from our base guests of honor at the World Light Heavyweight Boxing Championships, Roy Jones Jr. versus Antonio Tarver at Mandalay Bay in Las Vegas. Sgt. Haskamp shotguns the whole thing, making sure that invitations go out to Marines just back from Iraq and not base guys. Never will I forget taking a call at home from Don King himself extending a personal invitation.

"I'll introduce you to the Mandalay Bay," he says on the phone.

I think he means showing me around the hotel and casino, or, more likely, having a staffer do it. But he surprises the hell out of me by having me brought to the ring just before the title fight. Michael Buffer, who is known to fans everywhere, makes an introduction that starts, "Now, ladies and gentleman, it is my pleasure to introduce to you a man who can be recognized as a true world heavyweight champion . . . " People would be charged up by now, anyway, just before the main event, and this patriotic moment pushes them over the edge. When the commotion dies down, I present Don King with a plaque expressing our thanks. All told, 200 Marines get great seats, the cheapest of which has a $400 face value.

It doesn't get any cooler than this. After the fight, we circulate around Mandalay Bay, where all the guys from Two Nine get star treatment. On this night, no Marine waits in line for anything.

Later in May, Sgt. Haskamp calls and asks if I'm ready to do another interview, this time for television.

"Okay, where do I do need to be and when?"

"The CNN crew will meet you on the tank ramp at 0800," she says.

The sergeant tells me that the crew is filming for a segment called "Heroes" on the Lou Dobbs show. Now I really do have second thoughts. Overuse of the H-word—so cheapened by now that we ought to outlaw using it for at least ten years—happens to be a pet peeve. And, as ever, I dislike being singled out.

Next morning I show up on the tank ramp bound and determined to talk about anything but myself. First I walk the TV crew around an M1A1, telling how the bad guys have no answer for it. Take this tank into the fight, and they have no way to get it out. Then I show the CNN people around the ramp and introduce them to some of the tank crews and mechs. Finally, during the Q and A with me, I focus on the great successes I saw in Iraq, the courage of others, and the fantastic quality of medical care that I receive. Meanwhile I downplay my wounds and tell them my sole intention is to get back onto one of these iron monsters and back into the fight.

Not long afterward I do a repeat with another crew shooting for Inside Edition. Hey, this isn't so bad. Why would a guy who had RPGs pointed at him get nervous in front of a TV camera? And it dawns on me that people who tune in will forget my name thirty seconds after the text disappears off the screen. To viewers I'm every Marine, period—it really isn't about me. But this weighs a lot heavier than any worries about looking like an egotistical jackass. If—like guys I've seen—I come across as a show-off and phony, speaking lines straight out of "Full Metal Jacket" and "Platoon," or expound on subjects way beyond my area of operations or say things that bring dishonor to the Corps and our mission, people around the water cooler the next morning are not going to say, "Hey, did you see that Nick Popaditch on TV last night? What a dumbass." I could live with that. But no, they're going to say, "Hey, did you see that Marine? Those guys are dumbasses." That I cannot live with. On the other hand, if I do it right, they might say, "Did you see that Marine who got shot in Iraq? Those guys over there really believe in what they're doing." Some might think, "Maybe I should believe in it, too." That is my target, my end-state, my victory.

The more I get it, the more I feel how high the stakes really are. If we lose this war, it'll be because people lose faith, even while we defeat the enemy on the battlefield. If I had any hair, I'd be pulling it out over the disconnect between what I saw in Iraq and people back here talking defeat and surrender.

A leader of Marines whom I greatly admire, General James N. Mattis, told us to share our courage with the world. I get a similar message from my battalion commander Colonel Chartier after he presents me with my Purple Heart. After the ceremony he takes me aside and tells me to keep doing the public affairs stuff.

"I know you don't like it," the Colonel says, "but it's good for the Corps. It's not for long, anyway. Pretty soon the next group of guys will be back, and your fifteen minutes of fame will be done."

This is a highly original Marine colonel. Think Woody Allen in uniform, all wound up with that same New York-ish accent and no tolerance for those who lose their heads under pressure. For them he has merciless ridicule, which is often really funny. A few of us used to get big laughs repeating Chartier lines. My personal favorite: "What's next, locusts?" spoken after a horrendous sandstorm in Southern Iraq that stopped our division in its tracks.

But the colonel misses the mark with his fifteen minute prediction. Three years later I still do public appearances and cooperate when media people seek me out, which now and again they do, and I still do it for the same reasons. The media come to me, I think, because I don't just mouth all this good stuff about the Corps and our war effort. I mean it. People know bullshit when they hear it. When Sgt. Haskamp offers to let me know what press people are going to ask before interviews, I turn her down, telling her I'm a better Marine than an actor. I want to speak from the heart, not recite lines. Getting tripped-up or tricked is never a worry for me, because I stay in my lane, sticking strictly to what I know and what I believe.

There is a side issue concerning public attention that gets to me. A Marine would rather be remembered for the fights that he won and his contributions to greater victories. But I become a Poster Casualty, better known for getting shot than shooting 200-odd enemies. I know this oversimplifies, because people focus on my fight back from disabling wounds as a way to honor the thousands of veterans in the same situation, many of whom have much tougher fights than I do.

Still, it bugs me to be remembered for the one gunfight I lost.

17

FX

If I had gotten killed in Iraq, I'd want a memorial service just like this one for a captain from Two Nine who died in combat in Al Anbar Province within a few weeks of my return.

They hold his service in the base Catholic chapel, which is packed with Marines and wives, kids, family, and friends. Obviously this was a well-liked and respected company commander. All of us in the Corps wear dress blue deltas, blue trousers and pressed khaki shirts like recruiters wear. Trousers worn by NCOs and officers bear the blood stripe, a vertical band of red that is full of meaning on an occasion such as this. Our tradition holds that the stripe commemorates the Battle of Chapultapec during the Mexican War, where 80 percent of the NCOs and officers on the field were killed. The stripe signifies leading from the front whatever the risks. And the Captain we honor today did just that.

Though I don't know this man from Adam, I feel more and more like a friend. Marines who knew him get up and tell us about him, not in grand heroic terms, but about him personally, his quirks, jokes he liked to make, his habits, the things that made him both a good Marine and a good man. From the podium we get more laughter than tears, even from his family, who describe what a teddy bear and a pushover he was at home with his kids. The music, too, gives a lift. Though I'm a Protestant myself, I've got to hand it to the Catholics for having hymns with more oomph. The crowd really belts them out, too. Though April and I are pretty much strangers here, we are all united in spirit. I swear the captain himself joins us in the chapel, and he's smiling.

Moved as I am by the memorial, something darker and creepier comes into the picture for me. The light seems to bleed out of the chapel, though in fact it's brilliantly lit by sun streaming through the windows. It's like somebody slowly twists a dimmer switch toward "off." Nothing like this has happened. My changes in eyesight have all been from bad to better. And, except for my post-surgery comeback, they've happened so slowly that I have had a hard time telling that anything changed at all. Now things change faster than ever, and not for the better. This concerns me, not to the panic level, but closer than I want to get.

Is this it?

Is this fade to black?

Am I going blind right here and right now?

The dimming goes on through the end of the service, when I stand and whisper to April, "We've got to get out of here. Now."

"Nick, what's wrong?" April asks on the way out of the chapel.

"My sight. It's fading out," I say.

"Do I need to call the Keefes? Do you want to go to the base hospital?"

"No," I say, "I just want to go home and go to sleep."

Why sleep should be the fix, I don't know. But I'm sure of it. Weird thing is, sleep does correct the problem. After a couple hours dead to the world I wake up and things are back to what they were, like somebody pushed a reset button.

I still wonder what the hell happened that day. Did my sight really change at all? Or did the limitations somehow hit me new and fresh? We were seated near the back of the chapel, so maybe the effort of focusing on the front did something to my perceptions. Whatever it was, it rattled me but good.

I get other weird visual effects. On one of our drives to San Diego, I doze off then wake up suddenly and see a semi sitting crossways in the road like it jackknifed. Even knowing it isn't really there, I'm thinking that April should hit the brakes right now. God no, I don't mention such things to anybody, even April. I understand what's up, though. After 36 years of receiving full bandwidth visual input, the brain just has a hard time adjusting to the current loss of signal. It still puts up pictures where the pictures used to be. The docs call this Charles Benet Syndrome.

After a few of the full-on hallucinations, the visual tricks are scaled back. I occasionally see very elaborate mosaic patterns made up of little blue squares. To this day, I sometimes get weird flashes coming out of light sleep, like when I doze off on the San Diego trolley. It's either a white flash, like when the RPG hit, or a ball of red and orange fire. I swear my mind uses this stuff to wake me up and restore focus, like an alarm clock that makes images instead of sound.

Now that I'm thinking of it, I realize the strange brain-generated graphics go back to when I was still black blind in Germany. Wide awake in Landstuhl, I'd sometimes daydream the most complicated scenes, like being surrounded by twigs interwoven to the point they were almost solid. I could see every little twig in great detail and follow how each one went above and below other twigs. I also saw, surrounding me, shelves and shelves of glass figurines—animals, people, little buildings and geometric shapes—with light streaming through. None of the figurines stood higher than three inches, but I could make out the smallest detail. I didn't just see a glass dolphin, but its fins and eyes and blowhole and the breaking wave it jumped out of.

In actual nighttime dreams I will still have perfect vision for many months to come. Often I dream of Iraq but not in any particularly troubling way. I dream of day-to-day events with people I knew over there, who are still there. Sometimes I get a kick out of my enhanced visual capabilities. All day long I can't see shit, and I have fun with 20/20 eyesight in Dreamland.

18

Progress

Another touch from Sgt. Haskamp toward the end of May. This time she asks if I will appear at a ceremony for veterans on Memorial Day up by Palm Springs. There I will read aloud the roll of the fallen from our base, 23 Marines killed in action since Memorial Day 2003, a year prior.

I go to the Sergeant's office to meet the ceremony's organizer. He gives me a roster in 12-point type, which might as well be a blank sheet of paper.

"What if we blow it up for you?" he says.

"Let's give it a shot," I say.

It actually takes a few shots. Eventually we have one name per page in huge headline letters, 23 pages in all. Even with printing this big, I have to put the paper a couple inches from my eyes to read every letter. No way can I appear at the ceremony hunched over and squinting like Mr. Magoo, but I figure I can memorize guys' ranks, names, ages, and units, and then use the pages as cue cards. That way I can maintain the position of attention and show proper dignity and respect.

For a few days I rehearse what I'll say. Driving to the ceremony, April pulls the car over for a last-minute rehearsal while she holds the pages with names and checks my accuracy. By this time, I've got it pretty well nailed but still ask to firm up a few details. After one runthrough, I repeat, then repeat again.

I'm feeling pretty good about my level of preparedness. The better I know the stuff, the more smoothly and powerfully I can speak. Still, I stop here and there and ask April for confirmation of details about the guys.

After a couple of passes, she doesn't respond.

I ask her to give me somebody's unit and get nothing. Then I ask for an age. Ditto.

First I'm impatient. Then I'm mad, thinking, "Why won't you help me? This is important!"

Eventually I say out loud, and not too nicely, "What's wrong with you? Is this too much to ask?"

With an oversize blind spot, I have to traverse my head 90 degrees left to get a look at her. When I do, I can see why I don't hear from her. She's got the list in her lap, and her hands covering her eyes. Now that I'm not talking, I can hear her crying.

"Nick, they're so young. They're just boys," she sobs, "This breaks my heart . . . "

I get it, Beautiful, and I am so, so sorry. Here I am running down a roll of all these nineteen- and twenty-year-olds killed in action, trying to get the details correct and worried about how I sound, and you're thinking about them, too young to be dead, too much life that will never be lived.

A man never feels like a bigger asshole than when he makes his wife cry. I'm an even bigger asshole because I also got mad and spoke harsh words for no good reason, when she was in pain. April, God bless her, cares much more about the young Marines than my stupidity, which she barely seems to notice. After she regains her composure, she goes back to helping me. She, too, wants to make sure the reading comes off in a way that does the Marines honor.

Looking past what a jerk I was, some good news shines through here. I see words on pages. Sure, they're headline-sized, but not long ago I couldn't go smaller than billboard-sized, and then I had to struggle. And more light penetrates, so day looks like day instead of an hour after sunset. Night's still a bust, but so what? I see some progress. For a month I've been talking like I see it, but now I really do. This is huge.

April and I have protocols for monitoring improvement. After we wake up in the morning, she asks me questions.

"Can you see the clock?"

"Yes."

"Can you see what time it is?"

"No, but I can see the frame around the clock."

"Can you see the heating vent?"

"Yes."

"What about the grating?"

I can see that, too, a new detail that I couldn't make out before, like the frame on the clock. We'll have to buy clocks the size of manhole covers to do me any good, but making measurable progress thrills both me and April to no end.

I use landmarks outside to test myself, sighting on objects at known distances from various spots—the neighbor's car across our cul-de-sac, the PX two blocks down the street, the tank parked in front of the chow hall on the far side of the battalion grinder. Here, again, progress shows. Day-by-day it isn't much, but it adds up.

I see progress in chunks, one week to the next, at Nicholas' Little League Games. We sit in the same place, looking at kids in mostly fixed playing positions, so new results show unmistakably. I'd love coming to the games anyway, because that's my kid out there, but pushing back my visual horizons inspires me and confirms all my best expectations. Keep up the trend, and I've got a good eyeball in a matter of months. Gunny will ride again!

Little League is the best part of my week. Besides the vision stuff, I'm just glad to be here watching my son in person instead of looking at home videos of the games months from now like other deployed Dads. Maybe more than in the office, I feel like I'm back in our Marine community, setting up our chairs by the other families, drinking sodas, cheering. I get big laughs from the crowd when the umpire doesn't show and I stand up and volunteer.

At first Nicholas plays centerfield. I pretty much have to take his word that he's out there, because there's no target signature whatsoever. Even today I couldn't recognize my kid at such a range. After a few weeks, he moves to third base. Proud dad that I am, I assume his fielding skills have improved. Kid must have a cannon now because that's where the good arms go. Looking back, I have some suspicion that the coach moves Nicholas to third so I can actually see him. This favor comes the Marine way, though, with no hint that it's anything but a straightforward rotation of position. Here's one more Marine to whom I owe gratitude. Thanks, Coach Sigo, Gunnery Sergeant USMC.

While adding to effective range of vision, I lose meds like crazy. Every time I empty a pill bottle, I call up Mr. Dr. Keefe and say, "Hey, doc, do I have to refill this thing?" When he says no, I feel a great weight lifted and feel that much more fixed. If I don't need the pill, whatever I needed it for is resolved, right? One fine day—and soon—Gunny Pop will be Red Con One, up and loaded. No doubt in my military mind.

Stitches disappear along with the prescribed medications. Holes in my face close, and the strange leaks from various orifices dry up. Steel still emerges, but at a slower rate. When the swelling goes down a little more, I can get fitted for a prosthetic eye and look that much more like a human being.

On one of our trips to the hospital in San Diego, we stop at a gas station for sodas and a guy says to me, "Hey, buddy, what happened, did you get in a car wreck?"

"Aw, something like that," I say, walking tall and feeling cool like I just got carded on the way into a bar.

Do I really look that good?

19

In the Rear with the Gear

Aye Aye, Sir. I damn sure don't want to say it, but do so anyway, no bitching or grumbling, when the Ops O comes to me before the battalion PT run and says: "Gunny, position yourself at the rear of the formation and pick up the drops."

All week long I've been looking forward to this run, a one-hundred percent moto-Marine event. First the entire battalion, almost a thousand strong, stands in ranks on the grinder. Then everyone takes off for a three-mile training run, with the battalion commander and battalion colors in the lead, one company after another running in formation behind with platoon sergeants calling cadences that the guys roar back in unison.

Within this incredible show of First Tanks strength and unity, each company tries to show it's the best and make the others look like girls. First, the units try to outshout each other. There's more to the game than just making noise. A good CO pulls his company up so close to the one in front that the rear half of that formation can't hear its own unit leader so they can't sound off. This increases your unit's dominance and makes the other guys sound weak. But at the same time, the company to the rear does the same shit to you. The only defense is for your leaders to shout so loudly that your company's Marines hear and keep sounding off. That's why this is a platoon sergeant's game. Nobody else has the right kind of command voice, like a human semi-truck horn. And nobody can outshout Gunny Pop; I'm pretty proud of that. Even though I haven't used my

Gunny voice for more than a month, I've still got it, and I know where I want to be, pounding pavement next to a hundred guys double-timing in sync with me and yelling . . .

> M1A1 rollin' down the road
> Four-man crew and a combat load
> TC traverses, gives the fire command
> Sends another enemy to the promised land!

Just like us big-voice staff NCOs, the track stars have a role in our competition. The fastest guys grab their companies' guidons and run laps around the entire moving formation, a quarter mile in length. So in addition to the cadence contest, we've got a footrace, young Marines holding their units' rags high in the sky and trying to smoke the others.

The more years in the Corps, the more I took a leadership role, the more I grew to love and appreciate this sort of thing. All the lines of loyalty and responsibility that we live by and fight by are there to see, up to the battalion level and down to your own platoon and even your own four-man tank crew. The exercise gives the big picture to younger Marines who sometimes focus on their peers and immediate superiors to the point that they forget they're also part of much bigger entities. That's important to remember when orders come down that don't seem so great for you, individually, and your small unit, but which do make sense as part of a grand plan. Getting this separates the men from the boys, the doers from the whiners, and a massed battalion-level exercise, even if it's just a run, makes the concept real.

Only an irredeemable dirt bag could fail to get into the spirit, picking up strength from others and contributing strength. You don't just know you're a Marine, you feel it down to your core. You feel it, and you love it. Only one thing motivates and inspires more, which is a battalion-level operational exercise, everybody in their tanks and amtracs—rolling thunder, man. For practical reasons that doesn't happen too often, but the runs do.

So where the hell am I?

In the rear with the gear.

Never have I run here before. The pace on these massed runs is never too challenging, but here at the ass end it's a joke, barely faster than walking. I'm not even puffing or breaking a sweat. But I don't mind that so much as the sense of exclusion. Since I have to stay with the last sorry son-of-a-bitch who can't keep up, the quarter mile of physically fit Marines pulls farther and farther ahead. I feel left out—no, worse than that, left behind. But this is where the Major put me, and I'll do my best to motivate the drops and get them back up to speed. This requires a certain amount of judgment, because sometimes guys are legitimately hurt or sick and need to get on the safety vehicle.

"Hey, you'll just make it worse," I say in such cases, "Get on the truck and live to fight another day."

Usually this takes some persuasion, because legitimate drops always try to fight through the pain.

Hung-over Marines and just plain sorry individuals, who let their PT slide, call for different tactics.

"What kind of Marine are you?" I might say, "You're five feet in front of the safety vehicle and it's pushing you. That thing's for the sick, lame, and lazy, and you ain't one of the first two. Get the fuck up where you belong!"

In one case, I don't even have to say a word to achieve the desired effect. A Marine falls back, just shuffling along, and I run up on him.

"I shouldn't be back here," he huffs and puffs, "I'm a warrant officer, a leader. And I can't believe it's you, Gunny, who has to help me."

I don't know this guy from the man on the moon, but clearly he recognizes me, and having a recently wounded man pick him up bugs him. It also cures him of the slows.

After parting words—"I am so goddam ashamed"—he takes off and catches his unit. I don't see him again.

Maybe this is what the major had in mind, putting me back here. What could shame and motivate a man more than aid and assistance from a busted-up brother?

It also occurs to me that I don't really have a unit to run with. Charlie, to which I belong, is in Iraq. So having me pick up drops makes sense from an organizational standpoint.

Maybe, for that matter, I just happen to catch the assignment because somebody has to. Who better than an unattached Gunny?

Let's be honest, though: That officer probably put me here because he assumes that I can't keep up because of my wounds. That hurts, Major. And it hurts worse because the whole battalion sees where I am, making it easy for everybody to assume the same thing, that I'm damaged goods, that I'm not the Marine and the man I was, that behind the battalion, not in the battalion, is where I belong. This is like calling me a straphanger, a hindrance. I don't push the team any more. No, it pulls me.

To add insult to injury, I'm in pretty good shape. After a month of morning PT on my own, I could outrun most of the men in front of me.

It's my eyes, guys, not my legs and my lungs.

I hate this, just hate it. But never will I gripe or whine about performing an assignment.

What happened during the run, happens all over the base. Only this time I'm not trailing the pack; I'm staying at Two Nine while other units deploy to the war zone. More or less continuously, somebody gets ready, then ships out. I get why I don't go—I can't see yet. In the open desert a tank commander acquires targets with the naked eye at 3,000, even 4,000 meters, or just under three miles away. At this point I can't see Nicholas in centerfield. Rationally I know the score. There has to be a hell of a lot more improvement. But I also know it's coming, day by day, and will continue until such time as I'm fully sighted in my left eye. No sweat about the missing right, because all of a tank's optics—periscopes, telescopic sights on the main gun and machine guns—are monocular, so I never really needed more than one eye, anyway.

About this time I start going to the armory every week to see if I can focus on the front sight tip of an M16A2 service rifle. Though a tanker lives or dies by heavier armament, I will have to qualify with a rifle, an annual training requirement. All Marines, male and female, even supply clerks, bakers, and clarinet players, are riflemen. So far, I can't make out a rifle's rear sight aperture, maybe six inches from my eye, much less the front. Rifle in hand, though, I realize shooting the Marine way will come even before full recovery. We're trained to focus on the sight, not the target, which is blurry when you aim correctly. My bigger challenge will be to switch from right-handed shooting to left, and I start snapping in now to get the feel.

Normal-size words on paper and typewriter keys are like the rifle sights, well beyond my current reach. Now and again in S-3, this causes me to feel useless. The guys in the office work their asses off. If they tried to get me on the team, it'd take them way longer to teach me a task than to do it, and then they'd have to assign somebody to be my eyes. The best thing I can do is just stay out of the way. On the slightest pretext or none at all, I look for something useful to do elsewhere, among other things going to the tank ramp to motivate guys and play Guru. I don't need to see to know what's happening and improve efficiency. When a crew breaks track, I ask if they wrapped a chain around the torque-binder for safety, and how come that loader's just standing there instead of opening up the track jacks. Guys need somebody prodding and telling them to think ahead, and I do that just fine. Feels good, acting like a platoon sergeant. Of course they have platoon sergeants already, so I could, if I allowed myself, feel like a fifth wheel. I don't, though.

We have an expression: There's no such thing as extra in the Marines. More is always better. And I'm more.

In the same spirit, I do walk-throughs at the barracks. Obviously I can't look for ghost turds—dust mice to you non-Marines—and check the state of police, but I can conduct verbal inspections, like testing the duty NCO on his command of the eleven General Orders, which every one of us should know backwards and forwards. Amazing how guys fall down on the details, like when they're authorized to leave their posts. To a man headed into combat, it might seem irrelevant, but knowing all the rules brings clarity of thinking and faster action in all circumstances, including a fight. Knowledge that works for you in Two Nine also works in Iraq and Afghanistan, and I show guys why and how this is so. I walk up on a bored guy, killing time until his relief, and leave a motivated Marine who knows that by doing his job properly, he's also training for combat.

Everything's training. In my Gunny role, I remind guys of this truth.

Anytime I talk about actual fighting, I have an eager audience, and wherever I go, I do hip pocket training sessions, telling guys what to expect from the enemy and how to kick their asses.

Every other week, on average, I make the two-hour trip to March Air Force Base, where we conduct training in MOUT—Marine Operations in Urban Terrain. As an instructor of the day, I do a morning brief for officers and staff on our operations in Fallujah and then, in the afternoon, go out to where the squads do PRAC-AP, practical application of classroom instruction on mechanized urban warfare. Damn, it looks like fun, smashing out windows and generally tearing things up. Fifteen years in, I still dig the Rambo stuff. Nobody puts as much oomph into training as Marines, and I love being part of it, even as a schoolteacher. I go home from March AFB fully recharged and proud of my contribution. Maybe today I saved a life or helped somebody win.

Two ways to keep up personal morale and motivation:

1) Find a way to be useful. Not always easy, but I manage to do it.

2) Look to the future. What I can't see now, I will see. And what I can't do now, I will do.

In connection with 2), I keep my ear to the ground, listening for scuttlebutt about billets that will get me back into the fight. Timing is everything here. If I wait until I'm actually ready, physically, I'll be too late because combat units are put together months before deploying so they can train and build cohesion.

In this connection, I'm in exactly the right spot. It's in S-3 that new assignments are made and processed. The man in charge of moving around staff NCOs, Top Dangerfield, sits about 10 feet from my chair. We converse every day concerning work and bullshit, too. The more I know this guy, the more I like him. My respect for him goes back almost ten years, when I took master gunner training and he instructed. Now I feel a developing friendship, too.

With Bravo long gone, since a week after I got back, the next tank company in the chute is Alpha, due to ship out in about six months. Word gets out that Alpha comes up short on lieutenants and needs a Gunnery Sergeant who can command a platoon. If I dreamed up a position, this would be it. Still on a tank. Leading a platoon. But with no lieutenant to train! This is winning the Gunny Trifecta. Guys would kill for it.

No sense beating around the bush. The instant I hear about this, I march over to Top, who sits at his desk doing S-3 things that will forever be a mystery to me. Honest to God, I wouldn't even want to guess what exactly those guys do.

"I want that platoon in Alpha Company," I say.

"You're not going to Alpha Company," Top says in a flat sort of way. I can't read his face, of course, but his words come out with complete finality. The thing isn't off the table because it was never on the table. And it won't be, ever. Not the next time I ask or next week. Not if his first 60 choices don't pan out.

Okay, Top, I get the idea. But you should bet your ass you will change your mind. As soon as I'm fixed, as I fully expect to be before Alpha goes, you will get me into that company one way or the other. I'm too good a tanker to be left behind farting around Two Nine while the unit goes into the fight, where my talents and experience are needed. It's wrong, and it won't happen.

So this No doesn't sound so negative to me, however Top means it.

With three years of hindsight, I understand that he means it the way he says it. For him it's completely out of the question to entrust other lives, the guys in the platoon the new Gunny will lead, to somebody who currently has a hard time getting around S-3. On a day-to-day basis, he sees more of me than anybody else in the Corps. He sees that I don't recognize old friends until they tell me who they are. Even face-to-face, six inches apart, I often just don't know who somebody is. Top knows, too, that I can't read a word if the letters are less than a couple inches tall, and then I have to struggle. He's seen me fish around for the door handle of his pickup truck for a half-minute and find it only by feel. He's seen me fail to identify everyday items within arm's reach, like mugs of joe and three-ring binders. People ask me to hand such things to them, and I ask what they're talking about. Whatever optimistic words come out of my mouth, Top Dangerfield keeps his eyes on me and knows how degraded my vision still is. He knows more of the truth than anybody but April and probably more than I do.

When he speaks the truth, that I am not the guy for that billet, no matter how good I once was, no matter how badly I want it now and how badly he'd like to help me get better, he shows a lot of respect by speaking directly and plainly, no kid gloves, no sugar-coating. This is the Marine way, and also a real friend's way.

At the end of the day, this man was—and is—a friend.

20

Club Pop

N o matter that the staff NCO Club closes at 2300 on weeknights. We've got a place to go that never closes, and it has all the amenities—a pool table, cold beer, jarhead memorabilia, everybody's favorite tunes on a good stereo, a TV, and cool-looking little lights strung all over. The place even has a perfect floor, unfinished concrete so spills are something to laugh at.

Club Pop.

My two-car garage. It never has a car in it while it's mine. It's the scene of every conceivable kind of party. Going away. Coming home. Birthdays. New Years Eve. Major and minor sports events on TV. Barbecues famous for burnt meat because the host can't grill for shit but loves to cook out anyway.

But I'm talking about what was here, not what is, because my tanker buddies are all deployed, and even though I'm back Club Pop remains closed for the season. In and of itself this isn't sad, just a natural part of the deployment cycle. And the garage can still fulfill its other major function as Gunny Pop's Fortress Of Solitude.

The Fortress thing actually comes from Superman, but I picked up the term from a morning radio jock in San Diego who says that every man has a Fortress Of Solitude, the center of his own personal universe where he can be himself and never, ever be bothered. No matter if it's just sitting on the crapper, a man needs his own space and to keep his own company.

I happen to have the best FOS in the world, perfectly equipped and laid out to suit my particular needs. In addition to the above-mentioned rec room stuff to enjoy with others, I've got a weight pile with 400 pounds of Olympic-size plates and bars and a tilting bench for prone and incline presses. The weight rack adjusts all the way up to shoulder height for military presses and squats, and I can do a complete heavy workout all on my own. I do most of my lifting right here at my own pace and level of intensity to fulfill needs that are my own and nobody else's.

I have no idea why my garage has this alcove in the front wall, maybe 6-feet wide by 3 by 3, but it could have been designed to hold three Marine footlockers. In my three I keep all my deuce gear—field gear. Sleeping bag, canteen, shelter half, Kevlar helmet, war belt, tanker hot suit, and so on. I have passed many a happy hour unpacking, refolding, and repacking everything. Marine Strat Mobex doctrine says we have to be ready to go to combat within 36 hours, so there's some merit to what I do. Not much, though, because the stuff's always good to go. Mostly I just like handling it and maybe finding some way to improve the organization and make it all neater. It never goes back exactly the way it came out. Some guys build birdhouses or model airplanes. I fold deuce gear.

I can always pass some more time with my 1998 Suzuki 1200 Bandit, forest green with gold trim. It can't get any shinier or more well-maintained than it is, but I take a rag to it and check fluid levels and make adjustments anyway.

Sometimes I just walk around and take in all the stuff on the walls. This is my own personal Marine Corps Museum. I've got pictures of guys I served with, unit flags, a captured Iraqi flag, a sight off an old M-60 tank, the Welcome Home sign that our wives made for Team Bravo after OIF 1. The first thing I show new visitors is a piece of the big statue of Saddam Hussein that my unit pulled down in Firdos Square in 2003 after we took Baghdad. April made a really cool display of the fragment with a picture of me holding it next to the fallen statue.

Club Pop is perfect. When I've got the garage door open, guys I don't know from Adam stand and look in like they're hypnotized. Overseas, Marines talked about how we were going to come back and party in Club Pop.

In truth, I don't spend so much time in here since I came home wounded. I'm too blind to play pool. Once in a while I start up the bike just to hear it, but I don't screw with it so much now that I can't ride. I still do daily weight workouts on a four-day cycle—chest day, shoulder day, arm day, leg day—just like before, and every day I sweep and police the place, which is a monument to my anal retentiveness, extreme even for a Marine staff NCO.

April, God bless her, understands what this place means to me and gives me a present to help me enjoy it more now. This whole situation has to be a pain in the ass for her, but she always tries to make things better for me. Knowing how much I love my music, she buys a Sony carousel CD changer that holds 300 discs. The idea is that I can program the machine to play exactly what I like and not have to change CDs, which are hard for me to read and handle.

To get such a thing April has to go down the hill, as we say, driving at least an hour one-way to get to one of the big stores at Palm Desert. I'm thrilled. This is perfect, Beautiful! If somebody gave me the money, I'd buy the same thing. I bust the player right out of the box and take it to Club Pop.

No problem hooking up the power and audio output to the amplifier. Now for the actual tunes. The machine categorizes the CDs into eight different groups so I can have oldies and hard rock and Beatles albums, or whatever. And it has all sorts of advanced functions so I can program it to play individual tracks in any order. My own soundtrack fine-tuned to any particular mood here in my Fortress. This is going to be great.

If I could see, it would be, too.

But I can't read the instruction book, the labels on the CDs or the little LED display on the player. April could help me here, but no, I'm not asking anybody to come to my assistance. I'm a grown man and I'll do it myself. So here I am with a book I can't read in my hand and my eyeball two inches from the player's light-up display, which I can't read, either. This cheap-ass magnifying glass, which we bought at a drug store, doesn't do a bit of good. The blurs get a little bigger, but they're still blurs.

Okay, now I'm pissed off, and I don't have any idea in the world how to make the situation less frustrating and infuriating and humiliating. I know how to dissect and troubleshoot the fire control system on a $2.75 million main battle tank, and now I can't program a home stereo component designed to be idiot-proof. I struggle to see it, strain to see it, squint to see it, go farther, closer, look from different angles, and I still can't see what I need to see to do this stupid little job.

Desire and effort don't mean shit. More doesn't get me more. In my life, this is new. And I hate it. I'm what's broke, and I can't fix myself. Nobody else can, not here, not now. I don't even know how to ask to be fixed.

I chuck the stool I'm sitting on, bang stuff around so loudly that April can hear it in the house.

She opens the door and says, "What's wrong, Sweetheart? What can I do to help?"

"April, I'll be all right in a little while. But now I need some time. Can you just leave me alone?"

I don't raise my voice, but the question is not a question. I don't want her to see me sink to the level I'm sinking to. I don't want her witnessing this anger, because she's entirely innocent.

And I know who I'm angry at. My eyes. To be more accurate, my one eye, the useless piece of shit. Why won't you work? Why won't you get better? How can you let me down like this when I need you? Without you, I can't do one goddam thing for myself, not the stupidest little thing like this. And I can't be myself.

Gunny Pop has left the room.

Hello, Self Pity.

Fuck it. Fuck doing the right thing. Positive mental attitude. Courage. Honor. Commitment. That crap is work, and right now I'm taking the pack off.

Time to feel bad, sink lower than I've ever sunk in my life and stay there until I feel like coming back up. I need to bottom out.

To sink further, faster, I let in a previously unauthorized thought. Never before have I allowed this dangerous son-of-a-bitch anywhere near. But here it is: What if this is it? What if, like Dr. Death said, what I see is what I get, now and forever? What kind of life is this? I can't go out and play catch with my son. I can't ride that motorcycle over there. I can't shoot pool. I can't be a tank commander again, maybe not even a Marine. I can't be Gunny Pop, and that's who I am. I'm the kind of Dad I am because I'm Gunny Pop. And the kind of husband I am. And the man I am. But now I don't know who the fuck I am or who I'm going to be.

I want to break in here, from three years later, and say this is complete and utter nonsense. Of course I was the same man and the same Marine and still am. I just fight with different equipment in a very degraded environment. Marines will pick such a fight because we can perform in the most adverse conditions, which the enemy can't handle. But in the mad scene back in Club Pop, I let myself lose track of who I am. Why the CD changer triggers this episode, who knows? Maybe anything would have done it, because I recognize my own psychological needs and do some self-adminstered therapy without a shrink. In tanker terms, I perform a self recovery after purposefully getting stuck in the mud.

But I don't have to stay stuck for long before I get sick of it. If this is what the bottom looks like and feels like, it ain't for me. I make myself want to puke, wallowing like this. Once again, I am Gunny to myself, yelling in my head Get up, Get up, Pick up your pack, Marine, and move out. I feel so much better with the pack on again, where it belongs. Not only do I straighten up like a Marine, I pick up what I threw and police the garage. And I put my eyes back where they belong, on the future. Like Mrs. Dr. Keefe says, there's still no reason to expect anything but the best outcome, so why should I? A man who takes an RPG hit to the head and lives, whose one remaining eye survives a near-death experience, just naturally should look for more good things to happen.

By the time I leave the garage, I'm good to go.

April, understandably, is a little nervous, but she takes a look and knows who walks through the door.

"Had to get some stuff out of my system," I tell her, "But now I'm fine. Everything's going to be great."

This incident is so over. Neither of us will mention it until I start putting together material for this book. Eventually, with patience and persistence and a little assistance, I get the CD carousel up and running. Now all that music is on an iPod, which I use the hell out of.

21

The Bomb Drops

The only major improvement during this period mostly benefits the rest of the world, which has to look at my ugly mug. At Balboa, Dr. David, another jovial specialist who's a riot to be around, pops out the conformer—a temporary cap to keep my empty eye socket in shape—and fits me for my first glass eye. I ask for pure white with a blazing red crosshairs like a tank commander's primary sight. I expect the doc to shoot this down, but he loves it! "Maybe we can get a watch battery in there and make it glow!" he says. That was the first of a small collection of custom eyeballs, two of which bear the Marine Corps eagle, globe, and anchor emblem.

But all remains quiet on the other fronts. Come on Docs, tell me something new. San Diego is a long way to drive for a rerun, but that's what I get for a few weeks running. Mrs. Dr. Keefe, primary point of contact with my team of specialists, says we're now in a holding pattern until more of the blood in my eye clears out. A glob of blood still sits over a big piece of the retina. This obstructs the doctors' view of any damage or lack thereof. As Mrs. Dr. Keefe keeps saying, there's still no reason to believe that the blood camouflages trouble. In her view, no news is good news, or at least not bad news.

On the other hand the blood blocks most of my vision, and I'd love to get rid of it. Every week I ask if there's something more I can do, like eating special foods or trying new medication. Name it Doc, and I'll do it.

"Sorry, Gunny," she says, "Nothing will speed things up. I know it's no fun, but we just have to ride it out."

I know she tells me straight. And when she says "we," it isn't just doctor BS because she's in the fight with us. But I feel trouble. I feel it because I see it. For a couple months the light came back like a long-lost friend, and I was so glad. But the light didn't come alone. It brought reality. I still can't see worth a damn. What used to be blacked-out is grayed-out like somebody ran a chalkboard eraser over three-quarters of my field of vision. No color, no detail, no nothing, just gray. The gray sits right in the cross-hairs, my central vision, so the more I point my eye and try to look at something, the more I can't see it.

My little bit of brightness and clarity shows in the lower right quadrant. Look down at the tip of your nose. Right where the nose appears, that's the center of my usable vision. The upside is, I actually can use it. I can see all the way to the horizon and identify major objects. On the far side of the barracks stands Bearmat Mountain, so named for the call sign of the range safety post on top. I see cars in motion so I don't have to rely on drivers not to run me over. My area of operations now includes the entire base, with my movement limited by the brutal summer heat and not my vision. I can make out actual individual people in some detail, telling tall from short, recognizing distinctive motions. If I see guys salute an officer, I know to do it, too.

That said, everything appears blurry, and I still can't recognize most people I know. Reading defeats me totally. I'm not even close. But my Marine perceptions and responses are so hard-wired I give the impression that I see a lot better than I do. I help the impression along by the way I come back when people ask what's up.

"Hey Gunny, how's the vision going?"

"Oor-ah," I say, or "Semper Fi," or both, and keep walking.

The all-occasion moto-Marine responses are acceptable answers to pretty much anything. Having heard them, a guy will assume I'm good to go. Not stopping means I've got shit to do. Since I used to say "Oor-ah" and "Semper Fi" a thousand times a day, Marines hear and see the Gunny Pop they knew. I'm not evading anything, and I'm not lying. I'm just being true to myself and my rank and position. Gunny does not speak of his own problems. He solves the problems of others. And the details sound too much like a pitch for pity; I want nothing to do with that.

Another week or two in holding pattern and I don't want news from the docs any more. I think I'm looking at the truth now, and I don't look forward to hearing it from medical authorities. I especially don't want to hear it from Dr. Death, the no-fun retinologist. When Mrs. Dr. Keefe takes a look in my eye and says I need to go see him now, I know the score. Hello, Trouble. If there's something new and significant for him to look at, the blood has drained away. Now the docs can see, but I still can't.

But to hell with the downside. It's time to get positive and go to work on the fix. Surgery? Portholes? That's Marine for eyeglasses. The lens will have to be thick like a Coke bottle, but, hey, U.S. Navy medicine works wonders, as I know from first-hand experience.

Wish they gave these guys more floor space, but the exam room is so small you look at the eye chart in a mirror to give the needed distance, and April and I pretty much fill the place ourselves. Waiting for the doc to arrive, we talk about anything but the issue at hand. Why speculate and get worked up when the answer will arrive any minute?

While we wait, I say to April, "Hey, it's nice to be cool for a change. Why don't we go to the beach before we head back up the hill?" I really do want to go, and we're only ten minutes from Mission Beach, one of our San Diego favorites.

"Sounds great," April says, more to stop the conversation than to agree. With the rest of our lives hanging in the balance she could care less about the rest of the day.

Dr. Death sits down so we're all close enough to touch knees, not that anybody wants to. Don't get me wrong, here. I hold no particular ill will toward the man, who is a standout retinologist. No doubt whatsoever about his expertise and competency. I do wish, though, that he'd cheer up a little, particularly around April, who dreads spending time with him. We could really use some positivity right here and now, when he drops the bomb: "Your retina is permanently damaged," he says, "and your optic nerve has been compromised. I don't think things will get worse, but they will not get any better."

He goes on to explain that retinas and nerves don't heal, and there's no way to fix them.

"What about new glasses?" I ask.

"Won't do a thing. Your eye is like a camera with bad film in it. You can put the best, most powerful lenses in the world on it, and it will still take bad pictures."

"Will he be able to drive?" April asks.

"No. That's out of the question," the doc says, "Any activity like that will be beyond his capabilities."

Before I can ask about surgery, the doctor brings up an operation that he could perform to remove some of the scar tissue that impedes my vision. But he says it probably wouldn't do much to restore clarity, because the eye would scar over again, though possibly in a less drastic way. And it might not do anything at all.

"I don't believe the benefit justifies the risks," he says, explaining that going back into my eye could blind me totally and for good.

"Don't try to make a decision now. We'll talk about it next time you come in," the doctor says.

Fine with me, although I already know the answer. If the surgeon says he doesn't want to take the risk, I sure as hell don't.

Before we wrap up, the doctor tells us, "Within 10 or 15 years, given the changing technology, we may be able to rectify your problem. I wouldn't rule such a thing out."

Give the man points for doing the best he can with the tools he possesses. It doesn't come naturally, but he strains to give hope and comfort by talking about medicine of the future. In my case it actually works. I appreciate the effort and think about what he says for some time to come, picturing a fully restored left eye or maybe, what the hell, two good eyes, because doctors will know how to make replacements. Such thoughts give me reassurance when I need it, like when I have to sell my Suzuki. It doesn't hurt so much when I think that maybe someday somehow I'll ride again.

Our meeting takes ten minutes. Just like that, we go from before to after. Instead of hope for the future in terms of my vision coming back and our old lives coming back, we have questions that we don't even know how to ask. If life as we know it is over and done with, what now, what next? Coming out of that doctor's office, the future looks pretty much like three quarters of my vision. A great big blank.

Forget about getting to Mission Beach. I still want to go, but I keep my mouth shut out of consideration for April. She's taken much more of a hit than I have, because she didn't see what I saw and didn't know the score the way I did. My wife has just jumped into this pool, and I'm already used to the water.

No worries about the beach in San Diego, anyway. Before we get past the guardhouse at the Balboa medical center, I know we're going to a beach we both love even more.

"Nick, what's going to happen? What are we going to do?" April asks me in the car.

These are the first of a million questions for which I have no good answer. But saying nothing and doing nothing is never an option, not to a Marine. It comes to me, while we're still in the parking structure, what we ought to do next: "To hell with this, Beautiful. Let's spend a week in Hawaii. It'll be like last year, and we can figure things out, too."

"Okay," she says.

22

Rough Takeoff

Now who the hell could that be?

In the best of circumstances I dislike hearing the phone ring and do not rush to pick up calls hoping for an hour of happy blah-blah, which for some people is better than TV. I really don't want a call tonight in the aftermath of the blast from the retinologist. You can't see the wreckage and dust and debris, but believe me they're here, particularly for April. I will find out later she cried on and off in a secret sort of way while she drove us back to Twentynine Palms. Here at home there's room for her to go off by herself.

When the phone rings I have to pick it up, because this might be some sort of vital communication or call to duty. As a Marine, you never know.

"Pop!" yells a voice from 10,000 miles away. It's a voice that I always love to hear. On a monthly basis my good friend Top J, Master Sgt. Johnson, calls and lets me know what he and my buddies in Iraq are up to. I can't tell you how much I love these communications, which are more than phone calls.

"We're out on a mission, and we thought we'd bring you along," Top J says and then does just that. He and his crew never call pogue style from one of the phones at firm bases. Instead they use a satphone outside the wire while they're doing something that they know I'd enjoy like patrolling some vill or manning a vehicular control point. Being pros, they call when they're static and things are quiet, but still they're out where shit happens.

"What's your POS?" I ask.

"Cloverleaf," he says. Hearing it, I can picture the highway interchange on the eastern edge of Fallujah where we maintain an over-watch of the city and control access. When I was there I'd sit Bonecrusher and my wingman's tank right in the middle of the road daring somebody to come and take a crack at us. Since then, according to Top J, Marines have turned the Cloverleaf into a prepared defensive position with bunkers for the infantry and dug-in firing holes for tanks so they sit hull-down with only the turrets showing.

"What's the enemy SITREP?"

"Zilch. Nothing. I've got Palacios' section in place."

"How come you're not killing bad guys?"

"Last week we took out all the stupid ones. Nobody's showing his face today."

"Why are you fucking around outside Fallujah? Why not drive in and take out the trash."

Top J laughs and says, "You tell me, Pop, and we'll both know. I've been screaming for that since I got here." Then he busts my chops a little, "I hear there's some asshole in town who's a good shot with an RPG, took out a tank commander, some Gunny who's back stateside now milkin' it, man."

I laugh my ass off and come back, "At least I'm not jerking off at the Cloverleaf. I'm as likely to see the enemy here in my living room as you are."

Now he's laughing, even though I just said he's in a safe rear position like a pogue, a grave putdown for a trigger puller. We're such good buddies we have fun with our insults incoming and outgoing. And it's nothing short of wonderful to go back to Iraq, in spirit at least, and enjoy the company of high-stepping global warriors, fighting Marines who are my kind of Marines. After our opener, Top J hands the phone around for visits with the rest of the crew, which are mostly just "Hey, how you doing?"

When Top J has the phone again he gets serious and says, "How's everything?"

"Good to go."

"For real Pop, how's the eye?"

"I'll tell you the truth if you swear not to tell a soul."

"Done," he says, which is all I need to hear, because this man's word is better than gold.

"It's broke for good. Ain't gonna get any better. Looks like you're going to finish this one without me."

"Done," J says, "I'll tag and bag a few of them for you."

After that we say goodbye the Marine way, "Semper Fi. Out here."

What did I just say, and why did I say it? To this day I can't explain why I told the truth about my eye to this man in the combat zone on the far side of the world. After my conversation with Top J, I won't tell anybody else for weeks to come. At the time, Top J is my best friend in the Corps, but that doesn't really explain why I told him. Maybe the extreme distance helps and my absolute trust that he won't betray a secret. In normal circumstances I would never share anything so important over the phone, but maybe in this case the phone makes it easier, because I don't see J while we're talking and won't see him for a half-year so he's just a disembodied presence. But who the hell knows? I told him.

And the next morning I do not tell another friend even though I specifically made a commitment to inform him when my vision stopped improving. Top Dangerfield will, in fact, be the next person I speak the truth to, but I can't do it yet. Bright and early on the day after Dr. Death's big bomb, I present myself to Top at his desk in S-3.

"Remember all that leave I got stacked up? I want to start burning some of it," I say.

"When?" he asks.

"ASAP," I say.

"Where are you going?"

"Hawaii."

"Nice. I can put papers in your hands in a couple days."

"Thanks, Top."

Thanks really are in order because normally it takes five working days after a request like mine for the admin machine to spit out leave papers. The two days is perfect, because April has to pack and go online and make a game plan to get us on a Military Airlift Command flight to Hawaii. But there's another side of the fast-track leave processing that bugs me. If I made a big difference—or any difference—to the operation here, it wouldn't be so easy to let me go.

We could try to fly out of San Diego, but there's too little traffic and too few seats, so we make the eight-hour drive to Travis Air Force Base near Sacramento, which has the most Hawaii-bound transports. At least once a day a plane flies out of Travis to paradise.

To this point we've had great luck catching MAC flights. Day one at Travis isn't our day, though, and neither is day two or day three. If you're picturing a cushy civilian airport with nice seats and a variety of stores and restaurants and bars, forget it. Travis is a bare-bones military facility, and waiting is less than comfortable. They made it that way, I think, so people with Mac flight privileges, like military retirees, don't set up housekeeping waiting to catch the next free flight to some cool place like Hawaii. Procedures make the Mac flight experience less than optimal, too. If you fly, you park your car in the long-term lot, but only an hour before the roll is called for the flight you're trying to catch. If you don't make it, you have to pull the car out of the lot. So the drill is this: Put the car in long-term, walk the mile back to the terminal, listen to some airman read a list of available seats and assign them to people in order of priority. Every damn plane for three days running, seats go to others who either have higher priority status or got here before us. With all scheduled planes to Hawaii flying, we'd be out by the second day, for sure, but half the planes don't show up because of the heavy traffic to and from the war zones in the Middle East.

Military flights go out 24/7, forcing the whole mob of would-be travelers to camp out day and night in a place where sleep is pretty much impossible for grownups. With flights being scrubbed and the crowd growing, emotions go to the extremes. People who get seats carry on like they won Big Lotto while the rest slide into depression. At least one woman sobs openly, and infants and toddlers yell day and night. When you wait for less than a day and get a flight to anywhere for free with an optional $3 meal that really is a meal, the system rocks, but on these particular days in the summer of 2004 it sucks to an extent April and I couldn't even imagine. As I said, our MAC flight luck had been great to this point.

The Marine mindset, which does not accept the concept of cutting your losses, works against me here. Where somebody else would take one look and say to hell with it, I stick it out until my wife and son are ready to crack. By this time April has a line on a terrific deal for three round-trips from Oakland. It takes one last hike back from long-term and coming up empty on one last flight, but at the end of Day Three even I see the light. Let's go to Oakland.

Any other wife would have walked or gone insane and possibly attacked me with a fork from the Air Force chow hall where we took all our meals. But April, God bless her, sucks it up. And worse things have happened. The three days at Travis are only the second-worse vacation ordeal. The 9-mile forced march on a trail off the rim of the Grand Canyon holds the all-time record for misery inflicted by Gunny Pop on his wife. On the other hand, the Arizona Death March did not include a four-month run-up of personal trauma that began with me getting shot and permanently disabled.

That night, in a crummy motel in a borderline scary neighborhood near the Oakland airport, April raises her voice in anger for the first time in memory. You can't call this an argument because that takes two. Even though I'm pissed, too, I keep my mouth shut and answer in my head.

"I have to do everything!" April yells.

And I still provide for you.

"Research the MAC flights!"

Looking for free seats to Hawaii on an internet connection. Poor you.

"Find seats on a civilian plane!"

What else were you going to do when we were stuck at Travis? And who, may I ask, foots the bill for those seats?

"Book this motel room!"

So tomorrow we can go to the South Pacific on vacation. What a catastrophe. What a bastard I am.

I'm not proud of my thoughts, but there they are. In Oakland I just can't understand how somebody could miss the upside. I'm not dead, and she's not a widow, and I'm well enough and possess the resources to get the three of us to one of the most gorgeous places on earth. Looking back, I completely understand why April feels the need to uncork. This isn't about the last three days so much as the previous months, which have been hell on her. I take a walk outside and come back cooled down and ready to hit the rack.

Next day we encounter one last rough patch on the road to Honolulu. With plenty of time before the flight to get situated, we look all over the airport and can't find the check-in for SunCoast Travel, our airline. A horrible suspicion strikes—there's no such airline and we got ripped off. But then a woman comes out with a portable sign that says SunCoast and sets up shop. The airline is just too small to rate a permanent installation.

Next stop, paradise.

23

Nice Tan

I've got a thing about snooze alarms. Don't use them, don't believe in them. When reveille sounds it's time to get up, so get up. And what's not to like about morning? In the Corps the excitement—the fun—begins before sunrise. At Two Nine the early hours belong to Marines doing Marine things—guys running and calling cadence, military vehicles roaring up the road, rifle reports at the range snapping like microwave popcorn. By the time the civilians in our midst come out of their holes, we have exercised, cleaned up, eaten, and gotten a strong start on the workday. Even now, three years out of the Corps, I put the same sort of energy into my mornings.

The other day, though, I had a non-Marine moment and hit the snooze button. I just didn't feel like getting out of the rack and took the extra nine minutes. I doubt I'll ever do it again, because it didn't gain me anything. It did, however, make me think back to our Hawaii trip.

What we do, in effect, is hit a great big seven-day snooze alarm button, giving ourselves a week in which we don't deal with one single issue pertaining to my permanent visual impairment and what it might mean. Before we took off we spoke a lot about using our time away to figure things out, consider our next moves, and so on, but in Hawaii we act and speak as if absolutely nothing has happened. We've just grounded our gear, leaving the heavy stuff in California. Even the cell phone's back in the car.

So we go on Hawaii Time and do whatever vacation stuff we feel like. Swimming off a catamaran far out to sea is great. I discover, the hard way, that a person with a brand-new prosthetic eye should close his eyelids before pulling off his snorkeling mask, because the action can suck the eye out of its socket. Fortunately I do this on dry land and catch the thing in my mask. Apologies to any witnesses.

I should explain why, on Retina Day, our thoughts instantly turned to Hawaii, rather than some other idyllic getaway place. This is our own personal paradise. A little over a year prior, after my first Iraqi deployment, April flew to Honolulu to meet the Navy ship bringing me home. On my four days of shore liberty, April and I had the most perfect, beautiful time, like meeting and falling in love again except better. A good marriage beats dating, and we had the excitement of both. That happened to be the perfect time to visit Hawaii because the islands were still starved for tourists in the post-911 visitorship slump. Wherever we went people rolled out the red carpet. And it didn't hurt to be a warrior returning from the great victory that people celebrated whole-heartedly. In honor of us servicemen a Hawaiian musician at a luau did the best and most moving rendition of God Bless America that I ever heard.

Our 2004 trip can't possibly come up to the standard of the 2003 Operation Iraqi Freedom Homebound Honeymoon, but it's pretty good, even after the heinous first few days. And it provides a 100 percent snooze alarm break that we need, apparently more than we realize. After seven days the trip ends like the extra minutes in bed—nothing substantive to show for it and a week closer to a future we have no idea how to prepare for.

I report to S-3 and turn in my leave papers to Top Dangerfield, who says, "Welcome back. Do you need any more time? You've still got a lot on the books."

At the section's next morning formation, nobody does anything to make adjustments to my return. If I did much, whoever covered for me would be able to resume his usual duties. People would be glad I was back to lighten the whole group's load and fix the stuff that only I could.

In my old platoon the lieutenant would say, "Thank God you're back, Gunny. The tanks are all broken. The barracks failed inspection. The Marines look like shit."

The Marines would say, "Thank God you're back, Gunny. Our platoon pulled all the working parties. Company dumped everything on Sergeant Jones."

Sergeant Jones, who filled in for me, would say, "Thank God you're back because the full-time platoon sergeants have been fucking me over."

Never before could I doubt that I left a big hole behind me. Now, though, the guys in S-3 tell me welcome back and admire my tan. Could it be more obvious that I don't make a difference, that I'm along for the ride, taking up space? Two weeks ago, I could put up with a little uselessness because they just parked me here until I got back in a tank. The bosses believed what I believed. But now I know different. Just like Dr. Death says, what I see is what I get. And I don't see a tank in my future. No tank platoon. No nothing in a tank company. I don't even see a job here in S-3. Even if I wanted an office billet—which I never wanted and never will because I'm a trigger puller—I couldn't have it because I do not meet the mission essential task list prerequisites. I know everything in the Corps is waiverable, but this is too big. I can't read!

A job I didn't want, and I suck at it. This is not a formula for high self-esteem. Two weeks ago I knew where hope was. I had eyes on target. Now it moved out of range, with intervening terrain features that hide its new location. I can't pursue, not yet, because I'm stuck here with broken track.

24

Out of Sync

D*EAR MARINE CORPS ABBY:*

Help me get straight with my wife, who seems madder by the day.

In 2003, only two months after my return from combat in Operation Iraqi Freedom, I volunteered to go back but did not tell her. Without actually lying I gave the impression that I had been ordered to deploy again. In Iraq I took an enemy RPG to the head and lost one eye and most of the vision in my other.

Lately my wife has been expressing anger about our changed circumstances, and the fact that I volunteered is a major factor. What can I do to "de-fuze" the situation? I have never actually admitted to her that I did volunteer. Should I come clean about what I did, even though that was more than a year ago, and she already knows?

Please Abby, help me get us back in-sync. In 13 ½ years of marriage and two combat deployments before the one where I got hit, we've never had tension between us. Now you could cut it with a K-Bar.

TROUBLED IN TWO NINE

DEAR TROUBLED:

What I'm wondering is how come that good woman stuck with you so long. God knows she could do better.

Your trouble, Troubled, is lack of integrity. Didn't your wife stick with you through two previous combat tours? That's commitment, Marine. What the hell happened on your end that you couldn't tell her straight this time? You volunteered to fight when you raised your right hand and enlisted. Don't you think she gets it? If she didn't, she would have dumped you for an insurance salesman. "Without actually lying"—are you kidding me? If you don't tell the truth, you are a liar.

Exercise some moral courage and tell her the whole truth. Even though she already found out from others she deserves to hear it from you.

Now, don't get the wrong idea about the tension between April and me. The marriage never is or will be in trouble. It's just that things become unpleasant, and we have a hard time speaking our minds. This comes as a shock because we've always had the most harmonious, happy household.

Some of the stuff involved with the volunteering issue seems strange. For one, I spoke openly and proudly about it on the network interviews I did just a few weeks after I got back. I was and still am pleased that I could get right back to Iraq. I went where I belonged, and I'd do it again. On the other hand, I avoid the subject around home after I get back because I know it pisses April off. Here's a fight I don't want to get into. April, for her part, does not come out and say in so many words what bothers her. It comes out in bits and pieces. So something I talk about on CNN remains an open secret at home. Opsec, as we say, meaning operational security. You know it, but you don't talk about it. There's a great big elephant walking around 3202-D Ludwig Court. Though I know, at the time, we ought to acknowledge it and air things out, we won't until after I start working on this book.

A minute ago April told me she's fine with the fact that I volunteered. And I'm fine that she was pissed off.

25

Bizarre-O-World

We meet again with Dr. Death, supposedly to talk over the eye surgery that both he and I think is a bad idea. Instead we do sort of a post-bomb post mortem. He takes another look and then verifies his findings of massive damage to the retina with probable damage to the optic nerve, both permanent. I ask him if I should get a second opinion.

"By all means if you feel the need," he says, "But it's right there in plain view. I'm very sure of my diagnosis."

I guess I am, too.

"What does this mean? What's next?" I ask.

"Well, you're going to be processed on a PEB."

Thinking, "What's a PEB? What does he mean processed?" I keep my mouth shut, because the details can be had somewhere else. Who wants to prolong a visit with this guy, always an exercise in severe social discomfort for all involved. To give the doctor his due, he doesn't get paid to entertain, and he had the situation pegged four months ago and predicted the outcome with great accuracy. To this very competent specialist I owe both thanks and an apology because sometimes I felt like shooting the messenger.

On our way out of the hospital we stop at Admin to find out what the doc was talking about. Turns out there's a PEB office where I get pissed off at the first of many military retirees turned bureaucrats who guard even the simplest, most basic information pertaining to duty status, retention, and transition—am I in or out of the Marines and what will happen to me and my family?—like they're protecting the President's missile launch codes. I want in the worst way to punch this little shit who reluctantly lets us know that PEB stands for Physical Evaluation Board, which rules on issues concerning medical fitness for service. After that he dodges questions and gives irrelevant responses.

When I ask what happens to guys found unfit for service, he says, "Well, that depends. Let's say your disqualifying condition came about when you were drunk on liberty. In that case you would be processed out and receive no benefits whatsoever."

How can he say such a thing to a Marine with a fresh entrance wound in his forehead, dozens of smaller dings, and a patch over his eye? Come on, take a look and do the numbers. Isn't it a strong possibility that I'm a combat casualty? If I got this while drunk somebody threw a grenade.

Thinking Fuck this useless idiot, I say to April, "Let's go home."

Little do I know it, but we just entered an alternative universe ruled by employees of various agencies and departments that are supposed to help Marines in my position. Everywhere I encounter irritating air thieves like the individual we meet at the hospital PEB office. Uselessness in any form angers me, but the deal here really chaps my ass because these zombies used to wear the uniform and then got on-base civilian billets through preferential hiring. The logic must be that former servicemen will do the best job because they speak our language, understand the system, and care enough to go the extra mile. After all, we're their younger brothers. In this case, though, Big Bro has some serious issues. Obviously the retirees think we've got it way too easy. "We had to fight for what the system did for us, and it wasn't much, so fuck you"—one guy actually says so, omitting only the fuck you, which he acts out. Sometimes they're friendly but can't stand to admit they don't know something, so they make things up. Or they camouflage laziness as encouragement, telling me, "You'll be taken care of," with big smiles on their faces, while doing absolutely nothing and thereby ensuring that I won't be taken care of.

I can't remember how many times I say to myself "What an idiot," before it dawns on me—they're all like this! This really is Marine Bizarre-O-World where everything works backwards and upside-down.

The command philosophy goes like this:

— Avoid the mission.

— There's always a reason it can't happen. Find it.

— Keep your ass in the chair at all costs.

For all I can tell they've got a secret brig where they throw high performers and those who show initiative. When I eventually meet people willing to work hard and help, it feels like drawing an inside straight. Coming from my world this seems impossible, outrageous, reprehensible. But it's real, man. Anybody with military experience will say so. There's a secret brotherhood, the retiree civil service Mafia, sworn to do as little as possible to earn their paychecks.

The upcoming weeks and months will give me ample time to wonder how things got to be this way. Age has nothing to do with it, because in our world "retiree" does not mean senior citizen. Some of these guys are not much older than I am, and their years of service overlap mine. The oldest might be Vietnam Era, still plenty young enough to be sharp and put in a good day's work. Blame lack of oversight and accountability, maybe. So far as I can tell the retire-ocrats don't answer to anybody. And it would probably be tough to measure performance because doing nothing could be a perfectly good response when somebody tries to game the system. It could be that the whole thing is based on suspicion that we're looking for angles, trying to cheat the system and get breaks and benefits we don't deserve.

For a few weeks post-bomb, I attempt a leader's recon to scout out the battlefield and see what I'm up against, without giving away my position or my intentions. In non-Marine terms I make inquiries in a vague sort of way almost like I'm talking about someone else. My purpose is to answer a few basic questions:

Can I stay in even though I'm legally blind?

How do I fight to stay?

If I'm out of the Corps, what happens to me?

Since I'm short of the 20 years for full retirement, do my 16 years go down the drain?

Overall, what typically happens in a case like mine?

Everybody dodges and ducks my questions, particularly the last one. I understand why. Giving any kind of prediction could come back and bite them in the behind, because the people I ask just process the paperwork and have no ability to control the outcome. And guys in my position get pretty touchy where bodily damage and career and compensation and the entire future are at stake. Where big emotions run into apathy, rage happens. God knows it will for me.

To be fair I could be more forceful and demand answers and try to move things along. I don't though, not at first. I don't want to jump into the fight until I know what I'm getting into. Problem is, I won't get answers until I'm in the fight, because nobody wants to tell me squat in a general, speculative way. So I make a few PEB office drop-ins, beat around the bush, and get frustrated in a low-level sort of way. But I don't want to push hard and fast if I'm pushing my way out of the United States Marines, which I highly suspect could be the case. Why hurry up when I can wait, at least for a little while?

By now you know me well enough to know why. Screwing around does not suit me, and patience is not one of my virtues. If there's a fight, I want to get into it now.

26

Full Disclosure

"Hey, Top, let's go grab a cup of joe."

By this alone Top Dangerfield won't know I have news. Over the past few months we've become pretty good friends, and now and again we duck out for a few minutes.

I cut to the chase before we get to the espresso kiosk outside the PX: "Remember how I said that when I get to the point where my vision stops improving, I'll tell you?"

"Sure," Top says.

"I hit that point a month ago."

Top knows by the way I tell him that I wish I'd given him full information right off. He understands my position, though. After getting some details about the retina specialist's findings and what they mean, he wants to know what I need.

"So far, nothing, Top. I don't even know what I need to do and how this whole thing works."

"I'll see what I can do on that front."

"Thanks. I'm really in the dark."

"We've got to let the Colonel know so he doesn't get blind-sided," Top says, "Do you want me to tell him?"

"No thanks, I'll do it myself."

Going to the Colonel's office without a stop to see the Sergeant Major would violate protocol and show disrespect to the Sergeant Major, who naturally wants to know why I need to take the battalion commander's time.

"It might be easier if I just tell you both together," I say.

"Let's go," the Sergeant Major says, and I follow him, then wait until I'm called into the Colonel's office.

Assuming the POA I say to the colonel, "Good morning, Sir. Gunnery Sergeant Popaditch reporting as ordered, sir."

"Good morning, Gunny. At ease. What's on your mind?" says our battalion commander, who took the place of Colonel Chartier about a month ago. The new Tiger Six is Lt. Colonel Slaughter—greatest last name for a fighting Marine I know of.

After I report the situation concerning my vision the Colonel says, "Whatever the battalion and I can do to help, let me or the Sergeant Major know."

"Aye-aye, sir," I say. Afterwards the Sergeant Major extends his own offers of help. I thank him and leave feeling deeply relieved. No longer do I sit on information my superiors need and deserve to know.

And no longer do I sit, period. I might not like the consequences, whatever they will be, but no longer do I avoid them. The blood cleared. The damage showed. The truth looked me in the eye. So be it. The waiting game is over. Even when reality falls short of expectations it's real, and I can get real about it. I can quit loafing around S-3 waiting for a recovery that won't come and find out where the Corps can really use me. I won't be a tanker, but I can do something. I know it. No way can I be put out now while the Corps fights, while brothers in my own units do battle and die in Iraq. I can't shoot, but I can and I will fight to remain part of the fight. That I owe to my Corps and my country. I happen to believe in this fight with all my heart, but even if I didn't I would fight because the Corps is in it. Whatever the cause, whatever the mission, I believe in my fellow Marines.

And if, God forbid, I can't stay in, I will go in another direction. A direction I hate, maybe, but there I will go. I am happy right now because life without a future feels like living death, and now I have a future once again.

I start to beat the bushes. Every visit to Balboa I pump everybody and his brother and sister for information—corpsmen, doctors, clerks, the usual do-nothing, say-nothing-useful retirees. Though I do it all out in the open now, I still don't get the picture. How does this thing work?

Back at S-3 I tell Top about the information deficit. One day he says to me, "Hey, Gunny, I found out about a guy at the hospital who might be able to help you."

Top means the hospital here at Two-Nine, and he drives me over and introduces me to Rick DeLuna, PEB Liaison Officer at our base, who turns out to be my Miracle Retiree, the paper-pusher who actually does his job and helps.

Rick served as a Navy medical corpsman, a background that suits him well for his current billet. He knows Marines get broken in their line of work and need assistance. He also knows we have ten-percenters who malinger and try to shirk their duty. And he knows who's who. Like most of my favorite people he's a straight shooter and a little rough around the edges. No BS, no hidden agenda, nothing but the truth. If you're not ready for it, too bad. He doesn't care what you think of him personally, either. Right from Jump Street, I trust this guy and like him.

I lay out the situation, telling Rick what's broke on me and that the doc told me I've been submitted for a PEB.

"Do you understand how this works?" he asks.

"I don't have a clue."

Rick launches into a brief on the process I'm involved in. For me and every other unserviceable Marine it's all about PEB, Physical Evaluation Board, a panel that will rule on whether or not I'm fit for duty based on my physical limitations. If the PEB rules me unfit it will issue findings on how disabled I am, which will in turn dictate the terms of my medical retirement. The board comes up with a percentage of disability that translates into a percentage of retirement compensation. Fifty percent disabled means fifty percent of my base pay pension as a Gunny.

Right now, Rick says, the docs will prepare what's called a dictation, a report on what's broken medically speaking. Meanwhile my command will prepare a non-medical assessment concerning my performance as a Marine. It will answer the question, "Is this guy worth keeping?" Also, our battalion medical officer will do a Separation Physical, a top-to-bottom checkup of my current condition to be compared to my condition when I enlisted. This will show non-disqualifying injuries and physical losses—like, for instance, a missing finger or a toe—that might justify compensation when I leave the Corps but would not keep me from staying in. It's sort of like I'm a car that the Corps rented for 15 years, and now it has to make good for scratches and dings.

"Everything's important," Rick says, "but the meat and potatoes is the doc's dictation and how the PEB interprets it."

"Who writes the dictation?"

"The physician who called for the PEB."

"What are my odds of staying in? That's what I really want."

"You never know," Rick says, "Stranger things have happened." He explains that my command can do a lot to help by reporting my desire to stay in and telling how I can contribute in spite of the physical limitations.

"With eyesight like yours they better say you walk on water," Rick tells me.

For more than two hours he expounds and explains, and except for the occasional question I keep my mouth shut and soak up information that I desperately need to have a fighting chance of remaining a United States Marine. At this point that's my victory.

"What can I do?" I ask.

"A lot of this is out of your hands. Get your physical, go to your command for their assessment, and wait for the medical dictation to come back. When it does you look it over and sign it, and the whole package goes to the PEB."

Great, more waiting. Rick reassures me, though, that things should move quickly. PEB findings have been coming back in just 7 to 10 days after all the papers go in.

Rick says something that really hits me: "If this comes back the other way, that you're unfit for continuing service, you've got to be ready to go on short notice."

In other words if I'm judged unfit I'm out of uniform and out of a job and my family and I are out of our home—all in a hurry. Goodbye means not putting food on the table for April and Nicholas and goodbye roof over their heads, 3202-D Ludwig Court. The fast relocation doesn't bother me because the Corps is a force in readiness. If you're not prepared to rapidly deploy you're a poor Marine. Your family ought to be ready to change address, too, because that's part of our way of life. Always, though, there's a destination and one thing stays the same—you're a Marine and a Marine family. Now Rick talks about a deployment I never even considered—out of the Corps, off the base, out of life as I and my family know it. From First Marine Division, First Tanks, to First CivDiv. Just like that.

This I don't like hearing, but I need to know, and I appreciate Rick's forthrightness. I sign off feeling pretty damn good. The clouds have parted and will stay parted, thanks to Rick.

I go back to S-3 with a bounce in my step knowing that I have a new guide through the bureaucratic jungle. As to the final outcome, my ultimate expectation doesn't change. For all these years I did right by the Corps, and it will do right by me.

27

Super Pogue

Today is tomorrow. And I am Super Pogue.

I'm still not worth a damn at actual S-3 desk work, because I can't read, but I throw myself into collateral duties harder than ever. I order myself to love it, too. Got to make this whole thing work because I'm never going to get back on a tank. Feelings of loss aside, reality motivates me like strong coffee and main gun fire.

I start giving classes on combat leadership at the sergeants' training courses on-base, telling roomfuls of newly promoted Marines, from truck drivers to machine gunners, how to fulfill the responsibilities that the Corps has entrusted to them. In combat they will carry a heavy, critically important load, which starts right now, ten thousand miles from the battlefield and long before deployment. A sergeant must enforce the high standards of the Marine Corps tirelessly and mercilessly every minute of every day.

Wait until you get to actual combat to be vigilant and start acting like a leader, it's too late. You have failed your men. As I tell the boot sergeants, you can't pick and choose which regulations to enforce. Discipline starts with the little things. Let uniform regulations slide, next thing you know you've got dirty weapons and vehicles that don't run and Marines who don't follow your orders.

"If you can't make them shine their boots here in Twentynine Palms, how will you make them follow you into enemy fire?" I say.

I drum into the new sergeants' heads that they are the backbone of the Marine Corps, and that they should never allow themselves to become irrelevant by letting staff NCOs assume responsibility that rightfully belongs to them.

"If the Gunny's doing your job, what the fuck do we need you for? Then you're just an overpaid lance corporal," I say. The last remark is a gut-punch to sergeants.

For a closer I like to tell stories about young non-commissioned officers on the battlefield and the amazing deeds I saw them do in Iraq.

"I know you hear a lot of guys of my generation saying you newer Marines aren't tough. From where I stand and from what I've seen, that's bullshit."

This always fires them up, and I'm not just blowing smoke. I mean it.

The whole battalion uses me to bring reality to Marines checking into our units. Every week or so a platoon sergeant will come to me and say something like, "Hey Gunny, I got six new ones in from tank school. You want to give them the Welcome Aboard?"

"Where they at?" I say, eager to give the boots a big dose of The World According To Pop.

Getting the speech from a one-eyed, scarred-up Gunny helps scare them straight concerning the value of their Marine Corps training. Nobody could miss my two major points: A) Everything you've been taught so far works. B) You've got a lot more to learn here in First Tanks and not much time to learn it.

Always I tell the guys, "Open your ears. Ask questions. There's a lot of experience all around you."

I also tell them to come and find me if somebody says, "Fuck off, Boot," when they ask questions. I will crush a son-of-a-bitch for that. And I tell them to ignore the loudmouths who talk down the value of training.

"If some shitbird says, 'Hey, in the first 30 seconds of combat you throw the book out,' get away from him. He's incompetent. Two-hundred-and-thirty years of winning our nation's battles went into writing that book. Now some little two-year wonder is going to throw it out? I don't think so," I say.

This is fun. Passing down wisdom and knowledge that was once passed to me when I was boot. I could go all day on this stuff. All night, too. You cannot overemphasize the value of nuts and bolts training and enforcing standards. Be brilliant at the basics at Two Nine, and you'll be brilliant on the battlefield. Throw the book out when the shooting starts, and you throw out your best chance of winning. One guy does it, you've got a problem. If everybody throws the book out, you're done. An effective fighting unit becomes an undisciplined armed mob and a bigger danger to itself than to the enemy.

After scaring the shit out of the boots I let the sun shine in. "Welcome aboard," I say, and I really and truly mean it. The new guys leave feeling like part of the team but also well aware that they've got a lot to learn to come up to standard.

I spend more time down on the tank ramp and at barracks and give classes to the infantry on operations with mechanized units. I even become Gunny to the Remington Raiders in S-3, giving them talks on Basic Marine Skills. Busy as they are, I don't disrupt the plan of the day. Instead I give my talks prior to liberty call—quitting time to you civilians. Since I don't let them go until they've successfully passed a verbal quiz, these guys are model trainees.

Meanwhile I face my own test with results important to the PEB process. As part of the non-medical assessment my superiors are asked to verify that I can pass a PFT, Physical Fitness Test, which Marines take twice a year.

A verbal indication that I could pass would do the trick, but I want to run the hell out of the test and put the score into the assessment so nobody thinks I'm just limping along. I'm able-bodied and then some, and I want the PEB to know it.

"Let me take the test tomorrow," I say.

Commencing at 0600 with Top Dangerfield holding the stopwatch, I put max effort into a three-mile run. As soon as I catch my breath I do as many dead-hang pull-ups as I can before letting go of the bar and then do as many stomach crunches as possible in two minutes. The numbers escape me, but my overall score comes in First Class PFT, the highest category. The score is down some from previous highs, but I'm very proud of my performance. Not bad at all for a 37-year-old, especially one who got hit in the head with a grenade not too long ago.

At the Separation Physical Exam, the battalion MO leaves me alone in his office for a couple of minutes. Looking at the eye-chart I have a thought: I could just go over there and memorize the letters and pass the eye test with flying colors. Why not? It's wrong, that's why not. During the test I can't even ID the biggest letters on the chart.

I get an audiogram after which a corpsman rushes up to me. In a voice full of concern he says, "Are you aware that you have a serious hearing loss in your right ear?"

How could I not be aware? I don't crack wise, though, because the poor guy really acts like he's breaking bad news.

Another couple of corpsman have fun busting open smelling salt capsules and holding them under my nose to absolutely no effect. The same shrapnel that took out my right eye also cut the nerves from nose to brain and killed my sense of smell. Overall, though, I'm a very healthy guy, tiptop and good to go from the neck down. That ought to look good on the PEB, too.

I feel better and better about my situation until one day Top Dangerfield tells me to conduct a pre-deployment gear inspection on one of our platoons, which is just about to ship out to Iraq.

"Aye-aye, Top," I say, happy to get such a task. I built a reputation as an ace detail inspector, with my own signature moves to ratchet up the stress level during personnel inspection and see if guys really know their stuff under duress. Only bullies and punks break their Marines down for fun, but stress applied in a calculated way has legitimate purposes and training value.

The entire platoon stands on the battalion grinder, each Marine holding his personal weapon at order arms with his deployment gear laid out on his poncho. I step in front of the first Marine, who performs the first seven counts of Inspection Arms, and then snatch away his rifle in such a manner that if he doesn't let go he gets a butt stock in the nuts. So far, so good. I could do this in my sleep. I go through all the motions of rifle inspection, looking over the key areas—compensator, slip ring, chamber, bolt face, magazine well, butt stock. I look, but I don't see. In truth, for all I really know, this weapon could be covered with rust, a major disgrace and outrage, or altogether unserviceable.

Hey, I knew this was coming, and it doesn't worry me because at this point the platoon sergeants and squad leaders have done their own pre-inspections. So the personal weapons are in good shape. Bet on it. I could take a shot in the dark here and list some minor discrepancies like dust in the magazine well and dirt on the butt stock with a 99 percent chance of being right. Instead, I do some verbal follow-up.

"What's your BZO, Marine?"

He spits out his settings for Battle Sight Zero on this particular weapon, two clicks right and front sight post flush. I make a show of checking his front and rear sights and try to squeeze some more good out of this charade by asking pertinent questions like the target range of his rifle's settings—36 meters and 300 meters—and why we sight in on those particular ranges. I can remember not knowing why and really wondering when I was a boot.

The answer: the rifle's line of sight is flat, and it intersects the round's arched trajectory at 36 meters and 300 meters. But everywhere in-between, the point of aim and the point of impact are never farther apart than the height of a human torso. Bottom line—if you can hit the paper target here, you can knock down anybody on the battlefield within the length of three football fields, just by shouldering your weapon, aiming, and firing. The BZO is all about confidence in combat.

I've got other questions with answers that are must-knows in Iraq. How do you signal an Iraqi to stop? Do it the American way and you might have to shoot him because he thinks you want him to come to you.

On to the stuff on the poncho. Every single thing each Marine will carry with him to Iraq—down to the required six pairs of skivvies, razor with 15 blades, two toothbrushes, extra boot laces, and on and on—sits out in plain view. If it's not on the tarp the man wears it or carries it, and my job is to make sure it's all present and all serviceable, just like his weapon. To facilitate inspection the Marines all put out their gear following a template laid down by a unit leader. Fully sighted I could do a lot of the work standing, looking for vacant spaces and counting items. Now I have to get down and dig. No problem here pride-of-rank-wise. Gunny is Gunny on his feet or bear-crawling on the grinder. But the rate of progress does present a problem.

With over 100 items per man I would have to spend an hour with each guy to do my job properly by feel and picking up stuff and eyeballing it two inches from my face. I could do it, but it's slow go, and I have no choice but to start cutting corners, looking at one representative piece out of groups, like inspecting one magazine of the required six as if it tells me the condition of every other one. Guess what? It doesn't, and unprepared Marines try to game inspectors by hiding the substandard stuff. I know enough to look down in the stacks, but still one out of six does not begin to complete the mission. Even if the guy's not skating there could be problems that he lacks the experience to recognize. That's why we have a

Detail Inspector, and that's why he's a Gunny and not a corporal a couple years off the street or a Second Lieutenant fresh out of college. Mileage, man, experience—except today I can't get the goods to market.

And even cutting some corners, I can't keep up the pace of other Detail Inspectors who simultaneously go over other squads that make up this platoon. Each one of us starts with an assigned squad, moving down the ranks. When the other guys are done with theirs, they move into the unfinished squad—my squad—and start inspecting at the little end and move up. When we meet, every Marine on the grinder will have been subject to a thorough inspection. It'll all get done, but no thanks to me. The other staff NCOs do ten for my two.

The whole business takes a couple hours, and all the while I feel like less and less of a Gunny. If the unit's any good, and I believe this one is, the Marines have already been thoroughly inspected and nobody will die in Iraq because of something I personally missed. That's what's at stake, by the way, life and death, winning and losing. If a magazine we fail to inspect has a weak spring, and a Marine inserts it into his weapon, he's an unarmed man because the weapon will fail to feed and will jam. In a firefight, that Marine's rifle is his life.

With gear, just like with training and regulations, the little shit is huge. Think about bootlaces. Even the best rifleman in the world has a problem or at least a distraction if he has to duct-tape his boot to his foot on a dismounted patrol. That's a problem he doesn't need to have, which I could prevent if I had even one serviceable eye. I know I contribute, but today I fail these Marines on the grinder. And I become a drag on my fellow staff NCOs by going so slowly that they come over to my squad to pick up the slack. When did this ever happen to the old Gunny Pop? Never, that's when, particularly not during an inspection. I was the Hammer, the man who didn't miss a thing. The Marines were scared to even try to get anything by me.

I hate this, but I don't beat myself up. Like we teach Marines on the rifle range, once you pull the trigger the round's gone. You can't get it back. Even if you miss the whole target all that matters is the next shot. Move on. That's what I do when I step off the grinder, move and take my next best shot. Back in S-3 I start working up the day's lessons for the office guys.

Wake up the pogues.

Make better Marines out of them.

28

SMEAC

"Gunny, I'm done with them. Give them a Liberty Brief and cut them out of here," Top Dangerfield says to me at 1700, about an hour early for knocking off.

Maybe eight of the S-3 pogues gather around and stand in what we call a school circle, a semi-circular arrangement for informal instructional sessions. In a bigger group they'd sit-kneel-bend so everybody can see, and they'd form up without even thinking about it, so often do we senior Marines impart knowledge to groups.

Since it's Friday and they heard Top say the magic word "Liberty," they're more all-ears than usual. They've got the whole weekend off with myriad possibilities for overnights down the hill in LA, San Diego, Vegas and all points in-between. To these single young guys living in barracks, a free weekend is a major adventure. At their age I felt like I could cut loose and roam the world before Monday morning. With no bills except maybe my motorcycle payments I always had a pocketful of money and no reason not to blow it all. To my way of thinking, another good sea story, involving major fun, was a wiser investment than buying mutual fund shares or however boring individuals squirreled away their money. Who could be more carefree than a young Marine? Life was just unbelievably good.

And it's going to get good for the S-3 guys as soon as I finish my brief. Impatient as I know they are, they all maintain a professional demeanor, and I do my best to make good use of their time and attention. I could get away with droning out the required Liberty Safety Brief, a lot of blah-blah about things they already know: Don't drink and drive and so on. They've heard it all so many times, they don't really hear it any more. That won't cut it. Today my S-3 guys get a bonus lesson in Fleet Marine Force Knowledge, which happens to include the safety brief.

I open like so: "Why do Marines fuck up on liberty?" I answer myself, "Because they don't have a plan. Liberty is a mission, and you have to approach it with the same diligence you'd use to prepare a real-world mission."

I tell the guys their solution is to give themselves an Op Order—operations order—using the five-paragraph format that we call SMEAC:

> S) Situation. "You are a single Marine stationed in Twentynine Palms, California, where there are two eligible females, both diseased."

> M) Mission. "You must conduct a tactical road march to the City of Los Angeles or other target-rich environment."

> E) Execution: "You will travel in the buddy system by use of privately owned vehicle."

> A) Admin and Logistics: "Fuel will be purchased at the base service station prior to departure and chow at roadside establishments."

> C) Command and Signal. "You will depart upon hearing the command 'Liberty Call.' In the event that one or both of you become physically injured and incapacitated or are detained by local law enforcement, you will call your platoon sergeant."

I get some grins. Come Monday, I will build on their knowledge, challenging them to make up five-paragraph op orders for whatever they're doing. From there I can move on to fine points that Marines of their ranks don't normally get. But Friday is not the night to run long, so I deliver the brief in about 10 minutes.

I tell them when to be back: "Liberty secures 0530 Monday."

Then I say, "If you're 10 minutes early . . . " and they finish with me, "You're five minutes late!" If you work with me, you've heard it a thousand times.

And finally I say the words they're dying to hear: "Liberty call!"

Abracadabra, they're gone, just like Penn and Teller did a trick.

Last man working, tonight and always, is Top Dangerfield. As we often do when we've got the place to ourselves, we shoot the breeze a little bit, winding down from the work week.

Tonight he asks me about the PEB, and I steer us into a subject that weighs heavily on my mind.

"I think this thing may go against me," I say.

"What do you mean?"

"I think they're going to find me unfit for service and try to put me out," I say.

Top listens like a friend, but he's too honest to contradict me here.

"I'm thinking about fighting it and trying to stay in," I say, "How could I leave now, Top, when we're at war, when Marines are in the fight?"

"I'm with you, Gunny."

"If I go work in the schoolhouse, I'd free up an able-bodied guy for combat, right?"

"How can we help you here? The colonel told me he's on board, whatever you need."

"I've got to find a billet that I can fill where this eye thing doesn't matter."

"I've been giving that some thought myself," Top says.

At this point I find out that what weighs on my mind, weighs on his, too. Top thinks I ought to look into teaching at the tank school.

"I been thinking a lot about that, too," I say, charged-up because Top sees the possibilities for me at tank school, too. Not only that, he says he'll make some calls to Headquarters Marine Corps, where one of our old battalion commanders now works in Manpower, Enlisted Branch. He's the duty expert, the one to ask if such a thing is do-able and how.

"It's Twenty-Hundred Hours Eastern, so we'll have to wait until Monday," Top says. "You need a lift?"

On Friday I'll take it.

29

(Im)possibilities

B*illets I can Fill*

1) TANK SCHOOL
Fort Knox, Kentucky

Both Top's idea and mine, too, even before I got hit, although I pictured doing it during my twilight tour 10 years from now. What better way to leave a lasting legacy than to send the next generation of tankers out to the fleet the Gunny Pop way?

Top sees me going to the Master Gunner Branch, a highly technical and tough school for career tankers and leaders. But I want to go where the rubber meets the road, turn privates into Fleet Marine Force tank crewmen. Fresh out of Boot Camp they're clay ready to be molded. Everything I did and saw in a dozen years—hits and wins on the battlefield, and thrown tracks, blown engines, missed shots with the main gun, accidentally injured crewmen, and numerous and sundry screwups. Every success and every problem was a lesson that I can give to the basic armor crewmen and start them out right.

Hell yeah, I can do it. With my head stuffed full of tankology, it won't matter that I can't read. Give this a 9.5 on the enthusiasm scale, next best thing to 10.0, which is being back on a tank.

2) COURSE FOR SERGEANTS
Twentynine Palms

I'm already a guest teacher here. Not reading makes preparation slower and harder, but it's not a show-stopper. I also consider myself a duty expert on the two key areas of the sergeants' course, leadership and Basic Marine Skills. I love this stuff and love drumming it into guys who absolutely need to know it.

On a personal, family level, this one's good because we don't have to move, meaning one less disruptive school change for Nick Jr. And I can still walk to work, which is huge. 8.5. Minor deductions because the new sergeants come to me a little more cooked and set in their ways.

3) COURSE FOR CORPORALS
Camp Pendleton, California

Another very good fit and personally very appealing. Brand-new corporals are great to teach, and they need to master a lot of new knowledge and understand their new responsibilities. In the Corps a corporal is a non-commissioned officer and expected to lead. The curriculum is pretty much a basic version of the sergeants' and pure Gunny Pop. I love working with corporals, who will bust their asses to carry out a mission. If they fail it's because they don't know how to do it, which is, of course, the point of the course. I could knock this one out of the park. 8.5, a tie with 2.

4) TRAINING IRAQIS
Multiple Sites, Iraq

If the Corps thinks I'm too blind to train Marines, let me go back overseas. With the training techniques and doctrine I already know inside and out, I'll make Iraqis off the street into fighting men that our Marines will be proud to regard as allies and fight alongside. Those people could be almost as good as ours, lacking only the intangibles that other nations don't bring to a fight and Americans do. And I happen to really like Iraqis. They're friendly, funny, and generous in their hospitality like nobody I ever met. Solid 8. Exciting, but involves a move down to the minors.

5) RECRUITER
Anytown, USA

Most career Marines who don't become hats do a tour in a recruiting office, often against their will. I would love to spread the word about the Corps and bring young Americans onboard for the greatest opportunity to transform themselves into more responsible, disciplined, motivated, and all-around better citizens and human beings. For reasons unknown I'm already a walking recruitment poster. Even with the professional hazards on display, people want what I've got. Kids want to get next to me and start asking questions. Afterward Dads come up to me and say, "Great, now he wants to be a Marine. Thanks a lot."

You're welcome.

6.7

Down, because you can't get any closer to civilian. My appointed place of duty might be in the mall next to Cinnabon. I'll do it, though.

6) STATUS QUO
S-3, Twentynine Palms

So far I've been able to invent missions for myself that really matter in spite of performing no function connected to my actual billet and visual limitations that stick out like a monkey's ass in an office setting. Score's a lousy 4.9

Problems and Deal Breakers

1) TANK SCHOOL

I can't get around Fort Knox on my own. The base is enormous. Depending on others for transport bugs me to no end.

Though I can talk a great game, I can't see well enough to make sure my students do what I tell them. Boot tankers screw up details right and left, and if I don't catch mistakes and correct them, some NCO out in the fleet will have to bust his ass to undo the damage I cause. I can't demonstrate much of anything, either, because I can't command a tank.

If I can't do a good job, forget it.

2) COURSE FOR SERGEANTS

The billet involves a lot beyond platform teaching. An instructor also acts as squad leader to a group of students, responsible for, among other things, personnel inspection. We saw how well that went out on the First Tanks grinder. And what the hell do I do during nighttime exercises in the field portion of the schooling? Here I become an outright liability.

3) COURSE FOR CORPORALS

(See 2 above.)

4) TRAIN IRAQIS

If I can't see the little stuff, the crack unit I want to train will be undisciplined fuckups. And I would need to pack personal weapons. On me, though, sidearms are just decoration unless a bad guy walks up and introduces himself, then stands still so I can shoot him.

5) RECRUITER

No go, because I can't drive. A recruiter logs an insane amount of road-miles going to schools, kids' houses, meetings with parents, processing stations, and special events. The rest of the joke is a guy who can't read trying to prepare an enlistment contract, pages and pages of miniscule print.

6) STATUS QUO

I still don't have a clue what the rest of the guys in S-3 do. And how long can I rack my mind and exercise initiative to be useful before the well runs dry? The idea of irrelevance bothers me, and here I stand on a slippery slope.

30

Not on the Bus

Top Johnson calls from Iraq with big news.

"I got a Warning Order for you," he says.

"Send it."

"Get Club Pop ready. The company's coming back in a couple weeks, and if it's all right with you, I'd like to crack my first cold beer at your place."

"Done. But are you sure it's all right with Mama? That's your first night home."

"Hey, I'm not coming by myself. She and the kids are going to be there, too."

After Top J hangs up, I authenticate with his Home Six—check with his wife. I call his house and ask Kathleen Johnson if it's really okay to party at our house on her husband's first evening back.

"Sure, that's all he's been talking about. We'll have a barbecue, and it'll be fun," Kathleen says. If she felt otherwise she would put the kibosh on the plan right here and now. As a former Navy corpsman she can express herself as forcefully and colorfully as any of us. She and Top J have been married forever, just like April and me, and she's an outstanding Marine Corps spouse and mother of four kids.

Two days before Bravo Company's scheduled arrival, I throw a bunch of steaks so big they look like they came off a brontosaurus into an A-1 sauce marinade and lay in a load of Bud Light—full-on Bud would make us staff NCOs heavier than we already are—and a ridiculous amount of soft drinks and side dishes including stuff just for kids. To run out of anything would bring dishonor on Club Pop, which always lives up to its motto: If you leave here hungry or sober, that's your own damn fault.

Early in the day Team Bravo's buses pull up to Victory Field, where various groups of welcomers wait. First crack at the returning warriors goes to wives and kids, who stampede toward their loved ones while the base band plays. Once the hugging and kissing winds down, the guys have some business to attend to, like turning in weapons, distributing personal gear, and taking care of admin details such as barracks assignments. At this phase First Tanks guys like me feel free to move in and mingle. Since I can't tell who's who, I have to wait for friends and Marines I served with and fought with to come to me. But it's good to be with them. All the pride and good vibes are out here for all of us to share. Welcome Homes are great days.

Top J's private Welcome Home at our place takes it up a notch. Damn it's fun to reopen Club Pop for business and see my trigger-puller buddy back home and covered with glory. Here he stands, stuffed full of steak as only I can burn it, bottle in hand, telling my favorite kind of war stories—ones that I haven't heard before and that I know actually happened. Compared to earlier bashes we go easy on the beer and adjourn early. After all, J has a home to go to with his family, and we will have plenty of time for more drinking and shooting the shit.

A week later I get a summons to appear at Colonel Slaughter's office. No idea what he wants, but no worries, either. After the "Reporting as ordered, Sir," he tells me to stand at ease and says, "Gunny, I'm going out to meet Charlie Company at the airstrip. I've got an extra seat in the vehicle and was wondering if you'd like to come along."

Next day at Zero-Six we take off in a van for March Air Force Base, where Charlie's flight will land. I can't call the silence that reigns for most of the two-hour ride awkward, because Gunnies and Battalion Sixes don't make small talk. We've got lines in the Corps that we all understand and avoid crossing. Personally I like it like this, and I bet Colonel Slaughter does, too, even though in other circumstances we could be very good friends. This is my kind of guy, a regular Joe who doesn't have to show off his college vocabulary to prove he's the colonel and a trigger puller in spirit in spite of the current heavy desk time. Don't get me wrong. I like a lot of officers, but what I like about our Battalion Six is that he's not like the rest of them. Back when he was a company commander he earned my respect by punching out another CO who cheated him out of some tank parts. Sometimes a good old-fashioned ass-kicking solves problems better than anything else, and this man knows it.

CNN—what else?—plays on the big screen TV in the terminal building, strewn about with guys sleeping, playing cards, and otherwise killing time before their outbound flights. Meanwhile American Legionnaires hand out phone cards, magazines, and pogey bait—soda and junk food.

The colonel comes to me and says Charlie's plane just landed and walks with me to their hatch where they come in single file while we meet and greet, saying "Semper Fi" and "Welcome Back." A lot of guys I don't know so well because I came into the company just prior to deployment and overseas my platoon got detached to Fallujah, but I'm glad and honored to shake the hand of every single one.

All is not so upbeat, though. Things get serious when I talk Gunny-to-Gunny with a friend and fellow platoon sergeant who lost one of his tank commanders only a week earlier.

"Sorry about Sergeant Smith," I say. "I hear it was like the Wild West out there." I say this because I met a lot of infantry in the hospitals who got shot up in heavy fighting in his platoon's AO on the Syrian border.

"No man, they never messed with the tanks. They only shot at us twice, and the second time they got Sergeant Smith. On his last patrol, too. Doing right seat/left seat with his relief."

I can't believe the dead Marine's unbelievably bad luck. As my friend says, he wasn't even commanding his tank any more but showing his replacement the patrol route. And he got hit in a one-shot ambush. Somebody pointed an RPG, pulled the trigger, hauled ass, and the grenade killed him. Thinking about the fallen fellow warrior I see him in maintenance coveralls, sure sign of a hands-on wrench-turning tank commander. What I knew of him I respected and liked. For an instant I flash on the parallels between us. Two guys, both tank commanders who volunteered to go back to Iraq and got hit with RPGs. Bang he's dead. And bang I'm not.

Good guy. Too bad.

Now for the reunion I've been waiting for. In the general mingling I'm surrounded by guys from First Platoon, call sign Red Platoon, who had me as their platoon sergeant until I got hit. All the guys in my platoon belonged to other units before but volunteered to go with Charlie, our first tank company returning to fight in Iraq after the big push to Baghdad in 2003. And my God, have they matured. In January they walked onto a plane headed overseas, still a work in progress from my point of view. Not a day went by that I didn't wear them out individually and as a group. Now, eight months and change later, they hit the home ground swaggering—tougher, more confident, proud of who they are and what they have accomplished. Some of my guys wear new stripes that they earned the hard way.

One new sergeant, a corporal when I left Iraq, says to me, "Hey Gunny, I'm going to go see the career jammer soon as I get back to battalion. Man, I love this stuff, and I'm going back again."

He means that he intends to re-enlist and redeploy ASAP—this from a man finishing his first enlistment, fresh from eight months in the war zone, who's been in California for less than five minutes!

He comes off the plane with another sergeant on his second enlistment whom I've known for years, from when he was a brand-new private out of tank school. This is Sgt. Escamilla, my wingman in Fallujah, designated Red Three to my Red Four, in command of the tank that went with mine into my last street fight. With him following I never felt the need to look back and check his position. He was there. This says something about him, given the way I always went into hornets' nests and stirred things up to get the bad guys out where we could shoot them.

Sgt. Escamilla doesn't say a thing about going back, and he doesn't have to. He's hooked, a lifer, a believer, in the fight for the duration and in the Corps for the long haul. Coming home does not end the story for him. Right now he'll take a well-earned break, go home, get laid or whatever, and come back to get ready for the next deployment. I know it because I know my own kind.

Guys gather around me dying to tell me what they did.

"Gunny, I did my first patrol as a tank commander."

"I hit that asshole from 300 meters away."

"Nobody could touch Red Platoon, not even close."

It's like I'm Dad and they're the sons coming home from college with scholarly awards and sports trophies and first-place ribbons. Their pride fills me with pride. I'm proud to be connected to a team like Red, which makes me feel more connected to the entire Corps. And the guys link their successes to things I taught them and showed them.

"We turned into fire and assaulted into the ambush just like you told us, last thing in the world they expected us to do. Fucked them up bad, Gunny."

"Just like you drilled us, Gunny. We walked the track when we came in every time, and we never threw track. Those other lazy assholes did it all the time."

"I remembered what you said and used turboshaft oil on the machine guns after we ran out of CLP. It really is better."

"Washed my hands before I ate every single time, like you taught us. and I never got sick. The other guys were falling out with Saddam's Revenge."

Even when they're not telling me how such-and-such that I taught them really worked, I hear my own voice and own expressions being played back. "Don't be afraid to act." "Be a Zero Four Marine." "Keep raising the bar." "Be brilliant at the basics." Behind it all is an attitude and spirit I did everything in my power to strengthen: Team cohesion and mission accomplishment. Before we deployed I beat these and hundreds of other lessons into them. Even though they could say the right things, some of them struggled because they didn't understand or hesitated because they lacked the confidence to act decisively. Now they're leaders, doers, unafraid, independent—Marines in every sense.

"Hey Gunny, ride the bus back to battalion with us. Come on!"

"Nah, this is your show. You earned it. I'll see you there."

In my head I'm saying, "Negative. Absolutely not."

These things they will see: "Welcome Home!" signs and banners starting miles from the gate. People on the highway and locals who don't know any of the Marines from Adam waving and cheering and running up with cold beer and sodas. The local radio station following in its mobile unit and doing live coverage. Every man on the bus will feel like a hero, like he raised the flag on Mount Suribachi and personally saved the nation. After the bus busts the gate at our base the guys will hear a chorus of women's voices. You have no idea how exciting screaming and uninhibited American females sound after months in a chick-free zone like Iraq. I've already described the actual disembarking where the families are reinforced by volunteer ladies—huggers, we call them—who show up to say "Welcome Home" and wrap their arms around guys who don't have anybody waiting for them.

You earn this reward. Riding along will only remind me that I'll never earn another one again.

The bond between me and the returning heroes breaks. Just like that I go from one of them to outside looking in. And I know that I will stay outside forever. They will fight again, and I won't. Another trigger puller would understand perfectly how hard this hits. It kills me. Always, though, I keep my good face on. Even my best friends—even April—have no idea what goes on in my head and how I fight to stay on top. Never will I let my mood sink to the bottom, where it would have gone if I had gotten on that bus.

31

Homework

In a gentle sort of way I issue a standing order to April and Nicholas: "The best way to help me, is don't help me. What I really need from you is patience."

It's got to be tough on them watching Dad fumble and struggle to do the most simple everyday things around the house, from putting the key in the front door on in. God bless them, my family always wants to jump in and help. Much as I love them for it, though, warning lights go off. Let them do too much and make things too easy, I become dependent and stop extending myself to use what I've got. Believe me, it would be very easy for me and all concerned if I said things like, "Why don't you unlock the door from now on? It takes me too long," and let April and Nicholas cook and set the clocks and do the laundry and so on with no help from me. "Help" at this point is more like interference—I have no illusions about that, but I have to stay on the team, and my loved ones must understand that easy is a prison where I could be locked up for life. Screwing up until I get things right is my only key to freedom.

Here's another case where jarhead training does me good. No real Marine denies himself the opportunity to fail for the sake of achieving success. You never outgrow or outrank training, which is practically synonymous with fucking up in spectacular and humiliating ways in front of God and everyone. It doesn't take long to develop a hide like a rhinoceros, which embarrassment cannot penetrate if it's embarrassment in a good cause. Therefore, I don't mind the slapstick and pratfalls around home, where I develop a few basic tricks like scanning my head's arc of travel before I bend over and toe-feeling at the bottom of the stairs to confirm this really is the bottom. Mostly what I have to learn is that there's a hell of a lot that I can't see. Funny how I'm still catching on six months in, and the whole deal still feels unnatural and unbelievably frustrating.

Not reading infuriates me. I feel like I'm lost in some foreign country with a strange alphabet. I never was a big reader, but I sure miss it now. I look at the newspaper full of longing and anger that I can't even make out the football scores and league standings. I used to go through that stuff with a fine-tooth comb picking up all the latest developments and details and predicting next week's winners. The more facts I have, the more fun I have, and TV dishes up too much fluff, not enough usable intelligence.

But reading goes way beyond personal entertainment and interest. Without the benefit of written instructions, which come on pretty much everything around the house, I have a choice: Wing it or ask somebody to tell me what it says. This applies to tuning in radio stations in the car or working the cable TV remote or my cell phone. Push a wrong button on any of these things and I wander into menu-land with no way to get back to where I started short of powering down and trying it all again. If April's out and I microwave chow for the kid and myself, I must walk it on target like artillery, deliberately under-heating the food, then heating a little more at a time until we hit the desired temperature. I limit commands to the microwave to Time and Start and open the door to stop it because the multitude of functions are out of reach. It isn't one, two, three or even ten of the little pains in the ass that get to me. It's everything, in every facet of life. Those of you with good vision have no idea how often you rely on the written word.

Fortunately Nicholas' schooling is still pretty basic so I can draw on my own knowledge when he comes to me for help. I can do a lot of good with spot checks and Q&As just like I do with the Marines. Whatever the subject matter I satisfy myself that he has a good grasp of it and does his required work. A good father would do as much no matter what, but in our case we're obligated to sign off on Nicholas' homework. His teacher requires that a parent look over all the kids' assignments and sign sheets verifying that they completed the required reading and written homework. Each day Nicholas comes home with op orders and we conduct an inspection to confirm that the orders have been carried out. Some parents I know resent this and consider it laziness on the part of the teacher, like she's pawning off work on us, but I don't mind at all. To me, this is "Don't expect—inspect" on the home front. And parents ought to be involved.

In my case, I employ some smoke and mirrors to appear more involved than I actually am. Basically, it's the pre-deployment inspection on the grinder all over again, except now we have numbers and writing on paper instead of weapons and field gear. Apparently I have a much better command of Marine Corps BST than the sixth grade curriculum because Nicholas pulls a fast one.

One night he comes to me with the sign-off sheet, and our conversation goes something like this:

"What was your assignment?"

"I had to read Chapter Six in the Social Studies book."

"What does Chapter Six pertain to?"

"Religions."

"Okay, what are the major religions practiced in the world?"

"Christianity, Judaism, Islam."

"What about Buddhism and Hinduism?"

"Those, too, in India and Asia."

Sounds solid to me, so I move on to Phase 2:

"Was there any written work?"

"Yeah, I was supposed to answer some study questions."

"About what?"

"The chapter."

At this point he hands me a piece of paper covered with writing. Given my son's record of honesty, I assume it's legit. We repeat the scene—and my assumptions—the next night and the next.

But then comes a rude awakening. I arrive home from work, and April tells me that Nicholas has been lying to me and having me sign off on homework that he did not do.

The news hits me like a gut punch. I feel like half a father, which is even worse than feeling like half a Marine.

Had something similar happened in a barracks or out on the tank ramp I'd be kicking some serious ass with an accompanying show of fury. Anybody within a quarter mile would get a loud, graphic reminder how much you don't want to piss off Gunny.

Gunny doesn't live here, though. Dad does. Before I utter a word I send Nicholas to his room and work up my game plan to make sure that he understands the lesson I need to impart. At the same I take my own feelings out of play. It doesn't matter how much this incident stings. Believe me, it does. For the first and only time I feel handicapped. And I'm much madder at myself than at the boy. How could I let a 10-year-old dupe me? With two good eyes, it never would have happened.

Right here and now, reality takes a big bloody bite out of my ass, and I know I need so much more to make this thing work. For my son's sake, for my sake, I need to do a hell of a lot better than I just did. His problem we can fix in one sitdown. Mine, I just don't know.

It is mine, though, not his, which is why I take some extra time to get a grip before I go into his room to talk.

He sits on his bed. Even I can tell he's mopey and sad as only a good kid who did wrong can be. I pull the chair from his desk up close to him and sit so we're level and eye to eye.

"You lied to me, didn't you?" I say.

"Yes."

"Once you betray somebody's trust, that's a hard thing to earn back."

"I know it is," he says, and he doesn't make a peep while I lecture him on integrity.

"Do you want to be this sort of kid, whose own father can't believe the words coming out of your mouth?"

"No."

"Do you understand what I'm telling you? Or do I have to do something, punish you, to make you get it and remember?"

"No, Dad, I understand."

"Is this the last time we're going to have this conversation?"

"Yes it is."

When I stand up to go he tells me how sorry he is, which I genuinely believe. April later tells me he had tears of shame after the incident. A kid's a kid, so we will have more minor integrity issues from time to time, but nothing so serious. All in all, Nicholas is the most honest kid I know.

You probably expect a Marine Gunnery Sergeant to yell at his kid and have him cleaning the garage with a tooth brush and applying all sorts of psychological torture, if not corporal punishment. I always think of the Marine dad in The Great Santini bouncing a basketball off his oldest son's head, asking if the kid's really his favorite daughter. That guy sounds reveille in the morning and generally treats his children like a platoon. However, as I wrote many pages back, I leave my Gunny persona at work. Nicholas doesn't need a staff NCO. I do want to instill in him my core beliefs and develop in him the virtues that belong to Marines—integrity, accountability, courage, honor, and commitment. But I cannot employ Marine methods. There's no need. And God only knows what the results would be, treating your grade-school-age kid like a 19-year-old recruit who has to be ready to fight in 13 weeks. I'd face serious opposition from April, anyway, if I even tried.

Much as it hurts, this incident with Nicholas and his homework turns out to be a call to action that does us all some good. We are failing to address nuts-and-bolts problems brought on by my eyesight. After this we do a better job of acknowledging, at least, that we do have problems and that we need to deal.

On the fatherhood front I sub in conversation for the dad-son things we used to love so much, like playing catch and changing the car's oil. I used to especially enjoy quiet activity with Nicholas, because as Gunny I had to run my mouth all day. Now, though, talk is what we've got, and we have as much fun throwing ideas back and forth as a baseball. We discover all sorts of common interests that might not have come to light otherwise. The apple fell closer to the tree than I thought, and Nicholas doesn't seem to mind hearing my favorite Marine stories over and over.

We open up new avenues of communication about my eyesight, too. For the first time I try to give Nicholas a precise understanding of what I see. Sometimes we just look around while I describe my view. Outside I say I can make out the major elements of the landscape—mountains in the distance, neighboring houses, trees—probably almost as well as he can. But blurriness wipes out the details. Indoors I point out things like pictures on the wall but say I can't make out the images. Nicholas deserves to understand my limitations. But I also want him to understand my capabilities, which are greater than he thinks.

"See that clock on the wall?" I say. "I can't see what time it is from here, but I can walk up to it and read it myself."

In other words, he shouldn't feel the need to tell me the time.

We worked out a drill for providing Dad with assistance as needed.

I say to him: "Son, I'll make a deal with you. Don't feel like you have to look out for me and take care of me in any way, shape, or form. If I get in a bind I'll ask you for help. Deal?"

The essence: He's still the kid, and he shouldn't worry or feel strange. I'm his Dad and the same guy I used to be except I don't see so well. Looking back from now, three years later, it's hard to believe the first-phase awkwardness we experienced.

Bit by bit we work things out. I tell Nicholas that when he walks or stands on my right-hand side he's completely off the radar. Since that's my deaf side as well as blind side, he might as well not be there. Over and over I tell him where he ought to be so we can communicate. Since he's a kid, restless and maybe testing the limits a little, he still goes to my right side. One day I tell him, "Do you want to be invisible to me? That's what you are, over there." Problem solved. The issue never comes up again.

We also air out an issue that's been bugging me practically from Day One. This involves April, too. Both my wife and son like to direct my attention toward objects of interest, things they don't want me to miss, by putting their hands directly in front of my good eye and pointing. It works pretty well, but it annoys the hell out of me on multiple levels. For one, this is how you get a dog or a baby to look at something. And I just can't stand having somebody's hands come up in my face like this. If a man did it I might punch him out. Knowing the good intentions behind my family's pointing, I kept my mouth shut until this point. But I can't endure it for the rest of my life, and the rest of my life just started. April and Nicholas understand and have no trouble adapting to a new system that works for me. Basically, I teach them to designate targets the exact way we do on tanks, a clock for the direction and range—three o'clock and fifteen feet away, for instance—and also to employ major landmarks that they know I can make out.

Crazy, isn't it, how you can live with people and talk not at all about such important aspects of your lives? We've been doing it for six whole months, and even though it feels terrific and saves us untold trouble when we get straight, it takes an effort to do it.

In my case, the obstacle might be my old friend PMA, Positive Mental Attitude, which I use 24/7, particularly during the most difficult times. I need it as much as ever, but have to adjust fire so I don't blind myself to reality. Talk's cheap—this goes for self-talk, too. Saying "I'm good to go" doesn't make it true, not unless I start turning wrenches on my whole damn life. Problem is, at this point I don't have a tool kit or technical manual. Beyond the most obvious fixes, like not falling down the stairs and talking straight with my wife and son, I don't have Clue One. And I don't know where to start looking for it.

32

Dawn of Hope

To this point my screwed-up balance has occupied a second-tier position. But now that we've reached a steady state vision-wise, Mrs. Dr. Keefe sends me to a specialist at Balboa known far and wide as the Dizzy Doctor. He is one of the most high-energy individuals I have ever encountered. Even the fully sighted might see this guy as a blur, and he talks as fast as he moves, like he comes from some other high-speed dimension. April says he reminds her of the Mad Hatter in Alice in Wonderland. I like him, though, and he explains my vertigo very clearly.

"You've got three level vials in your inner ear that give you your sense of balance," he says.

"Oh yeah," I say, "Like the gyroscopes on tanks for yaw, pitch, and left/right rotation."

I think I just annoyed him by delaying the proceedings for five seconds. He resumes; "Most people's balance organs are full of a thin liquid like water. But yours on the right are full of mud. Since your left ear is fully functional, you lose your balance while the right catches up."

He says he has a procedure to take care of my symptoms. I picture something lengthy and unpleasant involving drills and new holes in my head, but he says it'll take about two minutes and he can do it right now.

"There's a catch, though," he says. "Afterward you must wear a neck brace and sleep sitting up for two days. Do you want to schedule it for later or go ahead?"

No inclination to delay, especially not with this guy. He has me lie flat on a declined table, head below my feet, while he and an assistant roll me right then left with my head and body in line like they're paramedics who suspect a victim's back injury. On each side they rotate my head more, and when they're done—in less than the advertised two minutes— I sit up and then stand thinking no way did this do anything. But Holy Shit, I am cured! I'm also out of the office, like the doc wants to set a world medical consultation speed record.

But in a week I wake up and Bam! the dizziness comes back. A second treatment doesn't take at all. The doctor talks about surgery, but can only tell me that it might help some. No thanks. Nobody gets to bust into my head again, not without some guaranteed overwhelming benefit. And I can accommodate pretty well. To this day, though, certain things make my head spin. Lie flat on my back and look up, I'm done. After a set of bench presses at the gym I have to sit up and get a grip for ten or fifteen seconds. If I stood right away I'd fall flat on my face. And once in a while dizziness just hits me out of the blue and makes me swerve like a drunk. Sleeping with my head up on at least two pillows lessens the problem. Thankfully I don't get seasick like victims of more serious vertigo. Given my aversion to throwing up that would be the Curse of Job.

With regular visits down to about once a month, April and I miss our sessions with Mrs. Dr. Keefe, my go-to eye doctor and the last one we regularly see. Even with no news she gives a big injection of positivity.

"Everything's still good in there, Gunny. The optic nerve looks healthy and the rest is fine," she will say after a look inside the eye, thus laying to rest any concerns that things are slowly and secretly going South. The eye cleared so slowly I barely noticed, and sometimes I worry that deterioration might sneak up the same way. With my vision as it is, I might not notice for quite a while.

Always the doctor makes conversation as she performs her retina and nerve exam, which takes five or ten minutes. Between reassuring statements about what she sees, she asks if I have other concerns.

On our late October visit I tell her I have a few.
"Okay, Gunny, what's on your mind?"

Even with her it does not come naturally to go public with problems, but after some grins and back-and-forth I get around to it.

First I tell her I still can't read no matter what store-bought magnifiers I use.

"Try this," she says, giving me the circular lens, like a magnifying glass minus the handle, that she uses to look into my eye. She also hands me a page with normal-size printing on it.

I expect another disappointment. After all, not one damn thing I've tried for seven months has worked. But an intelligible word jumps off the page. And then the next word jumps up at me. Hallelujah, after seven long months! I can't believe it! Instantly I flash on everything I can now read and the pleasure it will bring—the sports pages, motorcycle magazines, actual whole books. This is not to mention the mysterious stuff on paper at S-3 where I can finally find out what the other guys do. In point of fact my reading with the lens will be hopelessly slow and too laborious for anything beyond instructions, menus, and the like. But I'm having a moment. The journey can't begin without this step.

I say to the doctor, "Wow. Where do I get one of these?"

She hands me the lens' hard plastic case and says, "Take it."

"No, no, just tell me what it is, and I'll get one of my own."

"No, Gunny, it's yours."

"I'll put in a request."

"Don't be ridiculous," she says and points out that she can replace this one faster than I could ever get my own. She's right, too. Given the way wheels turn I might not have the lens yet. And I'm glad to hang on to Mrs. Dr. Keefe's lens because I don't want to give up my new capabilities. For the next year I will go nowhere without the doctor's generous gift. Medical-grade high-powered optics by Nikon can't be anything but very expensive.

"There are other, more specialized devices available," she tells me.

"Count me in, if they work like this."

"Actually, from what I understand, they work much better. There's one machine sort of like a microfiche reader. You put a book in it, and it projects the printing onto a screen. It can make the letters as big as your hand."

"I'd kill for something like that," I say.

"No need," she chuckles. She goes on to tell me about a low-vision training program set up to rehabilitate guys exactly like me at a Veterans Administration Hospital up in Palo Alto.

"It's for everything, not just reading. I have heard it described as life changing," the doctor says.

The last two words ring and echo in my head. Hope rises and explodes like a fireworks finale. Not to be sacrilegious, but I have something close to a Born Again moment. I now know that there is a key to a better life. No idea what it looks like or what exactly it will do for me, but I know it exists. Chalk up some of the emotion and tidal wave of optimism to months of starvation for a focus of effort, a mission, an objective of my own that fixes some of what's broke. It's one thing to be hopeful and positive on principle, which I always am, but somebody just told me where hope actually lives.

"I'll look into this some more and get you contact information for Palo Alto," Mrs. Dr. Keefe says.

Normally I walk out of her office feeling recharged and upbeat. This time I fly. As usual I stop in to spread some motivation among the combat casualties in the hospital's Marine ward. After the morale visit I drop in to BS with my buddy Staff Sgt. Cheney, platoon sergeant of the ward. I tell him what went on with the doc, and he says the most surprising thing.

"Oh yeah, I hear good things about that place in Palo Alto. Do you need the phone number for it?" This is not, by the way, the first or last time I see Staff Sgt. Cheney pull a rabbit out of his hat. The guy's knowledge and resourcefulness constantly amaze me.

Can the day get any better?

I walk back to tell Mrs. Dr. Keefe not to trouble herself finding the number for the Palo Alto rehab. What the hell, I might as well stick my head in at the PEB office and check on my paperwork. My route takes me that way, and my terrific mood will make it easier to face the stupidity and laziness I will surely encounter.

Wrong. The drones have very annoying news. Absolutely nothing has happened with my PEB, which hasn't gone in. They got all the material required from me and First Tanks a week after the process supposedly started, and now, two months later, that's still all they have. Not one scrap of paper has come in from the medical side.

Let's stop fooling around, people.

Either put me to work, or put me out.

I express my impatience to Mrs. Dr. Keefe, who is very surprised at the lack of action from within her hospital.

"Do you want me to write the medical dictation?" she asks.

"Are you sure? I know you're really busy."

Left: Nick in the 3rd grade at Warren G. Harding Elementary School, Hammond, Indiana.

Right: Freshman year (1981) at North Terre Haute High School in Terre Haute, Indiana.

Ready for the 8th grade school dance (1980). "This was my first date with Margaret Polock, who was killed by a drunk driver shortly after high school."

Top: April Popaditch, Nick's California beach dream girl, photographed in Oceanside, California, in 1990. "I carried this picture with me through Desert Storm."

The newlyweds, following a 1st Tank Battalion football game at Camp Pendleton, California, autumn, 1991. "I loved playing ball with First Tanks."

Top: Boot Camp photo, 1986, taken at the Marine Corps Recruit Depot, San Diego, California.

Right: Private First Class Nicholas Popaditch, home on leave from boot camp in 1986.

Left: "Busted up" in the field at the base of Mount Fuji, 1987. "Everything is training, and some lessons I learned the hard way. But I was just happy to be there."

Above: Lance Corporal Popaditch on his first overseas deployment in Camp Zama, mainland Japan, 1987. To his left is 1st Sgt. J. J. Carroll "on one of the few occasions that he wasn't yelling at me." In the background is LCpl. Patrick Flemming and LCpl. Estanol. On the right is one of Nick's friends, LCpl. Vinson.

Top: Nick's promotion to sergeant, Saudi Arabia, October 1, 1990. Above: Inside Saudi Arabia the day before crossing the border into Kuwait for Operation Desert Storm. From left to right: Cpl. Todd Chandler, Sgt. Bob Brennan, Cpl. Mike Robinson, and Sgt. Nick Popaditch.

Right: Sgts. Bob Brennan and Nick Popaditch (right to left) posing on the raised mine plow of a tank lovingly named "Bates Motel" at one of Bravo Company's many defensive positions in Saudi Arabia. LCpl. Brian Clark (far left) is seated inside the "Scud-Bunker."

Sgt. Nick Popaditch stands on the back deck of "Bates Motel" watching scores of oil wells burn in Kuwait, ignited by Saddam's retreating army. "Lance Corporal Brian Clark took this photo from the loader's hatch of the tank a few miles after the second minefield breach and the first battle with Iraqi forces."

A new drill instructor. Nick, April, Rich, and Nick Jr. (front), following Nick's graduation from Drill Instructor School in March 1998. "It was a very proud night for all of us."

Right: On the Physical Training Field near the rope climb at MCRD San Diego.

Top left: Nick in his apartment in San Diego, ready to report to the Recruit Depot for his first day training recruits. "I was as nervous as if I were reporting to boot camp as a recruit." Above: Nick supervising one of his "chosen ones," Rifle PT Recruit Callou (foreground). "I loved being a Drill Instructor."

Left: April, Nick Jr., and "Gunny Pop" in the Bravo Company office at 29 Palms a few hours before leaving overseas for Operation Iraqi Freedom. "My son Nick helped assemble my gear and load my magazines, probably to help avoid awkward silence as all of our goodbyes had by this time already been said."

Left: Riding on top of a Humvee in Baghdad just after the fall of the Saddam regime, "when Baghdad was a fun place to be."

Below: "Carnivore's" crew in a Baghdad suburb after the Diyala River crossing (sitting left to right): LCpl. Jeffrey Conkwright, Cpl. Schroeder, and LCpl. Vance Hagewood. SSgt. Nick Popaditch is standing in front of the tank.

The Palm Grove fight in Al Kut. The top photo was taken from the cupola of "Carnivore." Nick's crew took out an enemy T-62 tank, which is burning in the middle distance. "My turret is pointing back towards the road we were traveling on when we were ambushed. The canal the enemy unsuccessfully tried to escape across is on the far side of the berm running across the photo."

Below: Another photo from my cupola from the same spot, looking left. The M1A1 Tank is "Black 5," commanded by Lt. Chesla, Bravo Company's Executive Officer. "Chesla followed me through the palm grove. We are on the far side of the ambush site, the firefight is over, and we are turning around to return to the road."

The day after the Saddam statue was toppled. "I am holding in my left hand a piece of the statue that I cut off with a cold chisel and a hammer." Nick's tank crew divided this piece of historic metal four ways. Today, Nick's section is mounted in a frame on the wall of his apartment. "It is one of the most important mementos of my life."

"A gathering of friends in a park before we left Baghdad." The warriors, from left to right: SSgt. Mark Wilfong, MSgt. Alan Johnson (Top J), SSgt. Nick Popaditch, SSgt. Tim Duval, GySgt. Eric Benitez, and SgtMaj. Arthur Thompson (kneeling).

Above: Nick makes the front pages around the world again, this time anonymously. "We were in a 'mop-up mode' in Baghdad after the fall of Saddam. I am escorting an insurgent POW into an Amtrac, which doubled as a paddy wagon. He was one of nine led by a member of the Saddam Fedayeen. Locals, who identified them as 'bad guys,' formed by the hundreds to watch. These Iraqis cheered us for cleaning up their streets."

Left: Nick's return home from Operation Iraqi Freedom 1 at the Tank Battalion Grinder, 29 Palms, July 25, 2003. "A welcome home from a very beautiful April. Days don't get much better than this."

Nick packing his gear in preparation for the deployment back to Iraq. "I knew I would miss my family terribly, but I wanted to be back in the fight."

The "Bonecrusher" tank crew, from left to right: LCpl. Alex Hernandez (loader), GSgt. Nick Popaditch (tank commander), Cpl. Ryan Chambers (gunner, second in command), and Cpl. Christopher Frias (driver). "I could not be more proud of these Marines. Their actions that day saved my life."

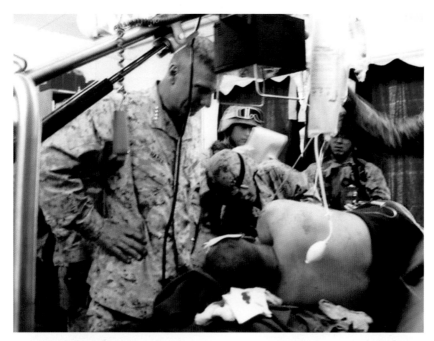

Above: On the table at the "Animal Hospital" in Iraq. "Standing next to me is General Michael Hagee, the thirty-third Commandant of the United States Marine Corps. Someone there took the photo and sent it to me in Twentynine Palms. I am very grateful."

Below: This photo was taken in Landstuhl, Germany, to make an ID card to replace my other ID that was in the pocket of my uniform cut off during medevac. "I still have this ID, and refer to it as 'the autopsy photo.' At the time, I was just happy to be alive."

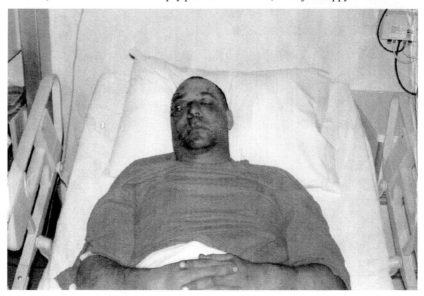

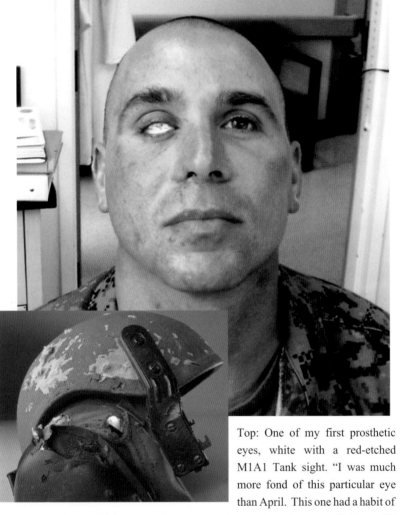

Top: One of my first prosthetic eyes, white with a red-etched M1A1 Tank sight. "I was much more fond of this particular eye than April. This one had a habit of falling out at times, which was much more upsetting to others than to me." Above: "The tank helmet I was wearing when hit by the RPG." The pieces were put back together for the photo. Notice the finger-sized hole in the temple area. Below: The shrapnel Mr. Dr. Keefe removed from behind Nick's left eye/optic nerve. "This piece entered my head through the right temple, traveled through my skull, and ended up behind my left eye."

Above: Capt. Michael Skaggs, GySgt. Nick Popaditch, and Col. Bryan McCoy in Washington, DC, the night before Nick's PEB hearing. "Col. McCoy was my battalion commander during OIF 1, and Capt. Skaggs was my CO during OIF 2. Both of these Marines stood by my side during the PEB hearing, as did April." Left: Gen. Richard Zilmer awarding Nick the Silver Star. "I was already medically retired, but proudly put my uniform back on for this ceremony." Below: "This is my favorite prosthetic eye, the Marine Corps' Emblem, the Eagle, Globe, and Anchor."

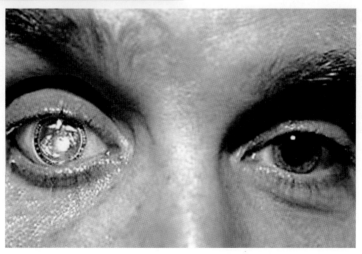

"One of the last times I put on this uniform as an active duty Marine."

SEMPER FI

"No problem. I just did for Corporal Lipe," she says. I know Lipe, who happens to be another member of the One-Eyed Jarhead Club.

The need to get moving on the paperwork—which will get me out of limbo, which I hate—defeats reluctance to take advantage of a friend, and I accept the doctor's offer.

"Give me about a week," she says.

That's all she takes, too.

33

Mister Popaditch

Come on, Top, it isn't that funny. Cut me some slack.

Top Dangerfield, however, can't quit laughing after I come to him and say, "Who do I need to see to get orders cut for this school for low-vision training in Palo Alto?"

"How long have you been here, Gunny?" he asks.

"Forever. Why?"

"You still don't know that we here in S-3 cut school orders?"

As a matter of fact, I don't, which doesn't embarrass me as much as it probably should, because I've always taken a weird sort of pride in my ignorance of routine paperwork. Considering my current billet the pride might be inappropriate, but there it is.

No problem getting the orders, but I have to wait for an opening in Palo Alto, even with my priority status as a fresh casualty from Iraq. I am, in fact, the first OIF/OEF vet with combat injuries to apply to the VA's low vision school.

Scheduling my schooling involves phone calls with an amazingly pleasant and accommodating woman named Lila Jaffrey.

To a career military guy like me the idea of being asked for input on scheduling instead of getting orders to report at such a time is downright bizarre. But Lila asks me, "What time period works for you? When would you like to begin?"

"Yesterday," I say.

"We can't do it quite that fast," she says, and offers a time slot in January.

She also says, "We have an opening next month, but I assume you want to be with your family through the December holiday period."

I do, but I want the school more, so December it is.

"I'll be sending you information. Would you like that in large print?" she asks. She closes, "Thank you, Mr. Popaditch."

A weirdness trifecta. Bing. Bang. Boom.

Large print. Does such a thing really exist? After seven months of degraded vision, I had no idea. What else do they have up there? This hits me like a glimpse of low-vision heaven where anything can happen— totally blind guys driving race cars by Braille, who knows what.

And the woman thanks me so sweetly and caringly, like helping me makes her day better. An angel amongst the drones.

And listen to what she calls me. Mister. I've heard it a lot out in the civilian world, where people don't address us in military terms. This time, though, I might be hearing my own name in the near future. It sounds naked, stripped of something very important to me, my hard-earned rank and Marine identity. Who is this Mr. Popaditch, and do I want to be him? Fuck no.

Moments like this make me want to go to that PEB office and shred my paperwork, then burn it and scatter the ashes and then figure a way to beat the system and re-up for four more years before anybody catches on. I just might be able to pull it off. Worth trying, isn't it? And what the hell's wrong with me, pushing things along that will most likely bounce me right out of the Marine Corps?

Signing up for rehab with a special VA program open to active military does not bear on my future in the Marine Corps. It might, in fact, make me more retainable by making me more effective and useful. Right now, though, it feels creepy. Most guys in the VA system are out of the military. It's like I just put one foot out the door.

Despite that I'm still dying to get to Palo Alto. But I've got more than a month to wait. Another five weeks gone, lost, sucking it up without knowing what I'm sucking it up for. It was one thing to vegetate in an office waiting for recovery. If I had to wait three years to get this eye back, no problem. I could do it standing on my head. But now I'm waiting for . . . what? Retirement? Death? Unforeseen events, as a result of which

Gunnies who can't see shit are suddenly vital to national security and the Marine Corps' mission?

Too much time to think, man. Too much time to go back and forth. Every time I look reality in the eye and make peace with the idea of medical retirement, something happens to snap me back. One day it's guys talking about somebody who lost a leg but now is back fighting in Iraq.

Some jarhead says, "Yeah, man, I saw that dude on CNN, and he's over there hookin' and jabbin', puttin' rounds down range." Everybody in the room oorahs the one-legged warrior, getting big motivation from his example. But I take this like a shot below the belt. How can I not be as tough as that guy? And how can I not find a way back into the fight like him? He ain't shining a chair with his ass, he's serving, really serving, out where the bad shit happens, where I belong. I don't need good eyes to fill sand bags, so put me on a firm base in Al Anbar and give me an e-tool. I could help clean weapons, dig fighting holes, string concertina wire. I don't mind getting shot at even if I can't shoot back. They can always use another body out there, can't they? So use mine. There's got to be a way.

If it isn't some dude getting hit, rehabbing, and going back in combat—and making me feel like a pussy—it's some other tale of individual sacrifice and courage. I've got to do more, and I cannot abide the thought of allowing myself to get put out of military service at this moment in our nation's history. A Marine goes to war, he doesn't go away from it.

But then my mind reverses polarity. I'm a pro and a realist, and I know that what I love about the Corps—this is the Tough Team, man—probably means the Corps needs to let me go.

Top Dangerfield, God bless him, never once tells me to shut up and knock off obsessing about where my duty lies and how much of a fight I should put up if the Corps wants to retire me. Given my sight, though, he's free to roll his eyes, which I'm sure he does in some of our one-sided conversations on this subject. He does the friend thing—he listens. And he does the Marine thing, making it clear that he'll stick by me no matter what. If I choose to do battle he'll jump in the fighting hole with me. And if I just accept the Corp's conclusions—which I am increasingly sure will not go my way—he'll watch my six and make sure the right things happen.

Too much time to worry, not on my own behalf but that of April and Nicholas. If I'm out how do I provide for my family? I can't quite bring myself to go to somebody and ask straight out, "How much money do I get if I have to retire?" Somehow this seems dishonorable. Even if I did ask, nobody could say for sure because the PEB findings, to be made by three officers in Bethesda at some future date, hopefully the near future, will determine my retirement pay based on how disabled I am in the board's judgement. So the answer is somewhere between zero and 75 percent of my current base pay, the highest possible retirement rate. The deal is further complicated by the fact that my monthly retirement checks will come from one or the other of two sources—either the Marine Corps or the VA, which handles disabled veterans retired for medical reasons in addition to providing its other support and services. In certain circumstances I could get retirement money from both the Corps and the VA, but who cares about that? The question is how much?

Forget about getting numbers from the VA. Our on-base VA rep comes around once a week. In his briefs I learn that he wants to buy a new truck and the VA has been fucking him out of his own benefits since the Vietnam War, where exposure to Agent Orange brought on his current diabetes. The disease I hear about in nauseating detail. He does give me one piece of actionable advice concerning applications for VA benefits:

Don't ever file your paperwork on Friday.

Another turd retiree. To hell with him.

I look to the Corps as the responsible organization, anyway. But even here among my own kind, the answers are not to be had. Up and down my chain of command I'm talking to fellow trigger pullers. And I don't really ask in a forthright manner. Somebody could get me an answer, but I will not push the issue.

"Hey, Colonel, can you take time out from training First Tanks to go into battle to tell me how much money I will get when I'm not a Marine any more?"

Does that sound right to you? It sure as hell doesn't to me.

This is, by the way, a reason good Marines and worthy soldiers and sailors get short-changed by the system. True believers can't stand to turn their service into a money thing. Meanwhile the turds kick ass and get more than they deserve because they have no problem putting out their hands and demanding and begging and showboating to get more.

In the absence of specifics or even educated guesses I feel compelled to run some numbers in order to answer one big, burning question: How much of a hit should the Popaditch family be prepared to take, in terms of losing our current lifestyle. Counting benefits like housing and commuted rations, our term for a monthly food allowance, I make the equivalent of about $60,000 a year before taxes, with terrific benefits and perks that a guy pulling down 60K in the civilian world doesn't get. Looking only at my base pay of about $3,200 a month, you might think we're among the working poor, but the pay is only about half of the package. And the life of a Marine Gunnery Sergeant is great. We are not, however, considering the many intangibles that are not germane to the issue here. We're talking money and what it buys.

Bottom line: No matter what, we will take a step down, unless maybe we move to some locale where we don't want to live, because dollars buy three times as much. Though we keep the good Marine health coverage and benefits, actual pay takes a nosedive. Retirement money is based on base pay and no other compensation, so even at the top rate I'm talking about 75 percent of half the compensation I currently receive. Disability benefits from Social Security, which I will also receive, will bump me up about $1,600, give or take. I figure that takes the place of free family quarters, so I call housing a wash. On the other hand, 3202-D Ludwig Court—two stories, three beds, two-and-a-half baths, two-car garage—would rent for twice as much or more in any half way attractive community here in California. Still, I feel pretty sure we can live in a nice-enough place.

There's another blank to be filled-in here. My future career. What does a guy who can't see well enough to read, whose only professional experience and expertise involve killing people while in command of heavy armor, do out there in CivDiv? As the past six months attached to S-3 makes abundantly clear, I hate not having a billet I can fill. So what's coming up next? Important question, but I give it very little thought at this stage, maybe because I don't like thinking about it, beyond the idea that a man with my strong back and initiative will find some useful occupation. Grunt labor, if nothing else. And even at minimum wage, steady work will help fill the financial gap and put us close enough to even.

All in all, I think we'll be all right, especially if the Marine Corps recognizes and fairly compensates me for my permanent loss of sight, hearing, and balance. This I take on faith, the same faith I have given to the Corps for 15 years, which has never been betrayed. Never, not in combat, not in training, not in all of life, have my fellow Marines let me down. Why would I expect anything different now?

Faith, in the absence of evidence. This gets me by on the long journey to wherever the hell I'm going. In some senses my position is much like that of a person contemplating death. Nobody can tell me what lies on the other side, because nobody comes back. Medical retirees are out of the Corps and gone, beyond my reach. These days I go around to hospitals and try to clue in busted-up guys about how the system functions and what to expect. No such person, though, comes to me. I don't even think to go looking for one.

One very important person does not share this faith of mine—my wife.

April knows me too well to challenge my conviction that the Corps will do right. I'd take it as a personal insult and a slight to the Corps itself. End of constructive communication. But every day, it seems, I come home and get 20 questions.

"How do they figure out what your percentage of disability will be?"

"If you have to retire, how long do we have before we pack up and go?"

"Can Nicholas finish out the school year?"

Most of the time I don't know, and April knows I don't. This is marital trench warfare. Without going on the attack April puts pressure on me to go get the answers that she needs. She knows my sense of obligation will drive me to do so. If every Marine deserves an answer, my wife sure as hell does.

Sometimes when I do provide an answer she pushes to make sure it's accurate and reliable. She's relentless, and who can blame her? She has as much at stake as I do, as does our 10-year-old. But she's even farther out of the loop, and I represent her only source of information. Hearing me tell her that everything's going to be all right, without providing details, must frustrate the living hell out of her.

At the time, though, down in the trenches, the questions feel like enemy machine gun fire, pinning me down in the one place I want to relax and get away from all that confusion and trouble.

Compared to full-on fighting couples we keep things pretty civilized and quiet. But we've got tension shooting every which way, and we both hunker down to avoid taking casualties.

Now and again the old conflict about why I volunteered also comes up. April starts taking the occasional verbal shot. "You tempted fate." "You volunteered for that." "You weren't supposed to be there then."

I sometimes snap back, "Would you rather this happened to somebody else? What's wrong with you?"

That's not right, though. She believes it wouldn't have happened at all if I hadn't screwed around with destiny. Such stuff has special meaning to her beyond the obvious implication that I caused our current troubles. As a Native American, April believes that you should never tamper with fate. It isn't my going to combat and getting shot that bothers her. That's the Marine deal, and she gets it as well as I do. She also knows I would have been redeployed to Iraq even if I didn't volunteer, and maybe something worse would have happened. April's bugged because I altered events as they were meant to unfold. Now we're living with the punishment I brought on.

One day she goes over the top and full-on attacks, saying, "You put us in this situation, Nick. It happened because you changed the order. You did this to us."

I counterattack, saying how sick I am of hearing this nonsense. Would she rather be married to a Marine who sat out the fight, who had to be ordered into combat to go?

"Yeah, I volunteered. I'm proud of it. Everybody else thinks it's great, like I did an honorable and noble thing. Everybody but you! And I'm sick and tired of being treated like I did something wrong, like I'm a dirtbag, in my own home. I don't want to hear one more word about any of this, ok?"

And I won't, either.

This is, incidentally, the first time I actually say out loud to April that I volunteered. It doesn't do us any good, though. The fight does nothing except maybe to remind us to stay out of heated arguments. It could be, in fact, things just got slightly more tense because we declared a major mutual irritant off-limits like unexploded ordinance.

These are not the best of times in the Popaditch household.

34

Shafted

Our differences about what to expect from the Marine Corps concerning my probable retirement have much less to do with the Corps than with the differences between April and me and how we look at life. Really and truly, she's not the least pissed off at the Corps itself for our current circumstances. She'd die if anybody had such a thought, because she loves the Marines at least as much I do. God help the person who expresses disloyalty in April's presence. When she hears about a Marine who fails to uphold our standards, she comes down harder on the guy than I ever would. She also takes a leadership role among base wives that mirrors my own position as Gunny.

When April doubts that things will go our way, that's just the way she thinks. As she herself says, when things are rolling along really well, she waits for the wheels to fall off. I, on the other hand, assume things will get even better. In my world nothing bad waits to happen.

Some people are optimists and some are pessimists, simple as that.

In this case, however, the pessimist turns out to be right.

The PEB guys at Balboa tell me that we need an addendum from an Ear, Nose and Throat specialist to add to Mrs. Dr. Keefe's medical dictation. I'm annoyed, sure. They've already got a couple pounds of paperwork, which I don't like because it's paperwork and which I can't scrutinize because I can't read, and we've been stalled since forever, so this had better be it. On the other hand, this gets Mr. Dr. Keefe, my ENT doc, into the mix, so I have the A Team on my side. I feel guilty about troubling him, because I know he's swamped with work and he already made an incredible effort on my behalf. I'd be totally blind by now if he hadn't operated on me with such courage and skill.

"Are you kidding? No problem," he says.

Thanksgiving comes and goes. Turkey, football, and nothing the least bit notable unless you flip back through the calendar. I got hit a week before Easter, the last major in-home family holiday providing I am home, which I wasn't. Count the months—seven-and-a-half since Fallujah, seven since my last important medical procedure and homecoming at Two Nine. After that I immediately became a broken pogue. In terms of my day-to-day routine on base nothing much has changed in all this time.

But here we go. Mr. Dr. Keefe tells me he's finished his addendum, and I make travel arrangements to go to Balboa to personally deliver the addendum to the PEB office and then sign off on the package and kiss it goodbye. Launch it. Get it gone. Be done with it.

First I do a little more vegetating because even for an official resident of S-3 it takes a day or so to generate the orders from scratch.

"Hey, Gunny, this call is for you," one of my officemates says. I pick up the phone and hear the voice of Chief Somebody-or-other, PEB liaison officer at Balboa, the guy who ought to be bird-dogging my case and watching my back, except I've never heard from him before. I don't even recognize his name.

"Your findings are in," he says.

"What? They can't be. I've got a medical addendum that needs to go into the package, and I never signed off on it like I had to."

"Well, they're here. I'm looking right at them. According to regulations, I'm supposed to brief you on the findings and what they mean."

Getting more pissed off by the second, and not wanting to deal with this lazy turd on the phone, I ask if he can fax everything up to our PEB liaison here at Two Nine, Rick DeLuna, and have him do the brief.

The Chief hems and haws. After three months of doing squat, less than nothing, you want to jump in and do your job? I don't even know your name, pal.

He doesn't hear what I'm thinking, though, just my insistence that Rick do my brief. And he caves, agreeing to fax the stuff right away.

I give Rick a heads-up and hoof the half-mile to his office in our base hospital. Incomplete PEB submission aside, I feel eager and upbeat. The answers have arrived, and I have no concern about what they are. Even without Mr. Dr. Keefe's addendum, the documents that did go in tell the whole story about my various conditions. Facts in hand, the PEB board members couldn't do anything but come through. The future has finally arrived.

By this time I count Rick as a trusted ally and a friend. I regularly come to BS and, if needed, get some PEB guru-ing. All I know on the subject I owe to him.

"I got it," Rick says, "Are you ready for your brief?"

"Hit me."

Reading from the document, he says, "The Department of the Navy has found you unfit for service." He goes into friend mode, saying, "Sorry, Gunny, but this can't be much of a surprise."

It isn't. Still, I don't like it. Hearing that I don't measure up anymore hurts.

I'm not going to bore you with the numbers and medical-technical Swahili he runs though, which all adds up to a number. Seventy percent. That's how disabled the board has found me to be. Their verdict says I have a full field of view in my remaining eye and okay visual acuity. In other words I have one good eye, not good as new, but serviceable. The findings don't even mention the damage to my right ear resulting in partial deafness and vertigo. Ditto the loss of sense of smell.

Insult to injury: instead of treating any of my conditions as permanent, as the doctors have told me they are over and over, the board has put me on the TDRL, Temporarily Disabled Retired List. This means I get put out and then, as a civilian, I have to go through the whole PEB rigmarole again.

So it isn't over. They get another chance to fuck everything up one more time.

"Does this sound right to you, Rick?"

"No, Gunny," he says in a neutral sort of way.

"They didn't give me a fair shake, did they?"

Rick gives me silent consent.

"I know what was in that package that went in. My whole medical record. My complete physical. Didn't they look at any of it?"

"Look, Gunny, you know the options. We talked about this before. If the findings aren't right you can refuse to accept them and file an appeal. Do you think that's an appropriate course of action?"

"Tell me where to start."

Professionalism won't allow him to say so out loud, but Rick, too, thinks I got royally shafted. And he's glad we're going to fix things together as a team. At the moment there are actually four guys on the team, Rick the solid pro and three Gunny Pops, of three entirely different minds. Number One is coming out of shock, not wanting to believe what just happened and what it means—they fucked me! Two is already pissed off, but only because mistakes were made. Number three is cool because mistakes can be fixed and that's what we're doing.

We are, in fact, in solid shape because Mr. Dr. Keefe's addendum gives us fresh, powerful ammo to start the appeal process and make the board take another, better look. It's down there in Balboa, good to go.

But I can't keep the other two Gunny Pops quiet:

"Did I blow out my knee playing softball?"

"It would take, what, ten extra minutes to really look through that stuff."

"If they needed something else, couldn't somebody call Balboa and get it?"

"How could they do this? I got hit in combat. They're dealing with my whole future."

"Lazy-ass sailors in the Navy Yard in D.C. Couldn't wait to punch out on liberty at noon."

Rick, a retired Navy corpsman, breaks in and sets me straight on the last one. "Actually, Gunny, the Navy and the Marines rotate positions on the board, two of one and one of the other. Your panel had two Marine Colonels."

Now I feel worse. I got run over by my own team bus. Fucked by Marines for doing the Marine thing. Let down. Betrayed. Unspeakable. Unthinkable.

Wait, though. I should get complete facts before I throw around such heinous accusations even in my own head. And this shit is too hot to handle. If it's unthinkable, I won't think about it, and I'll concentrate on the task at hand.

They didn't fuck me. They couldn't have. Somehow or another—and we'll find out how—they just dropped the ball. And that we will rectify.

35

Needs of the Corps

So what happened to fighting to stay in?

I've been talking about it for months. My PEB submission states in several places that I desire to remain on active duty. Now that the results are back, though, I accept without protest that I am medically unfit for continued service. At this point, if this were somebody else's story and he made as much noise about wanting to serve no matter what, I'd need to know why he all of a sudden accepts the board's verdict. Unless he accounted for himself right here and now I'd think he's full of shit. And I'd put the book down.

So tell us, Gunnery Sergeant . . .

Why do you give in so easily?

Why will you now go without a fight?

Five-word answer: Needs of the Marine Corps.

If you don't buy it, don't, but it's the truth. In my world, Needs of the Corps is the *bottom* of the bottom line. Nothing trumps it, supercedes it, gives room for further consideration, compromise, or appeal.

Why do I spend Christmas away from home? Why does my unit have to breach the minefield? Why are we the fixing force instead of the assaulting force? Why does my family have to stay in Twentynine Palms while somebody else extends in Pensacola where we would love to live?

It isn't fair.

Screw you, fair. The Corps puts you where it needs you. It's tough, but what do you expect from The Tough Team? And I would not want it any other way. The tougher Needs Of The Corps has been on me, the more I have loved the Corps and felt bound to it.

Well, now it needs me out. Nothing could be tougher, but so be it.

It has taken me a long, long time to recognize the truth and more time to accept it. I hate it and wish it weren't the truth, but I can't deny it. The longer I stay in, the longer I deprive the Corps of somebody it needs especially now that we're at war. The Marines need another fighting-fit Gunnery Sergeant leading tankers into battle. I belong to a small segment of the smallest branch of America's fighting forces. There's a set number of us, so the space I now take up really matters. One man makes a difference. If I put up a fight and managed to stay in—not easy but there's a chance I could—I would do the Marines and our cause a disservice, because for all my assets I bring greater liabilities. And I can't take more than I give. That I cannot live with.

I finally decide not to fight for the exact same reason I was sure I had to fight. Because I'm a Marine. I must submit to leaving the Corps to be worthy of it.

Like they say, the truth hurts. I don't like putting it down on paper because I don't like thinking about it. And if I want to look back and second-guess a decision I made, this one comes to mind first. Even now, three years later, I can relive the back-and-forth and wonder how a real Marine could not fight. I know I made the right decision for the right reasons, but sometimes I want to unmake it.

I believe I always will.

36

New Look at Life

Western Blind Rehabilitation Center
Veterans Administration Medical Center
Palo Alto, California

Holy Shit Moment (HSM) One

Rick Ludt, my mobility trainer, takes me out to the parking lot.

"Can you see that sign?" he asks, pointing at something a few feet in front of us.

"I can tell there's something there, and I wouldn't bump into it," I say, feeling proud I detected an obstacle before I bashed my head on it. That's the point of the exercise, isn't it?

Maybe not. Rick hands me a ball cap and sunglasses and tells me to put them on.

"Now look at the sign," he says.

Holy shit. Not only do I get a clear rectangular outline and the sign post, I make out the blue universal symbol for a handicapped-only parking space. Never since the RPG hit have I had such visual acuity. Less fuzz. Cleaner. Sharper.

Hello, World.

That's another handicapped sign next to this one and another and another and another. Whoa, this is different. Here the blue spaces are in the majority, which means unserviceable are, too. That's who lives here, and I am one of them, a thought I don't especially want to entertain. And I don't. Not a minute for anything but training with Rick, a true hundred-and-ten-per-center who works me like I used to work my Marines. This guy would make a hell of a platoon sergeant.

Rick jumps into an explanation of why his hat and shades just made a major fix. Most people's eyes are light-metered and self regulating like cameras with automatic adjustable apertures to keep excessive brightness from spoiling the pictures. My eye, Rick says, is pretty much stuck in the low-light, wide-open position, so I desperately need protection.

For me the hat's okay, but sunglasses go against the grain. A long time ago a platoon sergeant told me only dope smokers wear them. Always I refused to put them on when in uniform, even out in the desert, where the brightness and glare are truly heinous. Rick politely tunes me out when I tell him all this, giving me a half-dozen more pairs of sunglasses to find the optimum tint. Gray with anti-glare filtration seems to do the most good.

The instantaneous improvement makes me feel a little bit dumb. I could have picked up a hat and sunglasses at the PX long ago and enjoyed the benefits. Why didn't I? The sunglass phobia, in part. And all the time I had an eye full of blood I craved sunlight, the brighter the better. That was my fix. After things changed, it never occurred to me that yesterday's fix was today's problem. And now the worst problem—full-on brightness—just became my visual sweet spot. To this day I have maximal vision outside at midday wearing a hat and sunglasses.

Seems minor to you, maybe, but my world just got bigger. And it is my world. Training. Effort. More work, more results.

HSM Two

How many times have I been here before, having an eye doc give me an exam and then deliver a gloomy report. Serious, irreversible damage, retina, nerve, blah, blah, blah. Now tell me something new.

This eye doc does just that.

"Try to read the letter on the top line of the eye chart," says Dr. Jenny Woods, a Gen-X Texan who conducts herself in a very informal manner but also communicates competence. She's this Lone Star sweetie-pie with big brains and a tough, tough core.

Same as always I can't ID anything on the eye chart.

"Now try aiming your eye above the chart and to the left."

Holy shit, there it is, not pretty but recognizable.

"Doc, I can read it! It's an A!"

"Good," she says and explains that with my central vision and much of the peripheral wiped-out, I must learn to re-aim my eye in order to use what vision I have.

"I get it, it's like Kentucky windage for my eye," I say, assuming that a Texan will know enough about guns to recognize the slang for re-aiming in the opposite direction of your misses. You point the rifle off the target to hit the target, in my case high and left because my good vision is on the lower right.

"Exactly, now read the next line," she says.

"Three letters, no idea what they are . . . "

"'No idea' doesn't cut it, Nick. What are they? Try again. And point the eye away from the letters."

This time I see clearly enough to make an educated guess.

"It works," I say. "Why didn't I think of this? Why didn't anybody tell me?"

"You didn't think of it because it goes completely against human instincts to look away from what you want to see. And nobody told you before because you never met a low vision specialist before. We're a rare breed."

She puts glasses frames with swap-out lenses on me and tells me to take a crack at the next line down.

"Can't get it," I tell her.

"Are you looking up and left?"

"Well, no."

"This is work, Nick. It doesn't come naturally."

Now I get some results, which still aren't good enough for the doc, who pushes me to re-aim and give her more letters. She won't try another lens until she knows I give her max effort. This Texan is relentless. I get un-annoyed, though, when I realize that she shouldn't have to push like this. Embarrassing for a Marine to be told to try harder.

We work our way a few lines down on the eye chart—amazing since I couldn't get the big A to begin with. Then the doc gives me more lenses for other tasks. I love looking across the room with a little high-powered monocular that shows me details like I haven't seen since April 7. But there's no time for appreciation. As soon as she knows something does the job, Dr. Woods makes a note and brings out something else. I don't even care that she puts everything away and I leave empty-handed. New stuff and operational training will come from somewhere else, so what?

This works! After months of practically nothing working, my mind races, thinking about all the great things I will do when I get my own optical gear.

Check this thing out. A Stand Magnifier. Not an impressive device until the doc sets it down on a page and tells me to take a look. I've been let down a few times too often to expect much when it comes to the printed word. But Holy Shit, I see a whole line of words. A sentence, all at once! Something simple, like "The car is orange," but I am looking at a miracle. As my experience so far has taught, one word at a time, coming clear with effort, does not make me a reader. Now I am.

Come on, doc, let me read this line again. She says it's too easy and gives me another page with smaller print that's readable only if I struggle.

"Come on!" she says, and after I get it better, she gives me a tougher page and keeps pushing it. By this time I appreciate the action, like doing bench presses while my spotter keeps putting on more weight. It will end in defeat, but every new max breaks my previous personal best. More power with every rep. I can feel it. No, I can see it.

HSM Three

"What are your goals, Nick? What do you plan to accomplish in life?"

The guy asking is John Wood, easily confused with Dr. Jenny Woods but no relation. Officially my visual skills instructor, he also coordinates the entire team effort to rehabilitate me. He represents everything good about the New VA—young, highly trained and qualified, motivated, concerned, not the least bit bureaucratic and turd-like in the stereotypic Old VA way. I'll admit it: Even I, a gung-ho military true believer and optimist to the core, expected a lot less from the VA than I get. Whatever was broken about this organization got fixed. The taxpayers get their money's worth and then some for the incredible professionals who work with me in Palo Alto, typified in my mind by John.

I say to him, "Well, I've had this ambition for a long time. But it seems sort of ridiculous."

"What is it?"

"I've thought a lot about being a high school teacher, even before I got wounded. It seemed like something I'd be good at after I got of out of the Corps."

"Why is that ridiculous?"

"I have to go to college to do it, don't I? How am I going to do all the bookwork?"

This teaching thing really does seem silly, like saying I want to be an astronaut or NASCAR driver. You haven't read anything about it until now because I buried it pretty deep. God knows I didn't say anything about it out loud after I got wounded. Until this point, I never really looked a post-Marine future in the eye at all. I guess I didn't want to get real about it because I didn't want it to be real.

John, however, denies me a bypass. And he makes me feel silly about feeling silly.

"Nick, there are totally blind judges out there, for crying out loud. They went through law school, didn't they?"

I know this. I've been thinking about the miracle blind-guy stories since I got wounded. But John's asking me for my story, not theirs. He's giving me reality, not inspiration; not talk but action; possibilities. Do I believe I can do what I want to do? Go through four years of college at my age with a wife and kid and with who knows how much money coming in? And if the logistics work do I have the visual capabilities?

A Marine at jump school must feel just like this when he stands at the door of a plane for the first time. Do I commit? Do I take the plunge?

"Nick, I've got a team of people waiting to make it happen. All we need to know is what you want to do, and we will give you the tools you need."

Well . . . .

"You can do it. If we didn't know this, we wouldn't be talking about it."

Holy shit, I can do it.

"Okay, John, how do we make it happen?"

John, I can tell, is almost as happy as I am to have a mission. He tells me that all the team's efforts now will go toward preparing me for college. And I commit myself to the mission, totally and without reservation. It's been way too long since my last mission—to get better and get on a tank—failed. The drifting that followed beat me up more than failing. But it's over. I just got my life back. The world is big again. And I have a place in it.

A totally blind secretary processes my paperwork, her seeing eye dog parked next to her desk.

The director of the entire rehab center, Elizabeth Jessen, is legally blind like me, and it doesn't slow her down a bit. I love to go to her office and watch her churn and burn using her arsenal of adaptive equipment. No wasted motion. She moves fast out in the world, too, teaching Nordic skiing to disabled vets.

I meet a 70s-era Marine vet who has visual limitations a lot like mine and now works as a cook in Acapulco. Not just traveling but making his home in a foreign country. Time to quit feeling like I can't go places and do things.

The rehab team works the living hell out of me every minute of my daily four two-hour sessions, but the major payoffs come so often that nothing feels like work.

By the middle of Week Two I have my own stand magnifier, which John trains me to use. I brought a book by Col. Oliver North and a boat magazine from home, hoping—but not totally expecting—to get some good out of them. Now look at me go, man, reading for fun. Who thought I could love it this much?

Rick, the mobility guy, takes me out in the world whenever possible. With the college mission in mind he works my ass off on the campus of Stanford University. "Here's your mission," he says, leaving me in a spot with no map and nothing but a designated goal, like such-and-such a lecture hall. Every time the routes get tougher. Multiple turns, crowds, tunnels, outdoor steps that disappear in sunshine, busy streets, open spaces too big to see across. Rick makes me find a book in Stanford's huge and multi-storied bookstore. The thing is down in the damn basement. To this day, I use the skills that my mobility instructor taught.

Dr. Jenny Woods keeps checking me out on adaptive devices and ordering mission-specific gear, like a battery-powered portable CCTV, a scanner with a screen display that blows up text. This one sits up on a stand high enough for me to write under it so I can take it to school and do tests. I also get a bigger CCTV unit for reading at home. Jenny thoroughly equips me with wearable optics and scopes for all environments and challenges. For the first time I can enjoy movies, wearing these crazy-looking four-power portholes they call Beechers.

You want to see something funny, check out movie night at the Western Blind Rehab Center, a different kind of weird super-glasses on every guy.

Every working hour, a member of the rehab team kicks open another door for me, expands my world like blowing up a balloon. I learn to type. I use power tools to make April and my mom Christmas presents in blind-guy shop class, aka manual skills. I'm still too impatient to be any good at woodworking, but it's cool to know I could take it up if I felt like it. Every day John clocks my words-per-minute like a reading track coach and starts testing comprehension. Assuming I prefer military material, he uses stuff like an explanation of how a submarine's ballast tanks work. Submarine reading becomes our private joke. Meanwhile Rick pushes the mobility envelope away from the hospital. He even turns me loose in the San Jose airport so I can learn how to catch flights on my own.

I'm constantly amazed at how easy, how obvious, some of the biggest steps are, like Rick's ballcap and shades trick and Jenny's Kentucky windage. I expected lengthy struggles, deep mysteries, but it turns out I already know a lot of what I need to know. In fact, a Marine tanker makes an ideal candidate for catastrophic loss of vision. What I need to do now I did all along, like scanning by sector to get the big picture as Rick teaches me to do. I aimed machine guns off-target to correct for missing bursts, just like Jenny teaches me to aim my eye. And I went from the naked eye to more powerful, narrow-field optics to overcome detection challenges. Now I'm putting a monocular on walk signals and posted menus at McDonald's instead of putting the 10-power primary sight on a defilade tank 2,000 meters away, but what's the difference? It all works the same. I'm in the turret again with the hatches buttoned up, making the most of a severely restricted and degraded field of view.

Could the timing be better? Right when I finally accept the Marine Corps' judgement that I am unfit for service, I step into a new world where I am fit and get a mission that's a fit and a team of fantastic people to make sure I succeed.

Semi-embarrassing personal fact: Two years into college I send my grades to Jenny and John like I'm a kid. Anything less than straight A's would feel like I let them down after all they did to prepare me for this. I don't send the grades to Rick, because that would probably seem to him like a needless distraction and waste of training time.

37

McMoney

Side benefit of my VA training: I get to hang with Old School Vets going back to World War II. Unlike at Two Nine, where I'm an old man to the junior Marines, I can feel like a kid. After the 70s-era Marine who cooks in Mexico goes home, something like 20 years separates me from the next youngest guy in the low vision training class. For most of the men, the age gap pushes forty years. Since I live in an old-guy-free zone, I had no idea what a riot senior citizens can be. I also learn that Marines carry certain traits to the grave. Without exception the biggest loudmouths in our midst are jarheads. One of them, old enough to be Dr. Jenny Woods' grandfather, has the audacity to hit on her.

Bill is his name, and he tells me the story himself: One day he calls to set up an appointment with Jenny, who offers him a slot at 1400.

"Nah," he says, "I need a later one."

"Okay, how about 1500?"

"Still too early."

"Well," she says, "You tell me what will work for you."

"I was thinking you and me should get together around 2100."

Without missing a beat Jenny rattles off directions to some spot across town no legally blind Korean War vet could possibly find.

"Be there, and we've got a date," she says.

Laughing his ass off, he tells me how she talked so fast he couldn't even begin to write the directions down. Then he hands me his latest practice document from computer training, which happens to be a recipe for potato salad.

"Girls like it when you cook for them," Bill says.

My youth means I do all the heavy lifting, like cleaning our giant coffee maker in the deep sink at night and then filling it and prepping it for morning. If the joe isn't brewed by 0430, somebody comes knocking on my door. Early to bed and early to rise for the old guys except on Tuesday nights when a swing band shows up along with little old ladies from who knows where. They dance their asses off until midnight.

Normally I'd do the whole training program in a four-to-six-week shot. But I get word that it's okay to go home for Christmas through New Year's, when training will cease. April lines up a flight for me on Christmas Eve. Better and better and better.

One morning during the week before Christmas, before my visual skills session with John, a voice comes over the intercom saying I have a call. Since I'm still in my room all I have to do is pick up the phone to take it.

The caller IDs himself as Colonel McSomething, whom I will call Colonel McMoney. He's in D.C., responding to my PEB appeal, which went out when I flew up here.

The exact words escape me, but in pogue Colonel-ese he says he can fix everything for me right now over the phone with no need for pursuing the appeal any further.

He opens with an offer of an additional 10 percent disability for my facial scars.

What? That was on my medical record but we never tried to claim it as part of my disability, first time around or in the appeal. At this point my bullshit alarm goes off.

Ten percent takes me to 75 percent disability, which the Colonel says rounds up to 80 percent. This puts me at the max in terms of Marine Corps medical retirement money.

I can't believe it. The son-of-a-bitch wants to haggle, like I—my career, my honor, my war wounds, my life—am a trade-in at a used car lot. The Colonel even adapts that smarmy used car salesman manner.

"I'm offering you the max on money, what more do you want?" McMoney says, like he's doing me a favor that I'd be foolish to turn down.

"I want it right," I say a little too loudly, because I'm not just suspicious, I'm mad, and heading toward furious.

He asks me what isn't right, and I bring up the TDRL, the temporary disability status that means the board will review and rule again on my case in 18 months. What is temporary here? What can be fixed?

"If you have some miracle cure, you might want to share it with my doctors," I say. This, along with the blunt and increasingly salty language, takes me as close to insubordinate as I want to get.

The Colonel has the nerve to say this, voice full of concern: "The TDRL is for your benefit." In case things get worse, he says, the board can make adjustments, which is, of course, total bullshit because if I'm maxed out already, how do I get more maxed? Bullshit, bullshit, bullshit.

How much do I trust this smooth talker now?

Here's his deal:

Buy out Gunny today.

Fuck him later when he's no longer a Marine.

Here's my deal: The truth.

Everything that's broken on me straight up and complete and on the official PEB findings. Forget the money, which I'll get anyway. I want all of it on paper, you shifty beancounter. The whole truth. After all I did, I don't deserve anything less. And I won't take it. I did right for 15 years. Now you do right for the 15 minutes it would take somebody to straighten things out in D.C. Your job is a lot safer and easier than mine was. Do it.

It really chaps my ass that these guys in Washington took more time and trouble to track me down at an obscure training program outside the active military and pitch me this nonsense than it would have taken to do the thing correctly.

I do not, by the way, waste my breath laying out these thoughts for McMoney. I just tell him I want it right and get mad enough to do whatever it takes to make it that way. While he wheels and deals, I draw a line in the sand. I will go to D.C. and fight.

I tell the Colonel, "I want a formal hearing." Though the appeal is still pending, his call makes it obvious that it already went down the crapper, and a hearing before the PEB board will be my next step.

He signs off: "We really appreciate your sacrifice, Gunny."

Take your appreciation and shove it.

Somewhere late in the conversation John comes into my room. If I remember, it was just as I said. "I got hit in the head with a fucking grenade!"

John backs out. After I hang up he returns and says he wanted to know what's up because I'm missing training.

"I was worried, Nick. You've never been late before," he says.

I apologize, and he asks if there's anything the VA can do to help me with whatever problem I was yelling about.

"No thanks. It's got nothing to do with you guys. Let's go read about submarines."

38

Rage Week

I put fury on hold and have a Merry Christmas. How much more Walton Family can you get than returning home on Christmas Eve? I come back loaded with gifts, tangible and otherwise, from Palo Alto. Dad has a life now, a future. He can read the sports section again. This is great news for everybody.

And we've got the tree, April's terrific holiday cooking and decorations, a kid still young enough to get the magic. The base goes all-out, too, with parties and our own unique traditions like the guys who dress as Santas and cruise all around on their Harleys on Christmas Day. A stranger knocks on the door, says "Merry Christmas," and hands me an envelope. Before I can say "Thanks" or "What is this?" he walks away. My God, it's a check for $1,200 from the Injured Marines Semper Fi Fund, in which April and I will later become very active as volunteers. For once, I will find a way to give back some of what I got.

Now to hell with Ho Ho Ho. On Sunday night the boy falls asleep and April and I start to upload ammo. She's been waiting for this moment, biting back her own anger for weeks while rerunning the following conversation with me:

"Come on Nick. We need help. You know all these really influential people. Let's get hold of some of them!" She's talking about the many outside big shots we've met through media exposure and public appearances.

"The wheels turn slowly, but they turn," I say.

"People keep offering to help. Let them!"

"The system hasn't failed us yet. We have to give it a chance to work."

"Why? The writing's on the wall, Nick. They're already screwing us. You want to wait until it's too late? Why?"

"Because that's the right way," I say, "That's who I am."

Belay my last. That's who I was, not am. Click me off safe. After weeks and months of packing down my anger, I cut it loose.

"The Marines taught me to fight. Now they picked a fight with me," I say to April.

Look at her, so happy, like I just brought home flowers. She'll love the Marines/fight thing just as much the next 50 times I say it during the last week of 2004. I like saying it to myself, too, to keep up the fighting spirit.

More where that came from:

"If I had led Marines on the battlefield the way these Colonels did their jobs with me, I'd be in the brig," I say.

Think about it: A Lance Corporal comes to me in Fallujah and says he needs ammo. And I say, "Chill out, man. The next guy will get it. You'll be taken care of." Isn't that exactly what all those lazy, lying, incompetent idiots say to me—"You'll be taken care of"—without doing jack to make it true?

I follow other routes to fury, picking apart what I've been told, especially by Colonel McMoney in his call and a follow-up email. The man is either short on facts or a flat-out liar, either of which enrages me. And I think about the two Marine Colonels on the PEB board. Are they really that lazy, that they can't go over the documents and make a correct, truthful ruling or call a doctor if they need something else? Is it so much easier for them to gloss over the truth and short-change me, after all I did for the Corps and gave to the Corps?

Courage, Honor, Commitment—I lived by them and almost died for them, and these people in the Navy Yard in D.C. shit on our values and principles. What they believe in and live by, I have no idea. Maybe it's dollars, which fills me with disgust. How dare those beancounters wear the same uniform as I do? How dare they dishonor my service?

When the Colonels start to get old, I picture the useless military retiree bureaucrats and get just as torqued. We got fucked, so fuck you . . . If they're so bitter about the system, what are they doing in it, and why aren't they trying to fix it? And if they're so unbelievably lazy, they should make room for somebody else. All it takes is somebody who gives a shit and does his duty. True in combat and true for the paper pushers. God knows it was always true for me.

April and I always tried not to get mad at the same time and did our best to chill each other out. This changes during Christmas-New Year's week, to be known hereafter as the Week of Rage.

When I cool off a little bit April reminds my why I ought to be pissed off:

"They lied to you."

"They're treating you like you're stupid."

"After all you did, Nick, they give you no consideration at all."

Now and again she nukes me: "Nick, you've got to fight. If they're doing this to you, a Gunny, imagine what they're doing to those poor little privates and lance corporals . . . "

This last one never fails. It makes our cause righteous. Acting on my anger and demanding justice for me isn't really for me. No, it's for others, and it's the Marine Thing to Do.

Looking back, I realize that I work so hard to get furious and stay that way and justify myself because I don't want to use the only weapon we have at hand, or so it seems. That weapon is the appeal to powerful individuals outside the Marine Corps. April has wanted me to consider this ever since the PEB process started to go South. Even now that I've decided to proceed, it feels wrong to take internal difficulties outside the Corps. It feels like betrayal, nothing less. To live with it I must believe and constantly remind myself that the Corps betrayed me.

Another thing amps up the anger. I no longer have even a day-dreamable way to stay in. If I have to give up the life I love, it must happen in a way that does honor to me and my service. I was a damn good Marine. I don't get to stay, and you do, so you do this right. It isn't the money. It's the truth.

On Rage Monday, April and I get six hours of unbroken fuming in the car on the round trip between home and Balboa. There, at the behest of the PEB board, I get an electronystagmogram, a weird test involving a spinning chair that measures my loss of balance, which turns out to be worse than anybody thought. Lousy balance with lousy vision is a double whammy, and the doc expresses surprise at how well I manage to compensate. Once again I admire and like the medical pros at Balboa, which makes me even more furious at the PEB guys for being so bad at their jobs and wasting the time of the great docs and staffers.

By the time we get back to Two Nine, April and I have a mature plan of attack. I will write a letter explaining the entire chain of events, beginning with the RPG hit in Iraq and laying out every single way in which the PEB people come up short and the Admin process fails to function. We kick around contacting only a few important individuals whom we personally have met, but then I decide to maximize the range and effectiveness of our shot by doing a mass mailing. We'll start at the top, the President of the United States, and include the Vice President, all U.S. Senators and members of the House of Representatives, and Secretary of Defense, 548 letters total. Though they're all civilians, these people are officially in my chain of command, so I feel right about contacting them rather than business magnates and celebrities we've met, people who might also have big clout.

So I start prep on the letter, the first pogue-like function I perform since I got shot because I can now type and read. To get it absolutely right, April and I do extensive recon and gather intelligence. April, our internet duty expert, has already tapped into the huge body of information on the VA's website concerning disability ratings and compensation. The stuff gives me even more reasons to go up the wall. If the PEB guys chisel me down on my rightful disability status and ignore or understate what's broken, they're cheating my family and me for life. The reason, which I did not previously understand and appreciate, is this: Once I'm out of the Corps I belong to the Veterans Administration, which will handle my retirement and allocate benefits according to the list of permanently disabling conditions in the PEB findings. If the Corps provides bad or incomplete information, the sum total comes up wrong. And I'm fucked. And so are April and Nicholas. When that smarmy car salesman McMoney tells me not to sweat the details because it will all come out right, he's not only lying, he's selling us short.

The deal about temporary disability status, with a PEB re-hearing in 18 months, makes it all a hundred times worse. At first I was suspicious, but now I know that if I take it, I have signed up to get a worse fucking when my position is much weaker because I'm not a Marine any more.

I started this fight for the Truth. But now I know I also fight for my family's well-being. A few percentage points this way or that means thousands of dollars annually.

Our crash course in the wounded warrior bureaucracy keeps bringing us back to April's big point: If they do this to me, a staff NCO who's still on base and in the loop, what are they doing to junior Marines who get disabled, kids a year out of high school going home to Mom and Dad in Knothole, Missouri? Such people would never suspect that a nice-sounding Colonel on the phone misrepresents the facts and cheats them. Look how long it took me to cop to the truth. I, who made a living scrutinizing details and checking the work of other Marines, could have let myself get sold down the river—except, thank God, I smelled shit.

Midweek I get a call from a lawyer at the PEB headquarters in D.C. He says he will represent me at the upcoming formal hearing.

Listen to the next words out of his mouth: "You're already maxed out on money. What more do you want?"

The lawyer, supposedly on my side, tries to sell me McMoney's rotten deal. I tell him the same thing, that I want everything right, whole, and complete on paper and will go before the board to get it.

"You understand if you go into a formal hearing, you risk losing money. The process starts over from scratch," the lawyer says.

"Good!" I yell, "Maybe we can get it right this time!"

What is wrong with you people? You represent McMoney, not me. I can just see Navy Yard guys drinking coffee together, golfing, yucking it up at the O Club like some great big happy screw-the-fighting-men family. And all the while good Marines and sailors on the battlefield risk their lives and get hurt and die.

The lawyer stokes us up for the rest of Rage Week. No shortage of volatile fuel in our house.

At the same time we remain mindful of parenthood and act normal around our boy, who's still young enough to miss the underlying mood. We mainly operate by night. After Nicholas goes to sleep on Thursday, the night before New Year's Eve, we sit down at the computer and I bang out the letter laying out my case for our country's leaders. Though I'm driven by anger, the writing turns out to be a strangely calm process. After all these months, going public, bitching out loud so to speak, actually feels pretty good. The writing comes out easy and fast, too. I make a special effort to translate all the military stuff into non-Marine terms, but even that doesn't slow me down. With the thing already written in my head, all I need to do is get it down, and I do it in one four-hour shot.

After a lot of recounting events and PEB play-by-play comes the thrust: "I am proud of my sacrifice and regret nothing and expect no pity. I do not want anything that I do not rate. I want what is fair and do not feel as though I have received it yet."

And the sign-off: "All I'm asking is that the PEB do the right thing for me and all of the other Marines whose cases come across their desks."

Re-reading the letter now to do this chapter fills me with contradictory feelings. On the one hand I get pissed off all over again at the idiots who try to screw me and realize that I have every reason in the world to go ballistic. On the other hand, I feel embarrassed at the intended purpose of the letter, to take my Marine grievances outside the Marine Corps. This is wrong, wrong, wrong, and I'm ashamed that I even allow myself to consider it, shoddy treatment or not.

Don't think I'm holding anything back because you don't get the whole letter. All you're missing is a name or two that wouldn't add anything. By now you know the rest of what's in it, the whole infuriating enchilada.

Happy New Year.

39

Back in the Corps

We watch the ball drop at Times Square with the boy, who's been a major holiday junky since birth, and have some soda at our own midnight three hours later. As ever, I spend New Year's Day in supine position overeating and watching football games. Football happens to be the one thing that can suppress the anger and divert my attention from the live ordnance upstairs.

I don't forget, though. There the letter sits, all 11 pages, on April's desk. Come Monday, January 3, 2005, we'll go to the copy shop, stuff envelopes, and launch. I hate the thought of it, but I will pull the trigger.

Pro games on Sunday. Oh yeah. First, though, we go to the base's Protestant chapel and take our accustomed pew two-thirds of the way back and on the right. Top Dangerfield and family sit directly in front of the Popaditches per usual. Our ranks don't show, though, because we wear civilian attire. During after-church Fellowship I have found myself socializing with senior members of command, no idea who they were until later. We are all equal in the House of God.

As always I feel better after the service. I don't make a big deal of it in this story, but my Christian faith is deep. It goes hand-in-glove with my faith in the Marine Corps and its bedrock principles, which to me are tied to religious truths and morality. Though some believers say you don't get your religion in church, I do. Miss a service for some less-than-vital reason, and I feel lazy and guilty. For all that God gives me, the least I owe him is to show up at his weekly formation. And he always rewards

me when I do. On the rare occasions when I miss the reward, I know
which one of us came up short. Not God.

For me, Fellowship happens only during the NFL off-season so
we're headed for the car when we bust the hatch of the chapel and shake
the chaplain's hand.

In the mingling out front, a man approaches. Ten o'clock in the desert
brings too much low-angle light and glare, and my Palo Alto sight gear,
hat and sunglasses, sit back in the car, so I only get the broad strokes. The
man stands six-foot-plus and too straight and trim to be one of the
retirees.

"Hey, Gunny Popaditch," he says, "This is General Zilmer here."

I shake his hand. In civvies we don't come to the POA and salute, but
still I straighten up because this is our Base Commanding General.

"Good morning, sir."

"How are you doing, Gunny?"

"Good, sir." I say it without even thinking, as I would if the chapel
fell down and I were pinned in wreckage. Given where we are and the
casual way he asks, I make no connection between the question and the
Battle Of My PEB. And even if I did, I wouldn't complain in front of the
church. Wrong place, wrong time.

The General leans in a little.

"If you have any problems, Gunny, do not hesitate to give me a call."

"Thank you, sir," I say, and he walks off.

My God, what just happened? I stand stock still and replay what the
man said. Maybe in your world offers of help can be insincere, but they
never are in mine. The General spoke man-to-man, Marine-to-Marine.

How could I not take my problems to General Zilmer, ranking officer
on my own home base?

Why should the man himself have to tell me what I already know,
that I owe it to the Corps and myself to go to him?

I know it. I knew it all along. And I pretended like I didn't know it. If
I were in trouble on the battlefield, who would I turn to? My
Congressman? The President or anybody else on our mailing list? Hell
no, I'd turn to the men around me and above me, and they'd move heaven
and earth to help. Why don't I turn to them now that I'm in trouble at Two
Nine? How dare I even think of crying to people who aren't my fellow
Marines?

I say it to myself again. Get up. Get up, and get back in the Marine Corps.

Then and there, I do get back in. And never have I felt so good and so stupid at the same time. Right with God and right again with my Corps and a complete dummy for what I almost did.

Do it like a Marine. Go first to Top Dangerfield, then the Sergeant Major and our Colonel who will take my problems to General Zilmer. It happens Monday. Nick's with us in the car, so I can't tell April. The minute we're alone, though, I say to her: "I'm not sending that letter."

"Why?"

"I can't."

The next day I go to my own command at Two Nine and get the ball rolling, the Marine way.

40

A Fair Shake

Cut and paste from an email sent by a Colonel who is the chief of staff for the Commandant of the Marine Corps (CMC) to a lawyer at Two Nine assigned to my case . . . .

Subj: GySqt Popaditch
Date: 2/11/2005

> The purpose of this email is to provide guidance on CMC intent as it relates to GySgt Popaditch . . .
>
> Marines take care of Marines. Specifically, if they desire to stay on active duty we should attempt to permit that when possible. For those whose injuries dictate that they cannot stay on active duty, the intent is for us to do everything possible to care for them while on active duty, then to provide assistance to ease the transition to VA services, and finally to monitor and follow up even after discharge to make sure we do all we can for our Marines.
>
> I am familiar with GySgt Popaditch's case. Despite his motivation and positive attitude, the extent of his injuries appears to dictate that he must be discharged. In connection with that discharge we must do all that is possible to annotate and document all his Injuries. This is important for both his PEB hearing and disability discharge

rating, but it is also critical to ease his transition to VA services. As you are likely aware, different injuries are rated differently for active duty Marines and those being subsequently rated for VA benefits. I have discussed GySgt Popaditch's case with the Deputy Chief of Staff for the VA who highlighted this issue for me, especially with regard to loss of taste or smell. Documenting everything now will ease GySgt Popaditch's transition and prevent him from having to reestablish the existence of these disabilities when he enters the VA system.

Please ensure that the above is communicated to the PEB on 17 Feb. I stand ready to personally attend the hearing if that will be necessary/helpful . . . Bottom line is the PEB must fully understand the Commandant's intent that we do everything possible to assist our wounded Marines. I'm more than ready to do my small part by driving to Bethesda if necessary.

This Colonel also calls me up and personally offers to come to the board hearing on February 17, and even offers to see if the Commandant himself might be able to attend. I am deeply honored but take a pass. The Commandant has bigger fish to fry, and his personal interest as indicated above is more than sufficient. We have heard the Marine Voice of God. Not a chance anybody will screw up.

Long and short: The truth will be told in Bethesda. I win before I show up. And what I win is huge, a fair shake not only for me but for everybody in my boots. As I discover, the Commandant issued guidance on how to handle cases like mine in 2003. Had that guidance been followed I wouldn't have one damn thing to get mad about or fight about and we would not be going to a formal hearing. Now, though, the Commandant's office is mad, too, and for the same reasons—not because the system broke down but because some bean counters in the Navy Yard are half-assing the cases of wounded Marines and screwing up their benefits and their futures. Boy, would I hate to be in their Corfam dress shoes now. As a Gunny I am not privy to what goes on in D.C., but I know fires burn under some very lazy asses.

Actually I've known which way the wind blows for quite a while. Right after I go to my command at Two Nine I return to Palo Alto, where the Base General reaches me by phone.

"You just concentrate on your rehabilitation, Gunny," he says, "When you get back, we'll get the situation rectified."

Back at Two Nine my house turns into PEB Central, with calls coming in from base headquarters, D.C., and people in the VA who follow my case, too. One day I miss a call on my cell and am stunned to get this voice mail:

"Gunnery Sergeant Popaditch, this is General Charles Krulak, 31st Commandant of the United States Marine Corps. I have been advised of your situation, Marine. We are going to get this fixed. Out here."

April's faith in the Corps is fully restored, just like mine. But we continue to educate ourselves on every aspect of the PEB process and all the ins and outs of the disabled veterans' bureaucracy. I will not show up at a formal proceeding without full command of the subject matter, not any more than I would show up needing a haircut or shave.

All the while friends and allies come out of the woodwork. Capt. Skaggs, my company commander when I got wounded, wants to come to the hearing on my behalf, as does Colonel Bryan McCoy, battalion commander on my first OIF deployment. I respect and admire both men and accept their offers—the more the merrier, right? The lawyer from the General's office at Two Nine plans to attend, too. Best of all, April gets to go East with me because I rate an escort, like a seeing eye human being. I could get by on my own just fine, but I'm really glad that she'll be at my side, which is where she's been all along.

I show up for the hearing, held in the Bethesda Naval Hospital complex, a hundred percent squared away, my Service Alpha uniform razor sharp. My lawyer goes in first for preliminaries, then sticks his head out and says the board's ready for me, after which I march in, assume the POA, and say "Good Morning, Gentlemen. Gunnery Sergeant Popaditch reporting to the senior member of the formal hearing as ordered, Sir." The single Marine on the board, flanked by two Navy officers in whites, greets me and tells me to be at ease and take a seat. Though I'm on my behind, I maintain the rigidity and uprightness of the POA all through the proceedings. The board doesn't call for this degree of formality, but I want to represent myself as a Marine and conduct myself in an honorable and upright manner.

What little bit of anger I bring into the room quickly turns to pride, which swells throughout the hearing. Immediately I lose all adversarial feeling. The board members and lawyers and staff treat me in the most professional, dignified manner. They don't third-degree me as if they doubt the truth, and they don't try to chisel as if the truth ought to be negotiable. We want the same thing, the truth about my permanent conditions and degree of disability all properly documented in the board's official findings. They go over what's broken and what it means to me but without making me feel like less of a Marine. We could be talking about equipment damaged in combat, like a track split by a mine or a machine gun barrel bent by an explosion. It's damaged and it can't kill people any more, so what do we do? That's the gist of the inquiry, and I admire and appreciate the cool professionalism. The results won't be out for at least a month, but I know I'll get a fair shake because they're giving me one right now.

Afterward my lawyer shakes my hand and thanks me for reminding him what PEB proceedings are really all about. It happens that this is his last such case, and he's doing right seat/left seat with a young female attorney. He tells me he's very glad she gets snapped in today. A little later the colonel on the board tells me that my conduct made him proud to be a Marine.

Passing thought: Where do they hide the lazy yo-yos who screwed things up to the point that I needed to come here? I know this is a different board because the names are different, but I can't believe these dignified pros even come from the same unit. Maybe they don't. As I said, a Gunny only knows so much about how the wheels turn.

Colonel McCoy says to Capt. Skaggs and me, "Let's go visit the wounded guys on the ward."

Really glad the Colonel suggests this, because I have spent hours and hours making morale calls at Balboa, a good thing to do. This I know from seeing the effect, but more so because once I was the guy in the rack, and I appreciated every drop-in, even nurses and orderlies. Somebody, anybody to talk with. I also like that I excel at this particular duty, where my wounds are an asset and not a liability.

The last time I was here at Bethesda I was blind as a bat, so I rely on the other two to find a floor with Marine combat casualties. There the three of us get a guide, a Lance Corporal in cammies who says he's a patient.

"What's going on? What's broke?" I ask him.

"I had cancer, Gunny," he says.

"How you doing?"

"It's in remission, Gunny," he says, like Cancer ought to be scared of him, not vice versa. He goes on to tell me he's running and working on his PFT and will back out in the Fleet in a month.

I hope it's true, Marine, I think, remembering all the things I used to say about getting back on a tank.

"Oorah," I tell him, "Semper Fi."

Today we've got the Morale Call Dream Team, three trigger pullers who are familiar with the Sunni Triangle. Odds are at least one of us has been to the place where each guy we visit got wounded.

Colonels lead, so ours opens in a Colonel-like way, introducing himself and then the Captain and me.

"Just stopped in to see how you're doing, Marine," he says.

"Good, sir."

"What's your MOS, Marine?" the Colonel asks, referring to the guy's Military Occupational Specialty, his job.

If the guy says he's infantry, the Colonel says, "Hey, I'm a grunt, too." Whatever the answer, the Colonel makes the same sort of connection, and truthfully. As a battalion commander, he's got pretty much every kind of Marine in his unit and knows a lot about their specialties.

Job talk puts everybody on a more informal level, unbelievably cool for a 19-year-old PFC who never shot the breeze with a full-bird Colonel before. Colonel McCoy, with a distinguished record of combat leadership and a commanding presence, is something of a trigger-puller celebrity, which ups the coolness even more. Once they relax and get going, the junior Marines bend the Colonel's ear about where they were and what they did, puffed up and proud as if they're telling him things that Colonels don't know, like the ins and outs of manning a vehicle control point or un-jamming a Mark 19.

Captain Skaggs, a city cop before he joined the Corps, has a particular gift for drawing guys out. Having a company commander with his kind of street smarts concerning civilian populations did our team a lot of good in Iraq. It also gives him a lot to talk about with guys who dealt with everyday Iraqis last week.

If the wounded Marine says he used to patrol Route 10, say, the Captain comes back like this: "Oh yeah, Route 10. We used to have this problem, the civilian vehicles intermingling in convoys . . . ."

"Exactly, Sir. You know what we did? We put signs in Arabic on the back of every vehicle. Some of those locals are so bullheaded they still try to Bogart in."

"Tell me about it," the Captain says, and the guy does just that.

Finally, I jump in with the question the guys are dying to answer—How'd you get hit, Marine?—which the Colonel and Captain would hesitate to ask. With no hospital time themselves, they have no idea how great it is to tell people about your actual wounding. Having talked to a hundred or more wounded Marines, I have yet to meet an exception. For us today, this is the great leveler. It finally puts us on the same plane, four guys just talking about fighting in Iraq. The man still calls the officers "Sir" and me "Gunny," but it's all Marine-to-Marine. And always the guy is proud of the manner of his wounding, which he wears like a badge of honor. And he should be. There can be no doubt that a man minus a foot or an arm spent time outside the wire—out where the bad shit happens. And we're proud to be with him. I swear we get more out of this than the guys we visit. I know I always do.

Something strikes me about the Marine patients at Bethesda. Every one of them got hurt by the blast from a roadside IED—Improvised Explosive Device—now a household word in America but then a relatively new weapon of choice for the bad guys. On my first OIF deployment, IED wasn't even part of the vocabulary. On the second we knew what they were and kept an eye out, but enemy fire caused almost every casualty I know of back then. Now, as I work on this book, IEDs account for a heavy majority of casualties and have for a couple years. When I talk to guys going over now, IEDs are all they worry about. It's as if fighters with guns disappeared. When I talk about Fallujah in 2004, guys get downright envious because I had somebody to shoot at. In a lot of ways the troops in Iraq since then have a tougher fight.

One PFC tells how he lost his foot before he got anywhere near the bad guys his team was sent to kill.

He was a part of a Quick Reaction Team (QRT) on a firm base in the Triangle, dispatched to reinforce a patrol taking fire. His team took a wrong turn on the way to the fight, then had to retrace its route past a hazardous spot.

"We knew it was a danger area the first time," he says, "So we knew we were pushing our luck the second time. But those Marines called—we're coming."

I sympathize. It's a fuck story, but a Marine story. A bad spot at a bad time, and he had to go for the sake of somebody else.

"Hey, when you're QRT, those guys are counting on you," I say, telling him his team made the right call. A fight's a fight, even against an invisible enemy.

The kid's as proud as he ought to be.

41

Getting it Right

All we needed was a wire brush and an oil can.

Looking back, I believe the foot-draggers and do-nothings were nothing more than rust on the Admin machinery for out-processing disabled Marines. Prior to the spring of 2004, the machinery didn't have to run full-speed under a full load because we just didn't take that many casualties. I happened to get hit during the first post-invasion spike when the fight against insurgents picked up steam.

Now we're a couple years into a much higher volume of serious and disabling combat injuries. Even so, I am continually amazed at the high quality of treatment given to wounded Marines and sailors I visit on the wards at Balboa. All signs point to the same thing—Command has a deep commitment to taking care of its own every step of the way. Nobody gets shown the door until every possible medical fix has been made. And a bigger effort goes into retaining disabled personnel if they can do some good.

The commitment to wounded and disabled veterans' welfare is, I think, national and not just in my branch of the service. But can somebody still drop the ball? The screw-up at Walter Reed Army Hospital, biggest veterans-related scandal of 2007, says yes. But it also validates the system and chain of command, which straightened things out in a hurry and would have even without political grandstanding and a media frenzy. So far nothing like this has happened in our Department of the Navy medical system, and I doubt it could.

I'm very glad to say that I believe the Marine Corps PEB system gets much closer high-level scrutiny and supervision than when I went through it. In my opinion, the system now works very well. This does not, however, mean the boards get it right for everybody. Marines still get screwed.

I say this without reservation because I meet guys getting screwed right here and now. It happens for a lot of reasons, which have a lot to do with the nature of the people involved. Trigger pullers, particularly the junior Marines who constitute the bulk of our wounded, have not been trained to push papers. And they don't question and scrutinize the work of superiors. "That's not right, Sir," does not naturally come out of a young enlisted man's mouth. And, though he knows what's broken on himself, he has no clue as to the proper codes and disability percentages for his conditions. All his instincts tell him to trust the technical judgments of superior officers who are also duty experts, like the PEB people.

Any good Marine's instincts scream against making a fight at all. "I'm sorry, Sir, but I'm more fucked-up than it says here." Who wants to go around saying that, even if it's true? I know I didn't. I hated it. It felt like groveling, asking for pity, which we abhor. A real Marine will be his own worst enemy in such a situation, which is too confusing for him to see the right thing, the Marine thing, to do.

That aside, a disabled guy will want to get the bureaucratic bullshit over with so he can get on with his life. For a career Marine like me, ending active service brings such pain you just want to get it over, like ripping off a Bandaid. The quickest and easiest way out is to accept the PEB board's first findings. If it's close to the truth a lot of guys will say, "Hell with it," sign, and move on.

Is it the Marine's fault if he comes up short? No. Is it the fault of the officers on PEB board if somebody who's not a doctor fails to properly code and rate a disabling condition presented in medical technical jargon? No again. Even with the best intentions, human error creeps in. And, as noted in the letter from the Commandant's office, any discrepancies can cause major problems when vets go to the VA, which can only award benefits according to PEB findings. You say they're wrong? Well, we have a piece of paper with your signature saying the findings are correct. The only way to change your disability status is to start from scratch with a physical and new paperwork within the VA.

I probably could have straightened things out in a couple months. But if it happened now? Well, Mr. or Ms. discharged Marine, we'll take care of you but only after we see to the 50,000 others ahead of you. On top of that we have 60-plus years of vets in our VA system. Sheer volume now makes minor mistakes a big deal, particularly to the guy who has to wait a year or more to receive all the benefits for which he rightfully qualifies. Since he might be unemployable, at least until he rehabs and retrains, he—and his family if he has one—needs every penny he deserves.

It goes against my grain to point out problems in a system that did so right by me, a system that is full of people who made heroic efforts on my behalf, who I know are doing just as much for others right now. I'm nobody's whistle-blower, because I believe in the system. On the other hand, I can't deny reality. Many Marines are ill-equipped to protect their own interests in the PEB/disabled vets' paperwork jungle. Even with good people bending over backwards to help, they can get short-changed. To try to head off troubles like mine, I give briefs on the system in wards in Balboa. Not a month goes by that I don't personally counsel some new casualty.

Most recently, I told a Sergeant going into his PEB, "Hey, man, even if it's a tiny error, you have to make it right. And even if you don't want to do it for yourself, do it for the junior Marines who need you to show leadership, just like you did in Iraq. If you don't make the system work the way it ought to, who will?"

I tell him he'll hate it for all the reasons given above, but this is where his duty now lies.

"You're right, Gunny," he says and accepts the mission.

If you know a combat casualty looking at a PEB and possible separation, make him or her read this little chapter or at least pass on my message. Very likely they're misinformed. All the current media about disabled vets' problems point the finger at the VA, which is now better than it ever was.

This is unfair.

The VA gets stuck cleaning up messes made by the branches of the active military. The danger area for vets is the PEB and how you're rated.

If it ain't right, you got trouble.

42

Final Game

1900 Local
East Gym
Marine Corps Air-Ground Combat Center
Twentynine Palms, California

March Madness, Two Nine Style

For those of us with kids on teams that make it to the base championships, this final night of coed basketball gets more interest and enthusiasm than the NCAA. Fans follow the action from 10,000 miles away, too. Those aren't videocams that people point all around but proxy eyeballs for deployed Marines who want to see their boys' and girls' big game as much as we do. Some guys in the Sunni Triangle could be looking at digital pictures and highlight clips emailed later tonight. I can just see them coming into the Morale Center between patrols, punching the stuff up, and yelling like Dads and Moms courtside.

"Nice shot!"

"Hustle!"

I was never that computer savvy, but I always followed my boy's activities by phone and letter and asked him to send me things from his sports and everything else—team standings and scores from the base paper, report cards, school work, and so on.

Nick's team surprised everybody by making it to the final round. Chalk it up to hustle and good coaching and team play, because other squads in the 10-to-12-year-old division that they eliminated had them beat on talent. Our boy, who plays forward, pretty much takes the success in stride. April and I always try to play up the fun side of athletics. As I tell him, you can't have fun if you don't give it your best effort, but the points he makes and the team's final score count for less than the intangibles. Don't think for a minute that I'm one of these "Let's not keep score" fairies because I'm not. A kid must learn to win, too, but the right way. However the games go, I pull out positive lessons for Nicholas. I used to praise his baseball team, which was a catastrophe, because everybody struck out instead of taking walks. "I like that. You can't get a hit if you don't take a swing," I would say.

The only push Nicholas ever got from us is onto the team in the first place. Kids' sports and group activities have a greater importance in our world because they encourage contact between youngsters who might otherwise feel isolated. Rule of thumb says we change bases every three years. That really involves two moves. First to temporary civilian quarters while you wait for base housing—usually a matter of months— then the move onto the base. I can count six relocations and four school changes for Nick between kindergarten and 2005, his sixth grade year. Even when we didn't move, he lost friends left and right because other families got reassigned.

You can't blame a Marine kid for getting a little gun shy about connecting with his own age group. Nicholas, the only child in our house on Ludwig Court, tends to hang with grownups and stay inside a little too much, so we do our best to push him out the door. Once he gets involved, like he's caught up in our base basketball league, he loves it.

Tonight I pack my optical howitzer, a 10-power scope that I was trained to use at Palo Alto, and we take our normal observation post about halfway up the bleachers. From here I can follow the action, at least in a general way, and even track individual players. I miss a lot, for sure, but I see so much compared to before. Two months ago I'd be down at the sidelines and still unable to ID my son and make out any of the play. I'd fake it for the sake of others, but I would miss it all. Tonight, I don't have to fake anything. Dad will see and enjoy the game, which means a little more to me than it probably should. For all my stuff about stressing intangibles, I want a victory tonight a hell of a lot more than I let on. The other team, undefeated and favored to win, is heavy on sons and daughters of field-grade officers, the base big shots. Our squad, on the other hand, has mostly kids of Staff NCOs, a couple of them buddies of mine now fighting overseas. I would dearly love for our side to come out on top.

Before the tip-off, I get a huge shot of the good feelings that come to me every day.

I am so damn lucky.

Things could be so much worse, and they almost were.

A millimeter this way or that in the grenade's trajectory, and I'm dead or brain damaged.

My tank crew doesn't come through, I bleed to death.

One of my surgeons makes some microscopic slip, I'm black blind for life.

I don't find out about Palo Alto, and I can't use what vision I have.

The PEB findings and out-processing come through so quickly we're already gone before this game.

I could not be more blessed. And a big part of the blessing is the community life we see all around us.

All of Two Nine shows its face on game night. You see more infants and tiny kids in the bleachers than in the civilian world, because you can't drop the babies off at Grandma's or Auntie's when she lives eight states away. Single barracks Marines show up in civilian sweats waiting for the league games to end so they can play their own pickup games. Shooting hoops is the young Marines' diversion of choice in the evening. Older guys, too. I miss the hell out of my jarhead basketball, which I played until the RPG hit.

Even non-player junior Marines show up at the gym tonight, because this is the best show in town on a weeknight. You also see Marines in cammies coming in from training or taking a quick break from duty.

Also here, among us, are our Marines in other places. Every family minus Dad or Mom establishes a living presence, not an absence. Maybe they're in Iraq or Afghanistan or out in the desert doing night training. Wherever they are, they're part of this crowd, linked to us by shared belonging and duty. We're here for the same reasons they are not. And maybe they'll be here when we're gone. Some of us never come back, which makes our bonds, our community, stronger.

The reality of risk and danger in the war zones wipes away all the bullshit that gets between people. And it doesn't make us sad—it makes us happier to have fun together on an occasion such as this.

Nobody here is a stranger, not even fresh arrivals with names unknown, and we would not be strangers in some other place in the Marine World. Everybody present—six-month-old baby, private fresh out of boot camp, Mom, machine gunner just back from Al Keim—belongs to something huge and important that will outlive us and that reaches far beyond Two Nine.

We look out for each other. You see it in a hundred little ways. A kid screams, and a Mom two rows in front hands back a toy. If an older kid misbehaves when his parents aren't in sight, somebody will let him know he's out of line. When the parents come back, they'll thank whoever squared their kid away. This is the Marine way. We hold each other up to higher standards, and we not only tolerate, we appreciate correction, which means we care in a way that people out in CivDiv don't—not as far as we can tell, anyhow. I belong. You belong. We belong.

Marine rules apply out on the court, too, where games are clean. Refs' calls go unchallenged. If a player so much as shows an unsportsmanlike attitude, the coach squares the kid away and benches him or her until the lesson hits home. Star players enjoy no immunity. For coaches and the crowd, hustle counts as much as the score. Nobody here forgives laziness or less than 100 percent dedication to the mission and the team. All the intangibles add to the fun, too. We in the stands get a big kick out of seeing our core values running around, like our kids are mini-Marines in the ways that matter most. The word "cute" does not naturally come out of my mouth, but that's what this is to me. And it fills me with pride.

I do not, by the way, care if my boy joins the Marine Corps one day, but I'd feel like I completely screwed up the Dad mission if he does not possess our best character traits. He does, and we see it every day. Mom and Dad can't take all the credit, because for the first eleven years of life he gets an indoctrination from everybody and everything around him. His entire world brings him up the right way, the Marine way. He's as lucky as we grownups are, and I hope someday he passes on the gifts he got here to the youngsters in his life.

You're probably wondering what gives with the Big Game. Well, we got ourselves a thriller. The teams flip-flop the lead and stay within a few points of each other. Just by keeping even with the other team, our kids have exceeded all expectations. And they do it the Marine way. Good hustle. Strategy. Commitment. Desire. Heart. Above all, teamwork. As I said, the other side has us outgunned, and if our kids ever let up, the opposition would pull away. We stay on the attack, though. Relentlessly.

Nicholas gets his share of court time and puts in a good performance. Never a star, he always advances the cause with solid fundamentals and sticking to the game plan. Box out. Low post. Hands up on defense, always. He shines by not shining. On the other hand, he's not scared to take the shot when he's open, even though his instincts tend toward the pass. Every time he scores I stand up and yell, while making a mental note so we can talk about it at home. I note the misses, too, and will praise him just as much for good decision-making whether or not the ball fell.

No doubt Nicholas hears Dad cheering him on. As a staff NCO, I could yell loud enough to make all the babies cry, and other guys in the crowd could give me a run for my money decibel-wise. We Marines are loud by nature and by practice. After all, leadership means projecting your voice above engines roaring and weapons fire. But what we yell at games falls within the bounds of good sportsmanship. And people cheer almost as loudly for the other side as they do for their own kids.

The whole place goes especially nuts when a little girl on Nick's squad steps up to the free-throw line and makes her one and only point of the entire season. All along we've been pulling for her, because what she lacks in athletic ability—everything—she more than makes up in heart. However much she gets scored-on and hits zero percent of her shots, she never hangs her head or acts intimidated. When the coach sends her out, she plays, and we love it—even tonight when he sends her out in this squeaker season championship. Not the best winning strategy unless you define winning our way. And this time, by God, she actually does contribute to winning.

By the closing minutes we're looking at a win if we can hang onto our lead, which is way too close for comfort. The crowd raises the roof, especially the staff NCOs and enlisted dads on our team. Beating the officers' kids—how cool is this? A little bit of the sick sports father nonsense that I don't like, projecting my feelings onto the kids' game, but on this night it couldn't be any other way, could it? April, I know, feels the same way but also keeps it under wraps.

How sweet it is, when the buzzer sounds and we're on top.

We stand aside while the kids celebrate and then line up for the obligatory hand-shaking and congratulation of the other team. After that the coach gives our team some final good words, and they split up and mill around the gym floor. On the way to meet my son I do what the other dads do, giving compliments to every kid I pass. Then, glad and proud beyond words, I congratulate Nick for the win and for playing his heart out. I'm so thrilled and happy for him, that he did the right stuff the right way and had it pay off. I put my hand on my son's shoulder and keep it there while we walk out to the car. This contact is all we need, because Nick's no more of a hugger than I am.

This night could not have turned out any better. If we let it, a little sadness could come in because we'll never have such a night again. Not in this world, with these people. Though we know and feel the same thing—Goodbye to the world we love—we don't say a thing about it. We just love our world a little more, which makes us happier.

43

Snow School

April 8, 2005
Snowmass Village, Colorado
19th Annual National Disabled Veterans Winter Sports Clinic

Happy Anniversary, Beautiful Woman.

I'm pretty sure this one represents a big improvement for April compared to a year ago, when I called her from Germany blind as a bat and flying on pain killers and she held everything together at home with no sleep and everybody we know calling up saying, "Don't look at the TV," which, of course, made her imagine things were even worse than they were.

A year before that I called her from Firdos Square in Baghdad flush with victory while watching my unit pull down the big Saddam stature. The next day April saw my smiling mug on the front page of the paper, as did millions of others all over the world.

Though I don't rank such things, this one is way up there. Just check out the Rocky Mountains, which April and I admire from all angles including the outdoor hot tub and swimming pool. Soaking in perfect comfort next to a huge snowdrift, this is something new and novel for both of us. But there's newness all around. All week long these incredible volunteers bust my cherry on skis, both downhill and cross country, snowshoes, and a snowmobile. Even the concept of enjoying snow all these different ways seems foreign. Back home in Indiana winter mostly meant freezing your ass and waiting for spring. Then, in the Corps, ten feet of snow like we have here would have slowed down movement and complicated the entire tactical plan, from the supply train to command and signal, and generally been a major pain in the ass. Here, when we get a big new accumulation, people cheer and act like surf's up.

Gotta admire the guts of a guy named Bill who gets behind me on a high-powered snowmobile that goes like one of my old motorcycles. I'm wearing distress-signal orange signs that say I'm blind, but that doesn't bother him a bit even after I tell him I'm a road warrior and a speed demon.

"I'm going to wind this up," I say, "Are you cool with that?"

"Go for it," he says.

I do just that, having some near misses with trees and a mountain stream at considerable velocity. Damned if a snowmobile doesn't handle a lot like a bike. The joys of the bike come back, the kick-ass acceleration, engine whining at rpms that would blow out a car's power plant, wind rushing by the helmet so loudly I can barely hear Bill yell which way I need to go. Out in open fields the choice is mine, and I carve turn after turn, big sweepers, wide chicanes, hanging way off on the inside and feeling the Gs. What a riot, man. I could do this all day. I could do it all week. Bill must be holding on for dear life, but he never once says to slow down.

Afterward, I thank him and ask him how many times he thought about bailing.

"No, man, I wouldn't leave you," he laughs. What a great guy. What a great group of instructors, putting themselves out on their own time to give disabled vets some of the wintertime fun that the volunteers so obviously love.

Though I don't especially like cross-country skiing, I enjoy hanging out with the instructors, who keep themselves apart like they're some kind of Mountain Marines, proud that their thing is more physically challenging than anybody else's. It is, too. They make their own camp in a clearing above the lodge and let us know that different rules apply when we're with them. If you don't like it this hard, tough, because we're not going to change it. I love the attitude and everything about these people except what they actually do.

Maybe my favorite thing about this clinic is that nobody ignores the elephant in the room, our disabilities, and nobody tiptoes around peoples' bodily limitations. One instructor openly makes fun of the goggles I wear, with thick lenses, protective padding, and a blue head strap. Knowing that the things look ridiculous, I laugh, too.

One vet who's been here before, also with low vision, gives me the following advice after I tell him I'm blind: "Don't sign up for sled hockey!"

Naturally, I want to know why, and he says, "The wheelchair guys we play against, they got all that upper body strength. And they know you can't see shit, so they're cranking out slap shots at you. They show no mercy."

Mercy I don't want, but I take a pass on hockey, which I played when I was sighted, and pick only sports that I never experienced.

April, meanwhile, has a resort-style vacation. She could try all the activities, too, but doesn't want to tie up an instructor who might otherwise be helping a vet. Besides that, she really enjoys chilling out in the lodge and socializing with vets and their loved-ones and the volunteers.

Even without actual athletics, I think April gets more out of the Winter Sports Clinic than I do. It gives her the first good look at where this whole thing goes—where we're headed—which is a life where disabilities don't stop anybody from taking on new challenges and having a blast. To this point, she's seen only freshly wounded Marines at Balboa and Twentynine Palms. And she's seen a lot of them week in, week out, whenever we needed to go to the hospital. Every time, her heart ached for the guys we saw, young enough to be her own sons, struggling to heal and get used to their busted-up bodies. Marine-style hospital humor and positivity aside, the wards were very sad places for her. I never realize how sad until later.

Here in Colorado, though, April sees people with greater physical challenges than mine doing things that defy belief. One day a guy missing both legs parachutes into the ski village. Another day, the world's fastest blind skier burns up the slopes. The everyday vets are just as inspiring, and their upbeat attitudes infectious. Chris, Army airborne with a terrible speech impediment and impaired motor skills from traumatic brain injury, turns out to be a major comedian. April and I discover this in the evening when I play a game of eight-ball with him at the bar. All the while he gets off Army-Marine zingers on me. Very cool to realize he only sounds slow but possesses all his wits.

Our BS is better than the game. Any pool sharks present see no cause for alarm when a soldier with bad motor skills takes on a legally blind Marine.

It does April a world of good to see all these disabled vets forging ahead in new lives, out of uniform and into exciting worlds beyond the military. To this point, loss has loomed much larger for her than anything that we might gain. I've seen a little more light at the end of the tunnel than she has, so Colorado isn't so much of a revelation. Still, this is a shot in the arm, a week of nothing but new kinds of fun with people in the same boat as me, everybody having a riot and loads of laughs.

Snow school for the permanently disabled—this doesn't sound like the best place to celebrate a wedding anniversary. But it turns out to be pretty damn good for our Fourteenth. We don't do a lot to mark the actual anniversary day, which falls at the end of the week. It just blends into general celebration.

My favorite recreational moment happens near the end of the clinic in the lodge's pool, in my first shot at a sport that has nothing to do with snow. When I signed up for scuba diving lessons, I figured it wouldn't involve much actual scuba. But the instructor gets me into the rig with tanks and breather and mask and gives only a short brief on safety before turning me loose.

Hokey, but true—it's a whole new world down here. Everything in view up above, the snow, the mountain, the skiers, goes away, and I don't care. We got better stuff going on underwater. I have company, people turning somersaults, floating, swimming around on the bottom. It's like some grownup, zero-gravity bounce house, no rhyme or reason to anything we do except it's fun. Think about what a rush this is for guys missing a limb, or two, or three. But the water does me good, too. It acts like a magnifier, and seeing better is part of the reason I love this new environment.

The water also slows down thrown objects to the point that I can play catch. A guy and I start tossing a sort of underwater Frisbee. It makes a nice straight track but at a speed that I can anticipate, and I can set myself up to make the catch. The day-glo orange rim makes it jump out of the blue-green background. For the first time in a year I can pick up a moving target and get a hand on it, not just once, but time after time. Basic, simple, back-and-forth garden variety catch. I love it, and I haven't played it for more than a year. I never thought I would, either.

An instructor comes down and signals that I'm about to run out of air. My catch partner comes up, too, and I recognize him as one of my favorite fellow vets, a young soldier who lost a leg, whose attitude I can't get enough of. All day long he laughs and smiles, acting like there's no better place in the world than wherever he happens to be.

All the while he and I played Frisbee, April sat pool side with the guy's Mother, who told his story. The same explosion that took off his leg put him in a coma for more than a month. His Mom quit her job and went to him at Walter Reed Hospital, staying at his bedside around the clock. Once he woke up, she assisted with his rehab program.

The soldier's Mom told April stories about wounded who had to fight alone, ignored or even abandoned by loved ones. Spouses just walked away from their disabled husbands and wives in the hospital, saying they didn't sign up for this, and the vets had heartbreak and loneliness on top of their physical wounds. As best she could, the soldier's Mom became a mother to all of those on their own in the hospital.

The stories that lady tells makes April's heart ache, just like her visits to the guys in our hospitals. Like so many times, while I'm healing—and in this case, having fun—she feels the losses suffered by others. And I won't have a clue until much, much later about the pain she feels. Looking back, I wish I would notice at the time and thank her.

Better late than never, so I'll do it now. Thanks, Beautiful Woman.

And let me rewind to Colorado and say this one more time: Happy Anniversary.

Thanks for fourteen years.

I wish I could have made this last year easier for you.

44

Thanks, Marines

April 22, 2005
1000 Local
Tank Battalion Grinder
Retirement Ceremony For GySgt Nicholas Popaditch

Really, I'd be happier and a hell of a lot more comfortable if some Marine I respected and admired said "Hey, we were better off with you than without you," and shook my hand.

But Top Dangerfield said to me, "It doesn't matter what you want. This isn't for you, it's for April and the boys. They deserve it."

So here I stand, centerpiece of a complete formal Marine Corps retirement ceremony. A few hundred First Tanks Marines march onto the grinder and form up. The band troops the line, playing music on the march down to the end of the formation and back. The crowd loves it, but the Marines in the formation wish it didn't take so long. In truth, they wish they were somewhere else. This I know because I paraded at ceremonies—retirements, graduations, changes of command, awards— more times than I could ever count, and every parade was drudgery. Any Marine who says different is bull-shitting. Here's another reason I wanted to pass on the hoopla: to spare the guys so they can do something better. Today, though, the battalion marches in my honor the Marine way, as we have always done and always will. And it's great for the rest of us to see.

One thing here gives me a case of the jitters. I must stand up and speak to the assembled Marines and guests. I've faced bigger crowds many times but always with information to impart and some specific communication mission. Today I say whatever I feel like. Some guys half-ass their speeches, but I owe everybody a real effort, especially the Marines who put forth an effort for me, and I want to make listening to me worthwhile. I also need to be brief. One gold nugget for the First Tanks guys and move the fuck out. And I owe it to myself and all present not to get drippy and weepy. That ain't me, and I don't feel the least bit sad, anyway. I feel happy and proud and blessed and full of hope.

What I feel, most of all, is grateful. Practically all the words I speak, such as they are, are words of gratitude.

I thank my tank crew, all three here to see me off, for coming through under fire and saving my life.

I thank a retiree in the crowd, Top Graham, my first tank leader and the Marine on whom I modeled myself. He kicked my ass every which way, and after I earned his respect he taught me how to lead and make a difference and how to win no matter what, which is what Marines do.

He and dozens of others who showed me the way gave me the life the guys on Bonecrusher saved. What greater gift could I receive than this, a life worth living that means something and makes a difference?

I cannot imagine my existence without the Marine Corps. Nor do I want to, because life would have been so much less exciting and meaningful. In the Corps I traveled the world and did important things for the sake of my country and humanity. When you fight on the right side, as I know I did, you save and improve hundreds of lives for every life you take. When you lead, as I did, you can stop terrible things from happening. All that I did as a Marine, I am proud of, and every single thing I am that gives me pride and satisfaction, I owe to the Corps. I'm the man I am because I'm a Marine. The husband, the father I am. I'm proud to be the man that my sons and my wife see today. Whatever success and accomplishment comes next, I will owe to what the Corps gave me.

To the First Tanks Marines I give a little bit of The World According To Gunny Pop. Not Confucious, but the best I have today: You got good times in the Corps, and you got better times. The best times you're going to have are when the nation calls and you're out doing that real-world Marine mission. For First Tanks, cycling in and out of Iraq, this is such a time. Enjoy the ride, I say.

I tell the First Tanks guys how proud I am to have served with them, and I say the words I put in this book many pages back: Thanks, Marines.

Every Marine that ever was and ever will be.

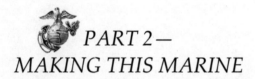

PART 2 —
MAKING THIS MARINE

45

Wrong Place

July, 2005
Monterey California
Popaditch Family Moving Sale

Easy there, civilian, don't be messing up my deuce gear. Show some respect.

When it mattered every single item performed admirably and upheld the highest traditions of the United States Marines. The canteen cup in your hand? Comforts of home, man. At zero-four I heated water in it over the exhaust pipe for hygiening and then cleaned the cup and heated more water for coffee. No finer way to greet the day than sitting on the hull of my M1A1 main battle tank, my own front porch, shaved and washed and with a hot cup of joe. You have no idea. The polypro kept my butt toasty. The cammies I marched in with other proud warriors. If you don't refold and square things away, I will do so out of respect and fondness and a sense of ownership that surprises me. I never imagined it would be so hard to let my field gear go.

But this is new. A female zeroes in on the military gear instead of April's household items and Nick Jr.'s kid stuff. She holds up a combat boot sole-to-sole with one of her own shoes and has a match.

My wife pulls me aside and whispers, "Nick, do you know who that is?"

"No. Why?"

"That horrible, disgusting war protestor!"

No kidding. April and Nick told me about this crazy radical artist who runs a booth in the city park and puts up really heinous, graphic pictures of maimed and dead Iraqi women and kids. I guess I should respond. Do I hate her, tell her to get lost? If I don't, do I dishonor the Corps and my country? What if she wants something?

"Were you a Marine?" she asks.

"Yes I was."

"Were you in Iraq?"

"Yes I was."

"It's horrible, terrible, what we're doing there!"

Good for you, lady. This beats the usual kiss-ass BS, "I'm against the war, but I love the troops." But then the protestor, who has never set foot in Iraq, tells me in great depth and detail what Iraqis want and don't want, especially how they don't want us there.

Oh really?

The last man I saw having his house pillaged seemed glad to have me chase off the criminals. Ditto other almost-victims of crimes, like shop owners who could open for business with my tank parked out front, and all the wounded people whose lives we saved.

I tell the woman how much I like Iraqis and say, "All the average Moe over there wants is what we want. I was proud to fight so people could have a shot at a decent life."

Protestor Lady seems surprised to meet a Marine trigger puller who is not a homicidal dumb shit. Surprise goes the other way, too. She's not a closed-minded jerk spewing propaganda and tuning me out. We actually come together on the subject of the maimed and dead people in her pictures. We both abhor violence against innocents and want to stop it, but we're 180 degrees apart on who perpetrates and who protects. It's stretching things to say we like each other, but I think we're both surprised by the lack of dislike. I don't mind when she touches my face where the shrapnel blew out my right eye.

All the time we talk she holds a pair of boots I wore in Iraq.

"Do you want them?"

"I think they might be good for my welding," she says. No doubt she means for some sort of wacko metal art that I would not like.

I pick up some gloves and say, "These might work for you, too. They're flame resistant. I wore them on my tank."

She pays for the boots and gloves and says "As Salaam Alaikum," Arabic for "Peace be with you."

I respond as I did a thousand times in Iraq: "Alaikum As Salaam."

God Almighty, did she really kiss my cheek?

*   *   *

No, I do not regret the move from Two Nine to Monterey, California, even though we fit in about as well as Bonecrusher on the golf course at Pebble Beach.

Say we go to San Diego the easy way, straight from the base using our retirement relocation benefits so the move doesn't cost a dime. Too effortless. Too obvious, too, because we've already lived here. Even if we're crazy about it, won't we always wonder if we should have made a bolder and possibly better move? And will we really recognize that SD is Home Sweet Home? Probably not. Sometimes you have to make a bad turn to recognize what's right.

And Monterey, in concept at least, isn't so stupid. We love the area, which we got to know on trips to see the motorcycle races at Laguna Seca. And we score a great deal on housing on the recently decommissioned Army base Fort Ord. Single-family home with four beds and a view of the ocean. Good VA facilities and support nearby. Loads of recreation. I get a mountain bike and a sea kayak that I can keep at a club right on the coast in town. There's a big gym nearby, so little-used that I can check out a ball and shoot free throws without bothering anybody. Everything, including a community college where I register for fall classes, is accessible by public transit or under my own power.

A better setup we could not have—except we can't stand it.

The whole Monterey experience brings to mind this big pine tree in our backyard. The thing stands maybe a hundred feet high with a trunk much too thick to reach around, and it sits just past the patio. When we first see the place we picture relaxing in the shade, drinking cold ones while listening to the stereo and watching the sun set on the Pacific, which the backyard overlooks. If this were Southern California, not Northern, it'd all be true. But you don't need a shade tree on Fort Ord, which is some kind of a fog magnet where you freeze your ass year-round. And the tree attracts birds that send down a constant rain of shit, so heavy we have to buy an umbrella and sit under it.

To me that's us in Monterey, hating what looked like paradise and trying to avoid all the shit—not from birds but from locals who shit on everything we believe in. People on the street pretty much live and breathe sedition and disloyalty– anti-establishment, anti-war, anti-military (in spite of still-active installations in Monterey), anti-President Bush, anti-American, anti-God, anti-fill-in-the-blanks . . .

Except when people tried to kill me I honest-to-God felt less resentment and opposition to me and my kind on the streets of Fallujah. Every so often I check in with the small Marine detachment at the Defense Language School in Monterey. When I ask the guys, "How can you stand living here?" they just shake their heads, like, "Dude, don't get me started."

Degraded vision spares me a lot of the daily affronts, like American flags flying upside down, unpatriotic bumper stickers, and loony political posters. And my day-to-day contacts with people are pretty pleasant. April, on the other hand, misses nothing, and the prevailing attitude drives her nuts. It isn't so much the opposing viewpoints, it's the snobbery and insult behind the radical left point-of-view that rules up here. Read between the lines and the message to people like us is not, "You're wrong," which would be fine, but, "You're stupid, and all your friends are stupid, too." This would get on your nerves, too, wouldn't it?

Maybe six weeks in, April comes to me and says, "Would you be mad if I told you I wanted to move?"

So here I am selling my boots to an antiwar artist chick. This is actually my first exchange of ideas with somebody like her. As I say, it isn't so bad. As time goes on and I meet more and more of her kind— particularly in college—I find myself more tolerant of radical lefties like the artist. Their beliefs, I am absolutely sure, weaken our country and endanger our troops overseas, but they don't see it that way and they stand up for their convictions, which I respect. The people I cannot stand shit on everything for no particular reason except they think it's cool and daring and smart.

Weasels.

Three weeks after I sell the boots, we settle into an apartment in the Point Loma district of San Diego, where I register for classes at the city college. We feel instantly at home in this very military city, which we already know and love. The day before classes start for the fall 2005 term, April and I do a very Marine thing, a leader's recon of the college campus to locate my classrooms and lay out my movements. The following morning I take a seat up front in English 101.

Right back where I started.

Twenty years ago I began my studies as a college freshman. But then the Marine Corps came and found me.

46

Accidental Marine

I do not live up—or down—to the two major Marine story stereotypes:

> 1) Everybody's all-American: I knew I wanted to join the Corps in the womb and excelled in everything to prepare for heroism in battle.

> 2) Gangbanger Redeemed: The judge saved my life when he gave me a choice, the Corps or prison.

I grew up on safe suburban streets in Indiana. The only gang I ever belonged to was the Physics Club at North Terre Haute High School. And I had no leanings whatsoever toward the military or glory on the battlefield. My daydream heroics involved discovering cool new things in a laboratory. I was your basic pudgy science nerd, spending an unhealthy amount of time with my face stuck in books and pulling down straight A's. I studied Latin as my foreign language, for God's sake, and knew how to use every button on my multi-function Texas Instruments scientific calculator. In my crowd the latest TI was cooler than a letterman jacket, which I had no prayer of earning.

Needless to say, I wasn't much of a fighter, although I feared no one and believed in sticking up for myself, a principle instilled in me by my father, John Popaditch, known to everybody, even his mother, as Duke.

If you want to get psychological about how such an un-tough kid as me became a player on the Tough Team, the Marines, here it is: Maybe I felt like I failed to measure up to my father, who was tough as nails. I don't mean in any violent or aggressive manner—although I would pity anybody that man went after—but in all the ways that count. Never did he show weakness. He never, not once, called in sick at work. Every day he busted his ass at a printing factory, first in Hammond, then Terre Haute, and came home and worked some more, fixing what was broken, squaring things away to make our house nicer. What better-paid dads did with money, he did with sweat.

All my father had in life he earned the tough way, and he provided a good home for my mother and five kids, three boys and two girls spread out over fifteen years. I was the youngest. My mom, Dolores, maiden name Thompson, worked my whole life, too. It couldn't have been easy to make ends meet, but I never heard a complaint at home, and I never lacked for anything I needed or wanted.

All in all, I had a perfectly happy, comfortable childhood. And I didn't leave Indiana to escape anything worse than boredom.

In terms of Popaditch family military tradition, my dad got drafted into the Army and saw combat as an infantryman in the Korean War. Though I'm sure he had war stories, he didn't tell them. He did, however, love to joke about how much he hated being a soldier. One of my two older brothers also went into the Army. He was already out when I was still a kid, and he, too, told about how much he hated soldiering. So at home I never heard a good word about the military, and God knows nobody pushed me to enlist.

After high school I embarked on my higher education across town at Indiana State University, where my good grades and book smarts earned me a scholarship. I still lived at home, though, sleeping in my same old bed. I hung out with my same buddies from high school, a lot of whom went to State on scholarships, too. Through no fault of the university, which is a good school, I failed to get in the fight as a scholar right from the start-point. I felt bored, like I'd entered some sort of super-senior year at Terre Haute North instead of striking out on my own and beginning a new life.

Lightning struck when I visited my best friend, Kevin Gilbert, who got to go away to school and live in a dorm at Indiana University in Bloomington. Everything I saw at IU, our elite state school with a huge campus in a really cool college town, made my own setup seem even more pathetic and intolerable. But I didn't have the money to go away and pay room and board.

Lack of resources pointed me toward the military, which I knew would pay for an IU-type education after one enlistment. I zeroed in on the Army, which provided the best educational benefits. After only two years, I could get out with a load of dough for schooling thanks to the Army College Fund.

Less than two months into my first semester I went to an Army recruiter and then dropped all my classes and withdrew from Indiana State. The recruiter took his time drawing up the enlistment contract and setting me up to go to the Military Entrance Processing Station (MEPS) in Indianapolis. If the guy hadn't foot-dragged, I would have been a soldier for sure. Maybe I would have been back in school in two years, maybe not. Who knows what would have happened?

Meanwhile, though, Corporal Delegal, a Marine recruiter in Terre Haute, called me up at home. He was working off a roster of recent high school grads and just happened to call me at this crucial juncture.

"What have you been doing since you graduated?" the corporal asked.

"Nothin'," I said, like a typical teenage mope.

"Have you ever thought about joining the Marines?"

"Actually, I'm in the process of joining the Army," I said.

"What do you mean, 'in the process?' Have you signed anything?"

I told him no, but I was scheduled to go to MEPS and sign up.

"Before you do that, at least listen to what I have to say about the Marines," the Corporal said, pushing me to set an appointment at the recruiting office.

I agreed, but only because I didn't know how to refuse. To hell with that, I thought. Even if I wanted to, which I didn't, no way could a guy like me meet the physical demands of the Marine Corps, which I knew to be the toughest of any branch of the service. At the time, I worried that I was too soft to make it in the Army.

I failed to show up at the appointed time, displaying any number of dirtbag deficiencies. Lack of discipline, respect, honor, possibly courage, too, because I hid out at home instead of facing that guy and his Marine Corps, which scared me. What can I say? I was still, as we say in recruit training, back on the block.

My home phone rang at the scheduled hour of the meeting, and even though I knew who was calling I picked up.

The recruiter spoke his version of hello: "Corporal Delegal from the World's Finest United States Marine Corps!"

Not stopping to hear any lame excuses, he said, "Stay where you are. I'm coming right over."

Now I felt trapped and more scared of the Marines than ever.

The corporal rang the bell, looking in-shape and squared away like a walking recruiting poster. We sat down on bar-stool type seats at the counter of the breakfast nook in our kitchen.

Nothing in his opening spiel sticks in the mind. His attitude does, though. Instead of reaming me out for the no-show, the corporal acted all relieved and excited, like we had a near-miss and ought to be happy that I still had a chance to hear about this terrific opportunity. "Lucky you, Nick!"—that was the message.

Corporal Delegal laid out name-tag-sized plastic cards in assorted colors, each with a different reward for being a Marine. He asked me to pick the three I considered most important and rank-order them. I made a pass to see all the options and then another, and finally laid out my winners:

1) TRAVEL & ADVENTURE
2) CHALLENGE
3) EDUCATION BENEFITS

The first one really did a number on me. Picture me partying in Hong Kong or the South Pacific, sitting on the beach and sucking drinks out of coconut shells with girls in hula skirts. Anywhere seemed far-away and exotic compared to Indiana, and I was ready to go.

The corporal went to work on number 2, which appealed because I really wanted to get tougher. On the other hand, I thought the Corps had way too much challenge. Between me and actual Marines I saw an unbridgeable gap, no different than the gap between me and a roster spot with the Chicago Bears.

"I don't think I'm physically fit enough," I said.

I will never forget what he said: "If you don't quit, we will never quit on you."

All I needed, the corporal explained, was desire and guts. The Marines would see to the rest. Just like that, what seemed so wrong flipped to right. The Marines had me.

The Corporal could have saved his breath and asked for my signature, but he talked a while longer. Interesting, isn't it, that dollars for college had already slipped to bronze? The issue then dropped completely out of sight. Corporal Delegal and I said not one word about educational benefits.

I went to MEPS the next day, signed an enlistment contract, then came home and told my mother. Poor woman didn't even know I had dropped out of school. I think that part, not the Corps, explains her yelling "Oh, God!" and weeping copiously.

When I told my Dad, he said, "Christ, Nick, are you sure?"

My enlistment became a running joke with my buddies. If we were shooting baskets, say, and somebody hoisted an airball, he'd run down the court yelling, "Oh no, I missed a shot, maybe I should join the Marines." Anything could call for a dramatic over-reaction and the "join the Marines" line, which my friends never got tired of. People would have been less surprised if I became a Hare Krishna or joined the circus.

Weird as my choice was, I got more and more excited about it during the two months before I would ship out to Boot Camp. In those days, such delayed entry was SOP. Thank God, too, because I had eight weeks to run and do pullups and lose some of the pudge. Corporal Delegal ran with me at first so I could learn the right way to pound pavement.

He'd say to me, "Wait 'til you get to Boot Camp, where you've got 500 recruits doing this together, boots hitting the deck at the same time. It'll sound like thunder!" Hearing his words got me so fired up. I couldn't wait.

The Corporal also made me work on pull-ups, which I practiced on the garage door roller track. He regularly called up my mom for progress reports. Brilliant motivation, on his part, because the last thing I wanted to hear was my mother telling me to get my butt in gear and do more pull-ups because the corporal said so.

In two months I went from zero to five pull-ups, two more than Marine bare minimum. Two years later I'd be cranking out fifty and change.

Like in many areas of life, the greatest difficulties arise at the beginning. Once you can do a few pull-ups, you're on the march to many.

47

Welcome to Hell

May 6, 1986
2200 Local
Receiving Barracks
Marine Corps Recruit Depot
San Diego, California

"

Get off my bus!

Stand on a set of yellow footprints.

If the set of yellow footprints in front of you does not have a body on it, move up to that set of footprints.

You will not look to the left.

You will not look to the right.

Your head and eyes will be straight to the front.

Place both arms out in front of you and make fists.

Place your thumbs on top of your fists.

Lower your arms to your sides until your thumbs rests along your trouser seams.

This is the Position of Attention.

You will never leave it unless you are instructed to do so."

The commands fly out of the skinny little drill instructor's mouth faster than you just read them. I can repeat them here because twelve years later I became a drill instructor myself. But to me the scared 18-year-old, the words hit the ears like the barking and snarling of a pack of wild dogs, bringing more terror and confusion than meaning. I'm one of many frightened prey animals trying like hell to stay in the middle of the herd and as far as possible from this maniac who roars at us nonstop.

There is no escape, though. He runs up and down the ranks yelling stuff like, "When addressing any Marine, the first word and last word out of your mouth will be 'Sir!'"

"Failing to obey an order is a violation of the Uniform Code of Military Justice, Article 92, punishable by fines and/or confinement in the brig."

And on and on.

I ask myself the question that every other recruit in the history of the Marine Corps has asked while standing on the yellow footprints.

What was I have thinking, that this seemed like a good idea?

Honest to God, the drill instructor machine-gunning words scares me more than enemies shooting actual bullets ever will. Why? Because he destroys reality as I have known it. I can't get a grip or re-orient under the bombardment of specific commands coming five times faster than I can mentally process them and twenty times faster than I could possibly do them. Hard to explain, but the situation creates the world's worse mindfuck, causing abject terror, panic, thermonuclear anxiety, the like of which I never felt before or since.

While I still try to assume the POA, the drill instructor yells out more commands, now employing weird new terminology: "Starting with the man on the front left corner of this formation, who will from this point be referred to as the first squad leader, you will file off through the double doors, which will from this point forward be referred to as a hatch. Turn left, which will from this point be called port. Then turn to port again. Go down the hallway, which from this point will be referred to as a passageway."

Halfway through the first sentence I join the stampede toward the receiving barracks while trying to rewind and replay: Thumb on the trouser seam or I go to the brig. That door's a squad leader. The guy up front's a hatch. What was the word for left? I should give no thought to routing instructions because all I have to do is follow the others toward the next maniac spewing out instructions at light speed. I do think about the route, though, because I can't help it.

Calculated application of anxiety is, by the way, the essence of recruit training, constructed to induce stress at all times in order to teach people to do the right things—follow detailed instructions and function coolly and intelligently—under extreme duress. We can't realistically simulate combat, which would involve killing recruits, so we try to create the same sensory overload and high level of mental challenge. Though most Boot Camp stories focus on the physical punishment, we hit the brain a hell of a lot harder than the body.

What follows makes the yellow footprints and intake seem like Kiddy Camp. After a couple days of processing, our platoon moves out of the receiving barracks loaded down with seabags and sundry awkward gear and then jams into the quarterdeck, a sort of entry alcove in our squad bay, our new home. There we meet the most terrifying human beings on Planet Earth, the three-man team of drill instructors whose mission it is to turn us into Marines in 13 weeks.

Having held all three positions—Third Hat (aka Stress Hat), the Heavy, and the Senior—I know the Senior's scripted opening comments word for word. Basically, he recites an ode to the Marine Corps and all its heroic virtues with no hint of the misery to come. The Senior closes with the words, "We offer you the challenge of recruit training and opportunity to become United States Marines." Then he turns to the other two and says, "Drill Instructors, carry out the plan of the day."

Just saying "Aye-aye, Senior Drill Instructor," the bigger of the two, Staff Sgt. Nichols, who is huge, fills me with terror. The guy roars like a locomotive doing ninety miles an hour a half-second before it smashes you flat. Once he and his partner, Sergeant Buffington, turn away from the departing Senior and face us, you know serious brutality is about to come down.

It does, too.

The arrival of recruits and grand entrance of the terrifying drill instructor is, by the way, one of the Marine scenes that Hollywood and book writers almost always get wrong. In the make-believe Corps, the three real-life DIs get knocked down into one, and the action always stops so he can intimidate and heap vile and profane abuse on one recruit. Ain't going to happen. Insults do, indeed, fly, but they're always at the end of orders that you're undoubtedly screwing up or following much too slowly:

"Carry your rifle properly, dumb ass!"

"You move like an old lady!"

"Keep pushing, mama's boy!"

The name-calling is nothing compared to the anxiety and physical pain. And while the storybook DI picks on one guy at length, what are the other 79 in the platoon supposedly doing? If it really happened, they'd be watching the show, just like the movie audience. Impossible, because the pain and anxiety comes non-stop for everybody. And standard depictions show pointless harassment, which is all wrong. Whatever happens, there's a purpose. Movie makers and whiny book authors, who were undoubtedly lousy Marines, don't get it. What they see as madness, is method, one hundred percent.

Like one of the staff sergeants at the recruit depot says to us, every single thing we do has a purpose. He says, too, that he doesn't give a fuck if we know what it is. Either way, Boot Camp works.

Please bear in mind that I went through seven cycles of training as a hat and only one as a recruit, so it's hard for me to look back and see things entirely from Stupid Clumsy Recruit Popaditch's perspective. To me now, the underlying training agenda stands out more clearly than the actual events, all of which are agony.

On the other hand, painful as it is to me the recruit, I start to dig Boot Camp almost from Jump Street.

In this weird hell-on-earth way, I love it.

48

Making the Grade

Question: How is a Marine Drill Instructor like a stage magician?

Answer: We employ elaborate tricks of the trade to create illusions in order to shock and awe recruits and generally mess with their heads—not for anybody's entertainment, of course, but to facilitate and accelerate training. Smoke and mirrors, man, to make things a hundred times more dangerous-seeming and stressful than they actually are. In reality, the depot in San Diego is a great place—really nice buildings and grounds, palm trees, view of downtown, the world's greatest climate—but we make it the Las Vegas of terror and pain.

Doesn't matter what time it is, somebody's awake and suffering.

Is anybody really trying to kill him?

Is he really less than a wart on a Fleet Marine's ass?

Of course not. But does he believe such? Deeply, because that's what all his senses tell him.

I'll pass on a couple of our open secrets. First, we don't deliberately destroy individuality in order to turn guys into automatons. Why would we? A robot in uniform is a liability. What we do is build individuals with the strength to use their talents and all their personal attributes for the sake of something greater and more important than themselves—their team and their shared mission. To rearrange thinking in a hurry, we have to obliterate the "me first" mentality, which non-hackers misinterpret as attacks on their very being. And getting stronger hurts. Why does this always surprise the whiners?

Boot Camp is very funny. A laugh a minute. Even funnier because nobody is allowed to laugh.

Picture this: A guy stands in front of a mirror pointing at his own image and screaming at the top of his lungs, "I'm not stupid, you are!" Meanwhile, the hat stands at his side, yelling, "Yell at him! Louder!" just like there is a third, really stupid, guy and the whole thing makes sense.

Meanwhile, out in front of the barracks, another recruit chases a seagull that he got caught eyeballing. If he puts out less than a hundred percent effort, he'll get a worse punishment, so he goes after the bird like his life depends on it. The bird seems to be in on the gag, because it sits still until the guy gets close, then makes short-hop flights all around our formation, as if to maximize the entertainment for everybody else, who better not get caught looking or then they'll have to chase, too. Or worse.

Absolutely everything in Boot Camp happens at a ridiculous hell-bent rate, like a movie speeded-up for comic effect, with things flying around and guys falling over each in impossible situations, such as trying to jam through the squad bay hatch, eighty guys all at once, while carrying rifles. And always, in the background, somebody gets smoked, doing absurd numbers of calisthenics and yelling out counts, or getting fixed in some outrageous manner like yelling at mirrors and chasing gulls. Unless it happens to you, it's a hoot, but you don't dare laugh or you'll get smoked and humiliated even worse. You will anyway, no matter what you do, but still you want to avoid the drill instructors' wrath.

Laughing on the inside while appearing not to notice what's so hilarious—this is an essential recruit skill. Drill instructors, as I later find out, need it even more.

Once in a great while the hat intentionally provides a lighter moment. Sugar, we call it. God help you if you so much as crack a smile, but it introduces a bit of enjoyment.

This, I think, is the case in one of my own Recruit Training Greatest Hits. Pretty late in the cycle, Staff Sgt. Nichols has us out on the grinder, rifles in hand, doing close-order drill. On this day he carries his NCO sword, which a unit leader uses to lead drill, employing very precise ceremonial positions and moves that have nothing to do with sword fighting.

By this point the platoon appears to operate like precision machinery, but all the individual recruit ever knows are his own moves. Eyes front, standing on-line in the first squad, I can't even see other recruits, so I have no way of knowing if everybody else screws up right shoulder arms, say, or if I hear the command wrong or otherwise fail.

Failure is all we've heard about from Staff Sgt. Nichols, who says we're the most pathetic, worthless, undisciplined, stupid turds he has ever trained, with no prayer of making it in the Fleet. Today, though, while we do halted rifle manual, we hear something never heard before:

Silence.

Nobody kicks our asses.

In Boot Camp, absence of punishment counts as a reward. And it's weird. Spooky, too, because we have learned to fear good things, which are always traps and set-ups for something horrible.

But now things get even weirder and spookier.

Staff Sgt. Nichols says to us, "You know, girls, that looked less retarded than yesterday. Not too bad."

As usual he bellows. But that was actual praise, man. The faces don't change, but every guy in the platoon glows, wallows in the man's approval.

"You must have been dreaming about drill last night, girls," he says, "I know I did."

Wow, the same Marine Corps dream. This from an individual who has never before acknowledged our humanity.

But now he waves the sword in my face and bellows, "You know what else, Popaditch? I dreamed I cut your stupid fucking head off! Hah!"

The "Hah!" doesn't mean he's joking, but just that beheading me gave him great pleasure and he'd love to do it now for real, and maybe he will.

You can see recruit training paying off. Not too many weeks ago, having this big brute maniac threaten me with a sword would have scared the shit out of me. Or, having adjusted to the fear factor, I might have broken discipline by showing that I appreciate the joke, as I know Staff Sgt. Nichols and everybody else does. But we keep our bearing, laugh on the inside, and enjoy the five-second break before we go back to work.

The reason I merit the beheading joke, along with much more than my share of daily smoking and verbal harassment from the drill instructors, especially Staff Sgt. Nichols, goes straight to the comedy issue. Very early on, I find humor in recruit training even while I'm terrified and in great physical distress. And I make the mistake of letting it show.

Just a few days in, the drill instructors put us hogs through the too-slow-get-back game, a timeless Boot Camp classic. We're too slow going from formation into the classroom so we have to run out and do it again, except this time we form up farther away. We're still too slow, which means we have to do it again, only from farther away, and then farther. Adding distance increases the physical effort and pain, which amps up the general panic of guys stampeding back and forth and smashing through the hatch, inflicting hockey injuries on themselves and others with their rifles.

Weaker-minded recruits wig out, pushing and screaming to hurry up as others cause their pain by going too slowly. How could they be so dumb? How could they not get it? Though I run and fight through the hatch as hard as anybody, I can't help but chuckle.

Out of nowhere a hand of steel clamps down on my left upper arm and yanks me out of the group. The herd thunders away. Wait, guys, don't leave me. A gazelle must feel the same way, suddenly alone and in the clutches of the lion. Sgt. Buffington, major predator of the moment, yells into my face, "You'd better stop fucking up, boy. You are easy to identify!" At each syllable he stabs his index finger into a birth mark at the side of my neck right where you'd stick a knife to hit the jugular.

I am a marked man. The damn birthmark, which has since faded, does destroy my anonymity. The real mark, though, is the chuckle and smirk, which give away a schoolboy sense of superiority, like I'm just a little bit smarter than the average bear.

In years to come I will encounter the same sort of wise ass who thinks his high IQ puts him above the game plan. Such an attitude infuriates a hat, and time and again I will do just like Sgt. Buffington—wipe the smirk off the recruit's face and then spend the rest of the cycle making sure it stays off.

So my drill instructors kick smug out of my ass in a hurry. Even after it's gone, though, I remain marked and catch much more than my share of hell. Such is my lot. I accept it, and, strange to say, I don't really mind. The upside of countless extra pushups, mountain climbers, bends and thrusts, and side straddle hops (jumping jacks to you non-Marines) is getting strong enough to do them. I feel myself get tougher and tougher. Nobody in his right mind would like the agony. But I love the results and, most of all, this amazing discovery about myself—I am tough. Steel emerges from under the pudge. No more calling me Food Blister and Fat-Ass. And whatever these drill instructors dish out, I can take it, better than most in the platoon. A new kind of pride, which I keep to myself, takes the place of schoolboy smug. I'm actually proud to get my ass kicked more than practically anybody, and I make it a personal game to endure no matter what.

Never will I forget the moment when I know I have won. Maybe a week before graduation, Sgt. Buffington wants to kill some poor knucklehead. He pulls the guy out and sends him to the quarterdeck for IT, Incentive Training. Up to that point, I'd go, too, automatically, because I was a Chosen One. Nobody went to the dirt without me.

This time, though, Sgt. Buffington says, "I'd smoke Popaditch, too, but it doesn't even bother him any more."

I wore him out wearing me out. Wow. I feel like the Sergeant just pinned a medal on my chest.

Never do I imagine that I'm some kind of hotshot recruit, bound for glory, but I know I make the grade, which is all I ever wanted or hoped to do here. I'm tough enough to get through Marine Boot Camp. Who knew?

And I make another amazing discovery. I really want to be a Marine. I showed up to prove something to myself and enjoy certain benefits—travel, challenge, college bucks, etc.—but now I want to belong to this entity greater than myself and live up to its great traditions.

This I owe to Staff Sgt. Nichols. Besides terrifying us and kicking our asses, he gives us visions of Paradise, this exalted realm for which we must prepare ourselves and become worthy, the Fleet Marine Force. He tells us about the Fleet and our heroic Marine traditions after lights out, when we lie in our racks in the POA.

Staff Sgt. Nichols tells us that we will face much greater challenges in the company of heroes in the Fleet, but we will be ready if we train hard and apply ourselves to learning here in Boot Camp. He also tells tales of immortal fighting Marines. Chesty Puller, most decorated man in the Corps' history, surrounded with Red Chinese at Chosin Reservoir in Korea, saying he likes the situation because he can shoot in any direction and hit the enemy. Dan Daly, awarded two Congressional Medals of Honor in two different wars. During the battle of Belleau Wood in World War I, when besieged, outnumbered, and outgunned, he shouts to his men, "Come on, you sons of bitches, do you want to live forever?" and attacks. The warriors we hear about span our nation's history, up through the Vietnam War and the present time. Never before have I heard of such men and their deeds and attributes. Coolness under fire. Fearlessness. Ferocity. Self-sacrifice. And this isn't some movie. When Staff Sgt. Nichols talks, it's real and possible—even for me.

Lying and listening in my rack, I get the idea that the Marine Corps exists out of time. The world changes, mostly for the worse, but the Corps remains the same, in its own realm, where right is right and men fight and die for the sake of what's right, and courage and honor matter more than anything. It's like long ago is now, like King Arthur and his knights still ride around Camelot. And nobody outside the Corps knows that there is such a time, such a place, as ours.

The world on the far side of the fence no longer matters.

I'm in.

49

Destiny

Everything's training.

Marines use this as a laugh line, usually in connection with tasks that seem stupid and demeaning and unconnected to any greater mission. If, say, you're a lance corporal and the corporal tells you to grab a can of diesel and burn the shitters, you say, "Everything's training," and thereby add a bit of levity and enjoyment.

Why not? As an NCO I would always tell my guys, "You can do it, or you can do it pissed off." Amazing how many choose the latter like it's smart to moan and get mad about the inevitable when all you do is mess up your own state of mind and lose the respect of good Marines. The NCO may give you a lot more to whine about, making things worse because your dirtbag attitude annoys him.

After a year or two in the Fleet you earn the right to employ another laugh line. This one comes in at times of max misery, like after you've been out in a freezing rain for five days straight and you don't have a dry square inch on your body and the op's only half over. At such a moment you turn to the cold soggy moe next to you and say this:

I'm just happy to be here.

As they say, though, humor also expresses truth. For the next four years—1986-1990, between Boot Camp and my first combat deployment in the Middle East—"Everything's training" and "I'm just happy to be here," are damn sure true for me, every minute, wherever I am and whatever I'm doing.

My classroom and formal field instruction, like tank school—which the Corps chose for me—is really the least of my education, which goes on 24/7.

Absolutely every Marine I meet has something to teach, even the most phenomenal dirtbags. Case in point—a certain unnamed lance corporal, with whom I do guard duty at Camp Pendleton while my first tank unit, Charlie Company, waits to be deployed to Okinawa. This guy hates the Marine Corps so much that when we go out to eat in Oceanside he saves up everybody's trash and then throws it out the car's window back on base. This gives him tremendous satisfaction even though we have to pick it up again because we police the roadside as part of our duties. That and similarly stupid and feeble acts of sabotage and silent protest on the lance corporal's part never fail to crack me up.

On the flip side, the guy knows how to do things right with the least possible effort in order to avoid extra duty. He teaches us boots, among other things, how to challenge the Officer of the Day, who always tries to infiltrate the post at night to test our vigilance. He teaches us to yell at the tops of our lungs. This favorably impresses the OOD because we're exercising great command and control of our post, and it also tips off the other posts that trouble is on the prowl. The lance corporal also tells us to put the OOD down on his face, if possible in uncomfortable positions in the dust. Again, very good procedure, but it makes him pay a price for checking on our particular post, so he's more likely to bother somebody else and thereby allow us to skate.

The motive is wrong, but the lesson right. The Corps has many guys like this, who hate everything they have to do. Push comes to shove, though, they're pretty good at it. I'd go to war with that lance corporal in a minute.

Question is, would he go with me?

Though guard duty and the working party stuff that comes with it are generally considered menial labor for boots, I constantly say to myself, and mean it, how glad I am to be here. Being from Indiana makes most places look good, but Camp Pendleton is great. You can see the beach and the Pacific from my squad bay. And in a few weeks we ship out to Okinawa—the Far East!—with rotations to other Asian nations and ports of call.

Okinawa gets pretty low grades from salty Fleet guys—too hot, too few women, limited nightlife, not enough room for training and shooting.

I, on the other hand, like it fine. Do we have lush tropical vegetation back home? Coral reefs by the beach on Lake Michigan? Exotic people with a different culture? Would I rather be here than in physics class in Terre Haute?

But then the really cool stuff happens after Charlie redeploys to Camp Fuji on the slopes of the fabled mountain up in mainland Japan. Living in for-real winter in a Quonset hut, busting our asses down on the tank ramp or out on ops in the snow, with a platoon sergeant meaner than a snake riding us hard as the hats in Boot Camp. I love it. Throw in liberties in Yokosuka and Tokyo, and I'm in heaven. This is what I signed up for.

Though training to be a tank driver, I, the boot, spend a lot of time on working parties while the senior guys do the actual tanking and weapons practice. Building targets and what-all irks prima donnas and dirtbags, who don't want to do any kind of work, but I don't mind because I'm paying my dues. Just happy to be here.

Though I want to learn tanking and do well, because that's my nature, I can't claim to have any deep feeling for heavy armor early on. The Corps, not personal passion, put me here, and I don't get enough hands-on experience to fall in love with the battle hogs. Then, in February 1987, on the snowy slopes of Mount Fuji, I look at our tank column and see Destiny.

As usual I stand down on the deck, a road guard, stopping civilian traffic where the column will cross. The show starts before the tanks come into view. First thing, at a distance, you hear tracks squeaking, followed by the snarling and coughing of the M-60 heavy tank's V-12 super turbo-charged diesels. Today's M1A1 turbines whine like giant home power tools, but these old-school machines make a mighty roar. From the road in Japan, you think monsters, huge and powerful, lurk in the woods. The noise gets louder and more complicated, like a monster marching band, hydraulic pumps racing, transmissions grinding, torsion bars groaning as they twist over uneven terrain, all the gear stowed up top banging and clanging.

Something wicked this way comes, and here it is. The cannon of the lead tank pushes out of the trees, traversing left and right. You can't help looking at it, the way you can't help looking at the muzzle of the gun an armed man carries, except you can stick your arm into the bore of this gun, and if it shoots, whole buildings fall flat miles away and many die.

The sight of the thing makes you feel small and easy to kill, like a balloon full of blood. It's looking to kill, too, moving as the crew traverses the turret to scan with their gunsights, the tank's eyes. If it sees you, it's aimed and ready to destroy you.

While everything else moves haphazardly as the tank jinks over uneven ground, the big gun remains steady, held that way by gyroscopes. The lack of extraneous motion shows lethal intent. I just watched a nature movie of lions on the hunt. The steadiness of their heads and eyes, even while their legs pumped wildly as they sprinted toward their victims, made me think of the gun tube of an advancing tank.

Coming side-on to me, the first beast shows its size and brute power. An M60 measures over twenty feet long from the cannon muzzle back and stands ten feet to the top of the cupola. Its 56-ton weight shakes unpaved ground, but its motion appears to be effortless. It's nimble, too, making quick turns down at the edge of the woods and climbing the roadbank. You want to step back in case it decides to pivot and crush you just for grins. One of these things would be awe enough, but sixteen tanks follow the lead, half with guns traversed left, half right, all scanning and searching. Look away from the cannons, you see more killing power in each tank's two machine guns. I've been around M-60 tanks for six months now, give or take, but today I watch them out and on the hunt, the way they'd look going to battle. And I have never seen such terrible magnificence. There are bigger machines, deadlier war machines, but so what? These things are so cool, man, so beautiful.

And no cooler dudes have I ever beheld than the masters of the beasts, the tank commanders. Look at them, above it all, out of the hatches from the chest up, each making his beast his own. What scares everybody else, obeys these men. Here's a guy with his arms resting on the hull, moving nothing but his mouth at the helmet mike to voice-activate his crew and bend the beast to his will. Another guy scans with binos. Another poses like General Patton and throws me a great big salute to remind me how insignificant my position is. Each man, in his own way, is larger than life and displays control and leadership presence that I suddenly want for myself.

I see what I want to be.

Right off I recognize that there's nothing about the job I can't handle, but I'll have to work my ass off to prepare and acquire the beast masters' knowledge. The difficulty of the task thrills more than discourages me.

Luck? Fate?

To this day I feel blessed that at this young age I come upon a mission in life that suits me perfectly. As the saying goes, find out what you want to do, and find what you're good at, and if they're the same thing you are a very fortunate individual. It will take some time to discover that I have an aptitude for commanding a tank. In the meantime, the quest fulfills me, and my goal drives everything I do.

And why is tanking so perfect? For one, it engages the sort of brains I have, particularly on the M60s. The old-school tank is dumb in terms of on-board data processing, so the commander must become a human fire control computer. Nothing but applied math, except more exciting than school because if you flunk in battle, you and other Marines die. Actual trigger pulling in the face of death constitutes a big plus. Tanks are brainy but not geeky in-the-rear-with-the-gear brainy. In all respects this is a man's game. You get greasy and grimy and sweat like a hog just keeping the iron monsters in operation. It takes a powerful dude to pick up tank parts and tools and an even stronger man to lead the bruisers best-suited to tanking. Like tanks themselves, these guys, now and again, require a tap with a sledge hammer. Even if you don't use it, you need a sledge in your tool box.

In this last connection, you can count my many fisticuffs with Lance Corporal McCloud—Ron DMC to himself because he's Ronald D.—as leadership training. We get put on the same tank crew after coming back to Pendleton from Japan. Though we got along fine before, now that I'm driver and he's loader on the same tank we have seriously bad chemistry and anything can start a fight. Since McCloud is bigger and meaner, my ass gets all the whupping early on. That never stops me from throwing fists again, usually the very next day. We fight out of anger, not hatred, and don't try to maim or kill each other, so I suffer no worse than bruises and pain and feel better off for it. Everything's training, right? Getting knocked around makes me tougher, and I improve to the point that once in a while I give better than I get, although McCloud takes the series by a huge margin.

Day by day the Corps makes me tougher in all respects. Whatever the extreme unpleasantness—heat, cold, fatigue, bodily misery and pain—I suck it up with the very best of them. At first I want to prove something, but the more I learn, the more I realize there are much more solid and even noble reasons to be tough.

Corporal Laskaris, our gunner, says something that sticks in my mind forever. One day, when we're both pissed off at a sunny-day pretty boy in our midst, he says to me, "Pop, this job's all about being a Zero-Four Marine."

At 0400, with rain pouring down and hunger and lack of sleep killing him, a guy walks his post. Not a thing would go wrong if he didn't, and nobody would know, but he does his job anyway because it's the right thing to do. That's the Zero-Four Marine who will one day become a leader and fight and win.

Self discipline, not enforced discipline. Every good Marine has some version of Laskaris's key concept in his head and heart.

Inner stuff like this counts for more than the actual education in tanking, which I learn more quickly than most. I become a dead-eye gunner, qualify for tank commander's school, and graduate first in my class, thanks in large part to acing tests the way I did as a nerd. I get my first command while I'm still twenty and let the Zero-Four Marine loose, running my guys through endless drills and dry runs. Engage target from a defensive position, from a short halt, from a moving tank, in a chemical or nuclear-contaminated environment, with main guns and machine guns simultaneously, and on and on. We learn it all in class, but school stuff ain't squat unless you can do it for real and in a hurry. It takes weeks to achieve simple competence, and after we do, I raise the bar. Do it in six seconds, great, let's go for four, now with hypothetical fire control malfunctions and casualties.

Nobody makes me do all this, but I do it because the Zero-Four Marine would. If other commanders let their crews off easy, that's fine. Fine, too, if some are better, as the salty senior guys are bound to be. We don't compete against anybody but the enemy we will someday face. We prepare for war, not to outshoot other crews on the range.

Or so I think until our first scored gunnery, a competition among all seventeen Charlie Company tanks to see who shoots best, fastest, firing at pop-up targets while moving around a prepared course according to radioed op orders. For a boot commander and crew like mine, passing a certain minimal standard of competency constitutes a win. I don't hope for much more, even after we turn in a performance that pleases me.

Almost right off I know we passed because we're told to proceed off the range instead of uploading ammo for another run. Good news, for sure, but I hand out more criticism to my guys than praise. We could have done better. While parked and debriefing, I send the gunner, PfC Klein, a former lance corporal who got busted down, to take a comm cable over to the position of the Master Gunner, who runs the range and calculates scores.

Now what's up with Klein? No idea what might explain the huge grin that he wears coming back to the tank. I prepare to be irritated, because it's undoubtedly something beside the point.

"Come on, Klein, mount up and let's get the fuck out of here," I say.

"The Master Gunner says I should tell that boot tank commander we just shot the range high," Klein says.

As it turns out, a hotshot sergeant's crew will beat us later in the day, but coming in number two with our level of training and experience is a grand slam.

This, a moment of supreme pride, is one of my lifetime emotional highs and defining incidents, occupying a place of honor in my memory equal to anything I accomplish on the battlefield. The combat successes will mostly confirm what I am—a good tank commander and a for-real Marine.

Here, though, is my moment of becoming, where my ambition turns into my future and a new resolve to become the best possible Marine tank commander.

Call it Destiny, Part II.

First, in the snow in Japan, I see what I want to be.

Now, after I work my way up and do the right things, I make it happen.

Days don't get any bigger.

50

Love and War

Master Sergeant "Top" Graham earns a special place of honor in my story, which I also give him at my retirement ceremony. I count it as unbelievably good luck to have him as my first tank leader and serve under him more or less continuously during my four-year education in tanking, which also happens to be preparation for my first shooting war, Operation Desert Storm in 1991. Top molds me into a better Marine the Marine way, no mercy, setting the highest possible standards and delivering countless precision-targeted kicks to the ass. He makes me do most of the actual kicking myself, which turns out to be more painful and instructive than your everyday yelling and abuse and coercion.

Though Top doesn't talk up his experience, he has some serious Marine mileage—two combat tours in Vietnam, Beirut, and rotations to pretty much every big-deal place in our world. And he has an awesome leadership presence. Though he stands under six feet, he overwhelms with physical power. This is one strong dude, a serious powerlifter and star athlete who qualified for the Olympics in judo. You wouldn't even dream about challenging Top, but he dominates much more with brains than with brute force.

By staff NCO standards Top is borderline mute, speaking words so few and simple that I have a hard time remembering any particular thing he says. The power comes back, though. I feel it from the first time he singles me out.

Early in my first overseas pump I half-ass an assigned duty I don't want to perform, clearing out the ditch that carries wastewater from our chow hall at Camp Fuji.

Top Graham later asks if I cleaned the ditch.

"Yes, Top."

"You did?" he says, looking me at me like he sees clear through.

"Yes, Top," I replied again.

"Then you won't mind doing a day of mess duty for every piece of trash that's still in the ditch."

Though I'm lying through my teeth, I stick to my story and hope for the best.

"No, Top, I don't," I say, and he leaves. So far as I can tell, he's satisfied, and I just dodged a main gun round.

Wrong.

Next day, when the platoon sergeant assigns jobs, he sends me to the BAS to get a mess physical for working with food. I get stuck in the galley for 45 days—six weeks of rear-echelon duty, dark to dark, seven days a week, while my buddies train on tanks and go on liberties in Tokyo and stand in the chow line to get meals served by me.

The deal is pure Top Graham. Instead of lighting me up in front of God and everybody, he makes me feel deep down what a sorry excuse for a Marine I am. He also makes me assign my own punishment, a day in the galley for every piece of trash I should pick up but don't. Can there be any doubt who causes me to suffer? No. It all comes back to me and my own deficiencies.

Though the details change, the mess hall incident happens a thousand times in my years with Top Graham, in Pendleton and Asia and the Mideast.

There's a hole, almost always of my own making. Top Graham puts me next to it and without actually pushing causes me to fall in.

There's a mountain. I climb, feeling really cool because I'm ahead of other guys my age with the same amount of time in the Corps. I make it to a big peak, sure I just conquered the mountain, and there stands Top Graham, pointing upward and showing that I'm nowhere near the summit.

Sounds a little cerebral, but that's how it goes: quiet, spooky, and brutal. The guy is the Zen master of the United States Marines.

Top, and only Top, never lets up or cuts me any slack after I become a somebody in our unit, the Charlie Tracks Boy Wonder. I'm not proud to admit it, but the success goes to my head somewhat, as if being great on a tank, which I love, means I don't have to try so hard at the stuff I don't like. And I get hung up on the wrong parts of the Marine tough-guy image and become a bit of an undisciplined asshole. Others tend to let it slide, but Top leads the charge on straightening me out, holding me accountable for everything and demanding more. No pats on the back or "Nice going," from him. Ever. Always he lets me know that whatever I achieve, I come up short. In combat, the only real measure of a Marine, discipline and character count for more than range scores and standing in tank school.

Top, a former high-school star and absolute fanatic for football, coaches our team in the Camp Pendleton league, on which I play. Until war actually looms, Top uses our sport as a sort of training seminar and practical demo for victory as Marines always achieve it on the battlefield. Winning, he says, is what we do. And if we do anything but, we fail. According to Top, winning is a habit—thousands of habits, actually, rolled into one. First you win small, in even the most minor, seemingly unimportant tasks and routines. And after you build all your winning habits, you don't change them. When you get to a foreign country or a new battlefield, you stick with the routine and drilled-in habits. That way the unknown never threatens or screws you up, because there are no unknowns. And you can't help but win, because you don't know how to do anything else.

Same shit, different place—Top Graham's Wisdom of the Ages regarding staff NCO-level military leadership and success in both peace and war. It works. It always has. And it'll work again next time the country needs Marines to go someplace and kick somebody's ass.

Trying to anticipate where the next war zone might be is, by the way, a pet peeve of Top's. He hates it when our CO gives speeches about geopolitical developments and hot spots where we could be sent.

Top tells us, "Don't waste your time reading the newspaper, trying to figure things out. When it comes time to fight, it'll be something you never saw coming in a place you never heard of. Who the fuck ever heard of Vietnam, before we went there?"

Or in our case, whoever heard of Kuwait? I know there is such a place, of course, and remember some school-boy facts about it having the highest per-capita income in the world. But I never dream that I'll go there to fight. Nobody does until we do.

And if I go to the fight ready, heart and mind, body and soul, credit must go to James Graham, Master Gunnery Sergeant, USMC.

Thanks, Top.

After acknowledging this great debt, I must blame the inner nerd for keeping me behind the curve in an area unrelated to tank warfare. April, at any rate, says the chubby bookworm Nick of years past screws with my self-confidence and prevents me from exercising initiative with females. Don't get the wrong idea—I've had girlfriends, sort of, and done what you do with girlfriends, but in dating and mating I mostly hold myself in reserve.

Even when I observe the ultimate objective—my dream woman, the most incredibly gorgeous female I have ever beheld—I don't jump up and get into the fight. No, I wait until the objective comes to me. And then I don't get what's happening.

I first lay eyes on the love of my life and wife-to-be in 1990 in Oceanside at the Black Angus, not just a restaurant but a very popular night spot with a DJ and dance floor. One night my buddy Sgt. Bob Brennan and I stop in, and he starts hitting on this raving beauty named April. It takes more than one no to convince Bob, who is bolder around women than I am, that she really doesn't want to dance with him. April has a friend who does, though. They go to the dance floor, and I admire April from afar.

I don't want to dwell on looks, but I'm young and let's face it: This woman is scary, traffic-stopping hot. She stands five-six. I'll find out she's a single mom with a six-year-old boy, who's with his dad right then, but motherhood does not show. She has the California beach girl thing going, with impressive female terrain features. Her complexion, obviously dark to begin with, has been cooked deep brown by the sunshine, and her face knocks me out, even at a distance, with black hair, big brown eyes, and high cheekbones. Her smile makes me happy before we even say a word to each other. No idea what kind of Pacific people go into the mix—Polynesian, is my first guess—but we for sure don't have girls like this in Indiana. April has all-American roots that go back thousands of years here in California. She belongs to the Pomo tribe of Native Americans and grew up on her tribe's reservation north of the Bay Area. So she's exotic, on top of hot.

Do I want to speak to her?

Affirmative.

Do I?

Negative.

A few days later Bob says to me, "You know that girl at Black Angus the other night, the one in the black shirt with the girl I danced with?"

"Yeah, so what?"

"She wants you to take her out."

"Bullshit."

"I'm taking her friend out, and April wants you to come along, too, with her."

I get it. I'm a convenient warm body to make it a double date. I'll take it, though. And April and I have a fantastic time. She turns out to be very nice, unassuming, not the least bit stuck on herself. Though she clearly enjoys herself, living by the beach and loving it, she's also smart and mature. I respect her. I like her.

In the following days a serious relationship sneaks up like a stealth bomber. Kapow. I'm in love and deeply committed. We never actually talk about becoming an exclusive item. We don't need to, because what else could we be, spending every off-work moment together? My God do we have fun, taking off on my motorcycle at a moment's notice for rides into the hills, trips down to San Diego for movies, nights on the town, strolls in the park. Doesn't matter what, we enjoy it.

There's a Bob Seger number, Hollywood Nights, that we love to listen to and sing. In the song a hick from the Midwest comes to California and hooks up with a glamour-girl.

She took his hand and she led him along that golden beach

They watched the waves tumble over the sand

They drove for miles and miles

Up those twisting turning roads

It's us.

A few months in, my unit gets orders to go to Fort Irwin, California, to take on an Army unit in combat exercises. I love it. And I don't mind putting some miles between April and me. It takes us to the next level. For a relationship with a Marine to work, you have to be as good apart as you are together, and I really want to see how we manage a separation.

Meanwhile, the deranged dictator of Iraq decides to invade Kuwait, forcing the U.S. and its allies to send troops to defend Saudi Arabia and prepare to kick the bad guys out of Kuwait. Top Graham moves over to First Tanks Bravo Company, readying to deploy to Saudi within weeks, and brings over some of his Charlie Company guys, including me.

Somebody asks Top if he's moving his best football players from Charlie to put on Bravo's team. Top looks at the guy and says, "We ain't going to play football, boy. We're going to war." One day we show up for football practice, and Top wears his cammies instead of coaching gear. Practice cancelled, he says, and reality hits. Holy shit, we are going to war.

In late August, 1990, before we ship out, I have a heart-to-heart with April and try to do what seems right—cut her loose, no obligations.

"After all, we're not married . . . " I say.

And she says, "No, we're together, that's the way it'll stay."

I fall even harder for April in Saudi. Every single day I write her a letter telling her what's going on and expressing my feelings. I write things that I'd have a hard time saying, and the exercise puts her right next to me. Nothing wipes the miles away like writing letters. Even on the recent Iraq deployments, with all kinds of instant contact via email and satt phone, I still prefer letters. I'll use the high-tech stuff, but words on paper mean so much more.

In our back-and-forth April and I close on the same target, but we won't even say what it is. I write how, when I get back, I will take care of her and do right for her. This is shy-guy code for, "I really want to marry you," but I can't say so, much less pop the question in a forthright manner, because I don't want to hear no. April hangs back some, too. She's worried about our age gap. She's five years older, which she thinks might bother me. Then, finally, thank God, she expresses what's on both our minds.

Unbelievable. I'm engaged to this wonderful, gorgeous woman. I also will become an instant father to a six-year-old named Richard.

Press accounts play up the boredom and discomfort suffered by troops on the Saudi-Kuwait border during the six months we build up to launch Operation Desert Storm. Heat, sand, plague of flies, cold, and lack of movement aside, I count this as one of the happiest times of my life. I'm exactly the guy I want to be—a bad-ass Marine 10,000 miles from home, in command of a tank, with thousands of heavily armed men on the other side of the line we defend. Pretty soon my fellow Marines and I will fight. Pulling triggers, man. It's only a matter of time. Until then my

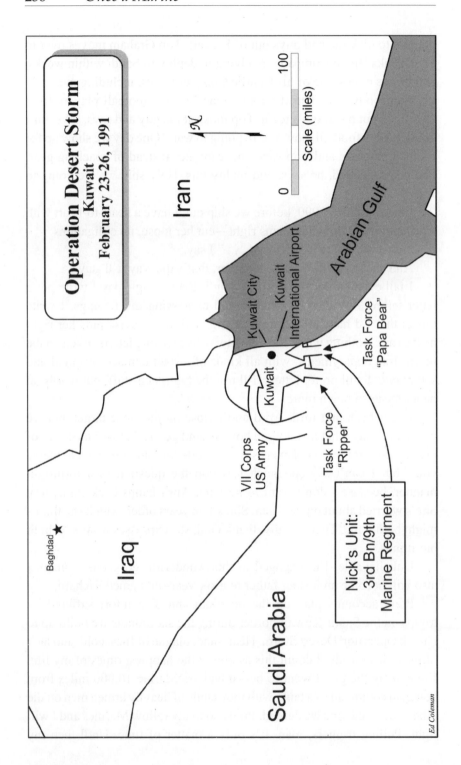

buddies and I have a riot. You can only turn wrenches on tanks so much, so we have time to lift the hell out of the weights that Top Graham orders up from the combat engineers. Also, on a daily basis, we bash heads on the gridiron. It's like we've got a football training camp with battle tanks.

The thing feels like a family affair, too. I'm with my Marine Corps father figure, Top. And love for April, my bride to be, wraps around everything. Now that we're a true Marine Corps couple, it isn't just my fight, it's ours, and the 10,000-mile separation for who knows how long ties us together. With someone I'm dying to go back to, I like being here more, and I'm more ready than ever to face death. Dreams do come true. First love, first war, in my 23rd year. What more could a Marine want?

Not long before offensive operations begin, I'm going through the chow line and my first sergeant speaks:

"You're getting promoted tomorrow."

"Who, me?" I say.

"Don't you think you rate it?" he says, like in his opinion I'm a pussy because I'm not sure.

"Hell, yeah. I just wasn't sure the Marine Corps knew it yet," I say, a little bit smart ass because the first sergeant, rumored to have harpooned a guy with a pool cue, never rattles me. In my opinion, the bark's worse than the bite, but God help the guys who show weakness.

So I will fight wearing a new stripe, a professional NCO.

51

Fire!

Sunday, February 24, 1991
South Kuwait
0800 Local
First Contact With Enemy On First Morning Of Ground Offensive
Operation Desert Storm

Another place, another time, you'd think the haze and clouds mean rain. But that's smoke closing over from oil well fires up ahead; Saddam Hussein's welcome to Kuwait.

The lieutenant comes on the radio and says, "White, this is White One. TCs up, my POS. Out." This means for tank commanders to stop, dismount, and come to his tank, where he gives an enemy SITREP based on the latest and greatest intelligence, using a section of radio antenna to draw on the ground. Constructing a sand table, we call this. The guy briefs like a pro, no drama whatsoever as he sketches out . . .

An AT (antitank) mine field.

Three entrenched infantry companies, two in front, one to the rear, in triangle defense.

A mortar company.

A dug-in tank platoon.

No mark but a by-the-way—self-propelled artillery far to the rear.

One, two, three, four, five interesting challenges. The minefield slows us down so everybody can shoot at us. The enemy infantry has SAGGER wire-guided missiles that can kill tanks at 3,500 meters, well beyond our own long-shot range. For up close, they've also got armor piercing RPGs, satchel charges, even grenades that can do damage. The mortars represent a much bigger threat to our own infantry, following us, than to the tanks, but a lucky direct hit would be fatal, and maybe they'll shoot chem weapons. Same situation with the self-propelled artillery, which can shoot from out of our line of sight and way beyond main-gun range, then haul ass and keep shooting.

None of this comes as a surprise. We've been practicing for months to breach a minefield defended by a combined arms team and then assault through and destroy the defenders. Basically, it's a beachhead landing with no water, a very Marine operation. In the desert, tanks lead, and I belong to the assaulting force. Tip of the spear, right where I want to be.

I walk away from the lieutenant's brief struck by a new feeling. Reality. This is not a drill. We're about to meet an actual enemy who won't just sit there and wait for us to kill him. No, he'll think, evade, move to where he can kill us first. We will be the targets' targets.

Of all the causes for concern in the lieutenant's brief, one won't let me alone. All I can think about is number four—dug-in tanks. Not good. Until very recently I commanded a dug-in tank, waiting to kill any and all comers. You sit with the hull below ground line. When you pull up to shoot, only the top of the turret and gun tube are exposed to the enemy, and those effectively disappear in the dust kicked up by the shot. Before the dust clears, you retrograde, putting the whole tank below the ground line and out of sight. When you're really well dug in, you have room to move and shoot from another spot. You get it all, man—cover, concealment, and a nice stable, stationary shooting platform. Meanwhile, the attacker hangs his ass out, exposing his entire tank and shooting on the move.

If that was us over there, we'd have the entire battlefield measured and sign-posted like a giant driving range for golfers. Visible marks and reference points would show ranges in meters, and we'd have pre-registered on-call targets. The attackers come to a designated spot and Bam! the artillery hits it, no bracketing necessary.

Can't miss. Can't get hit. Every little thing dialed in. Honest to God, I'd kill a whole tank company on my own and keep destroying targets until I ran out of ammo.

Except now I'm the other guy, the one hanging his ass out.

Am I scared?

Not nearly as much as you'd think.

Am I nervous?

Big time.

Do I show it?

No way on this earth. Not any more than the lieutenant showed it. We Marines are masters of the poker face. This goes for high ranks and low.

I get my three-man crew up on top of the turret and pass word like we're going to walk track or clean the weapons. Plan of the day, that's all. Nothing to get wrapped around the axle on. They don't, either.

What a great team: Gunner, Corporal Swanson; Loader, Lance Cpl. Clark; Driver, Lance Cpl. Howell.

Great and somewhat weird, too, both individually and as a crew. Swanson knows his tanking, but he's boot to his rank and doesn't know how to act like an NCO yet. He comes across soft to the other guys in the unit. Clark got busted down from corporal. Don't know why, and don't care, because he's not screwing up now. Howell came to me under his own personal black cloud because he once drove a tank over a cliff, an accident that caused fatalities. Guy was boot, not negligent, but the rest of the company treats him like a leper. Clark, too. Nobody else wants any of these three guys. We didn't come together until we got overseas, so we've had a lot less time to build team cohesion than the other crews. But hard work makes up the difference, and the guys have hidden reserves of character. I wouldn't want to be here with anybody else.

We actually take pride in our underdog status and weirdness, which I use for motivation. I nickname our tank Bates Motel.

No idea what goes on in the guys' heads right now, but I would bet they're thinking about how much they don't want to mess up and let the team down, just like me and everybody else out here, top to bottom.

The command to advance comes over the radio, and I say, "Driver, move out."

Bates Motel lumbers a tank-length back and maybe 50 meters out to the left side of the platoon commander's tank, which leads our giant wedge formation. Looked at from the air, we'd be an arrow, the tanks forming the arrowhead and columns of amtracs carrying infantry making the shaft. Down on the ground, the sight makes an unforgettable impression. Rolling thunder. Unbeatable power, on the move, far as I can see. And up ahead of me, nothing but empty desert.

Coming up to the last rise that gives us cover, my heart pounds like it's trying to bust out of my chest. 'Roided up butterflies slam-dance in my stomach. Eagerness beats anxiety, though. Pick up the pace, guys. Let the games begin.

I say a silent Warrior's Prayer, made up spur of the moment:

> *God, grant me skill in battle.*
> *God, grant me strength to be up to this task.*

I would never say to God, "Please don't let me fuck this up," but · that's the essence, and I want all the help I can get. I don't pray for courage, because I don't feel any lack thereof. And I don't pray to stay alive and unhurt, because that's not right and actually way down the list of concerns.

It's amazing how many times I can repeat my prayer in ten seconds. I can't stay out of the here-and-now any longer than that. My little interlude is plenty, though, because I'm not asking God for anything but the tools to do my own work. The rest is up to me.

Short as it is, the prayer works wonders. I'd be lying if I said I don't feel nervous any more, but I'm less so and feeling not so alone, and I'm ready as I'll ever be. No part of me wants the thing about to happen not to happen.

Here we go. The top of the rise opens up a clear view of a long, wide valley. Everything the lieutenant drew in the sand sits out in plain sight, much closer than I expected. Right there, big as hell, is the minefield, marked by wire and sign posts, starting maybe 1,500 meters out and stretching across the horizon. It's shallow, though, no more than 100 meters deep.

A few hundred meters beyond lie the enemy trenches, zigzagging like the pattern on Charlie Brown's shirt. I can't believe how much goes on down there.

Shit burns everywhere.

Soldiers swarm around by the hundreds, their numbers undoubtedly drastically reduced by weeks cut off from supply, followed by nonstop aerial bombardment that peaks right before our attack. Terror and death from the sky—gotta love our air power.

Even from a mile away you see the confusion and disarray. Some wave white flags and assemble in big block formations, obviously getting ready to surrender. They must have prepared, because they have an amazing amount of white cloth. At the same time, though, hundreds of other guys dart around the trenches and bunkers, getting out of the open and into fighting positions. Unbelievable, how the two factions take opposite courses of action right next to each other and without interfering. No hard feelings, apparently.

At the time they're the enemy, plain and simple, but I find out later that these units belong to the Regular Army, mostly moes who got conscripted and probably hate Saddam Hussein as much as I do. Knowing this doesn't alter my willingness to kill them, though. Tough shit, you're on the wrong side. Surrender you live. Fight you die. Either way, your war will end today.

After taking it all in, I look for something to shoot. First thing, I scan for the tanks, every one of which cooks in its hole. Good shooting by Marines in Cobra helos armed with Hellfire missiles. So I go for the number-two most dangerous target, one of the sand-bagged bunkers that sit on the trench lines. They rise only about three feet above the deck, but that's where they keep the crew-served weapons—the heavy machine guns and tank-killer missiles. Missiles wouldn't show, but I make out two machine gun muzzles in the black-shadowed firing slit of the bunker I pick, range two-two-hundred—2,200 meters. I know it's manned because the guns move. With two three-man machine gun crews, I know at least six guys are in there.

Almost simultaneously, these things happen:

I reach down and grab the tank commander's override, moving the turret to get the gun into the ballpark and put the target in view of the gunner, who looks through a narrow-field, eight-power sight.

I say, "Gunner, HEAT, bunker," meaning the loader needs to change out main gun rounds from armor defeating to High Explosive Anti-Tank, which are also our bunker busters.

The gunner, Swanson, yells "Identified," which tells me he sees the target and will arm the electrical trigger, set the ballistic computer, and aim the main gun.

Just for insurance, I say to the loader, "Clark, hurry the fuck up and change out that round." Within five seconds he yells back "Up!" meaning he did it, which I already know because I can hear it happening, a series of metal-on-metal sounds ending with the heavy CHUNK of the breech, which weighs more than 100 pounds, slamming shut.

The instant we're ready to shoot, the CO comes on the net and says, "All right, Bravo, let's start knocking out some of these targets."

"Fire!" Swanson pulls the trigger before I spit out the entire word, just like I trained him. Those of us in the tank miss the concussion and tremendous KABOOM outside, but the gun still puts on quite a show. Down in the turret its chamber slams back from recoil, after which the breech drops straight down violently and throws out a burning-hot shell casing two feet long, a hazard to all, especially the loader, who has to ignore it and stuff in a new round. Meanwhile, the gunner and I keep our eyes in the sights but can't see anything until the driver moves us out of the obscuration. I would love to tell him to gun it and take off, but we're part of a formation. We wait forever, tracks going ch-ch-ch-ch while we creep forward and my eye stays glued to the sight.

The cloud's gone, and—yes!—so is that bunker. A mile-and-a-half away but close in my optics, it shows a wound like a gunshot to a man, with only a small entrance hole in the front and a massive exit, roof and back wall blown off and debris strewn all over. Clothes. Gear. Pieces of weapons and human bodies. Whatever was inside is out now and ripped all to hell.

"Target!" I yell, tanker-talk for "We got it." Howell doesn't key his mike, but he oorahs so loud I hear him over my helmet's sound suppression. He keeps it up while the other two join in.

You bet your ass we're happy and proud. We just made a great shot for an M60 main gun, especially firing a HEAT round, a slower projectile with arced trajectory. And this is actually the first main-gun round we ever shot as a crew. Swanson, who just got promoted, never even pulled the big trigger before. First shot, first kill, at 2,200 meters. How great is this?

Immediately I look for the next target, feeling all the weight and worry lift off my shoulders. No nervousness, no anxiety, no nothing, not now or ever again. From here on out, preparation will concern me much, much more than anything that happens on the battlefield. You win in training. When the shooting starts, I will relax a little, because a fight's all about acting and reacting.

After a breaching tank opens our lane through the minefield—big thanks to the commander Sgt. Bob Brennan, the same buddy who set me up with April—we get into the trenches and make a mess out of the defenders crazy enough or stupid enough to want to fight. Over the few days on the way to our northernmost position in an overwatch outside Kuwait City, we kill three tanks, five armored personnel carriers, and a few dozen more infantry. Swanson, my supposedly soft guy, turns out to be an all-star killer on a tank. He has the gift, no doubt about it. And the other two turn out to be kick-ass crewmen, not just good but good Marines, proving all the guys who thought they were turds to be wrong. And me, I find something I'm good at. What do you know, I command a tank in battle pretty damn well.

Top Graham, our combat guru, was absolutely right: You don't have to have done it before to be good at it.

52

Hot Tub of Horror

Y ou can partially blame the next big event after marriage—leaving the Marines—on newlyweds carried away with newness.

After our wedding, just two days after I got back from overseas, it seemed like our new life together meant we ought to leave behind the old, including the Marine Corps, where I did everything I came to do and then some. I felt like I'd never been anything but a Marine. Time to spread wings and fly. So on May 5, 1992, I was honorably discharged, and the Popaditches set up in San Diego.

I got a job in construction and had a near miss as close as the one I later had in Fallujah, but with no lasting effects. Another guy and I lost consciousness and came within an inch of dying from breathing solvent fumes while working inside a tank (the kind that holds liquids). This led to my first televised medevac, a big surprise to April, who tuned in the news and saw me on a stretcher. The incident had nothing to do with my leaving construction in less than a year, though. For me, the work led nowhere beyond the next paycheck. After the birth of Nicholas I needed solid family-man employment.

My dad told me I could get work as a guard in a prison back home. Guards got good state-government benefits, and in Indiana we could afford a house with a yard for the kids to run around in, an impossible dream in SD.

To be honest and fair, I did meet a few honorable, committed, motivated individuals working at the high security prison near the

Indianapolis Airport. But they did not significantly raise the appalling, dirt bag average. On the upside, I excelled at subduing and talking sense into dangerous felons. This involved using cool new moves and physical control techniques (joint manipulation, pain compliance) that would do me a lot of good back in the Corps. My verbal skills also improved, because I couldn't hope to physically dominate some of those monsters. Even our celebrity inmate, former heavyweight boxing champ Mike Tyson, used to get leaned on.

Challenging and fun, but again I didn't see a future. And my California girl April couldn't stand Indiana. We both felt out of our element, homesick, in the wrong place among the wrong people. This really hit home one night at a party held at a fellow guard's house. We had no idea, but it was a hot tub party, and we were supposed to take our clothes off like everybody else. We don't do group nudity, because we're not that kind of people. And, as April says, those people had absolutely no business running around naked.

Get us out of here. Let me back into the Marines.

On September 15, 1995, I re-enlist. Who cares that I go back in as a lance corporal? I'm back on the team and in tank school, this time for the new M1A1 Main Battle Tank. In December, 1995, I report to Alpha Company, First Tank Battalion, at Twentynine Palms, California, where I command a tank and get promoted to sergeant, right where I left off.

Pop rides again. Thank God and the United States Marines.

I take pride, by the way, in the fact that every occupation I have held as an adult, up to this point, requires me to wear a helmet.

53

Making Marines

$\mathbf{M}$y becoming a hat has two things in common with joining the Marines back when I was eighteen.

Number one, I do it for the wrong reasons. In this case, I volunteer for drill instructor training because I do not want to be a recruiter, as I almost surely will be if I don't sign up for something else. In 1998, with nine years in, re-upping as my prior enlistment runs out, I will have to take what's called a B-Billet. Hat and recruiter are the biggies, and I pick the one to avoid the other.

Number two commonality with my first enlistment: I will love my new occupation, which is really a whole new identity and life, more than I ever thought possible, and I find new strengths within. If we didn't go to war against Iraq in 2003, my three years making Marines at the recruit depot in San Diego probably would mark the high point of my military life. It definitely makes me a better Marine than I was. Nothing in peacetime brings the same level of 24/7 commitment and challenge and reward. Just like combat, drill instructor duty brings out the best in you or crushes you.

Volunteering for DI school doesn't get you in. That's up to the chain of command, which minutely examines your military record and personal data. You must be a proven leader. Any history of bad judgment or problems like screwed-up personal finances, you don't get in, because you have to be completely trustworthy and free of any distractions from the mission, which will dominate your entire life like no other mission short of making war. The duty is so demanding and all-pervasive that marriage counseling is part of the preparation package.

Training, which lasts 13 weeks just like Boot Camp, involves absorbing an unbelievable load of info and rules and SOP. We get PT that's actually tougher than recruit training. It has to be, because we will run way ahead of the kids while carrying additional equipment and calling cadence and making it all appear completely effortless. Absolutely nothing a hat does can look hard, except maybe the effort you make to restrain yourself and not kill some knucklehead recruit. The latter, of course, is theatrics for calculated effect. No, I didn't just betray a trade secret. Even if you know this, a hat on the warpath will scare the shit out of you.

We have to be more than just smart and tough—witness a guy who gets put out because he belts another student who fails to execute an assigned task. Gone by the end of the day. No way will they turn a man loose with recruits if he can't control his temper. Ditto prima donnas, who think they're bigger than the mission of making Marines. Half my class, made up of proven leaders from the Fleet, fails to reach graduation from the school, the all-around toughest training program in the Corps.

Scared that I won't pass muster, I give everything a thousand percent and surprise myself by graduating third in the class, which is down to 28 guys from the original 55. I don't really click on the job, though, because school doesn't give a real feel for it. Nor does my first 13-week training cycle with recruits, where I feel pretty much lost, doing my best to watch and learn from the senior DIs. It's like I'm a young lion that mama quit bringing meat to, and now I have to do like the older predators and help kill our lunch. But I still manage to make a lot of noise and inflict pain and generally terrify the recruits, which is the essence of the third hat's job.

Second time around, I get it. What we do here is critical to the Marine Corps and the recruits themselves. Do it wrong, and we set young Marines up for failure and create problems for the team. Do it right, we fix problems before they happen and send new fixers and problem solvers to the Fleet. I start loving the job and decide to do everything in my power to excel on the drill field the way I did on the tank ramp. Every drop of sweat, every waking minute, which includes a lot of time when I ought to be asleep, all my brains and strength and ability, I will devote to making Marines.

Like a lot of brand-new converts, I get wound up and overzealous, coming down a little too hard on recruits in an uncalculated manner. With more time on the job, a good hat actually gets much more vicious, but in ways carefully designed to hammer home whatever lessons recruits need to learn. Early on I also drive myself a little too hard. Fortunately, I've got superiors to rein me in and show me how to do things right. It mostly happens behind the scenes, but we drill instructors are subject to harsher, more constant correction than our recruits. If you don't have a thick hide and don't want to address your own deficiences, better go back to your old unit.

One of my favorite bosses, First Sergeant Jackson, makes me tape a picture of my family and a corporal's chevron inside my campaign cover and checks to make sure I keep the stuff there. You might think the picture in my hat is supposed to remind me to go home once in a while. In fact, 1st Sgt Jackson wants me to remember that other people feel the consequences of my actions. Screw up here and I get busted back to corporal, which will hurt my wife and kids, too, because I lose a pay grade and throw away all ten years in the Corps. With so many years in, a guy who's only a corporal cannot re-enlist. That's what's at stake.

Pain, or implied pain, and learning are often one in the same on the depot. The thinly veiled threat comes with a lot of valuable instruction and assignments with more senior DIs who can teach me. One absolutely brilliant boss, Staff Sgt. Siaw, shows me over and over that you must be cruel to be kind. Go a little easy, let somebody off the hook, and you betray the trust placed in you and cheat the guy by not teaching him and pushing him to his limits. In our business, fighting, this can be tantamount to killing him and killing a lot of other good people, too.

After I spend a training cycle with Staff Sgt. Siaw and really take his lesson to heart, I turn loose the inner rabid grizzly bear and become the merciless, uncompromising, endlessly demanding, loud, threatening, famously vicious leader that I will be for the rest of my time in the Corps. Those who know me afterward probably can't imagine that I was ever anything but. Many would have a hard time believing I possess any compassion at all. In fact, I have loads of it and despise pointless cruelty, which is for cowards and weaklings. But if being vicious and intimidating does some good, sign me up. In this line of work, nothing does more good so thoroughly and so fast.

Tough love. Marines are laughing their asses off because I used this fruitcake expression. But we really and truly care about our recruits and look out for them every step of the way. And we take such deep pride in them, watching them toughen up and grow into Marines. One of my proudest moments on the depot comes watching a certain Recruit Garcia, dumb as a box of rocks, so slow on the uptake that at first I think he doesn't understand English. Out on the bayonet assault course, a long and brutal ass-kicker that involves running and crawling and stabbing, he comes to the last dummy and jabs it in the throat so hard that he beheads it. This ought to be impossible, because the thing has a metal skeleton inside and is built to be stabbed a thousand times a day. Proud as can be, like he's my own kid bringing home straight As, I nevertheless stay in my role, yelling at him for standing and looking because what he did surprises him, too.

"Why are you not still stabbing, Garcia?" I shout, "He didn't fall down yet, did he?"

In fact, he never will, because a frame holds the dummy upright.

It seems Garcia was more like scared stupid in Boot Camp, because he becomes a good Fleet Marine, a tanker, too, and ultimately an NCO. Hundreds of success stories like his add up to a feeling of tremendous achievement and one of the best and most fulfilling periods in my military life.

By 2001, I've held all three drill instructor billets, Third, Heavy, and Senior, and sent my last platoon across the parade deck. With no more training cycles in my future, I process out recruits who get dropped from training and sent home. Compared to the insane hours I've been working, this 9-to-5 job is a dream.

Early on Sept. 11, 2001, I get up to go to work and turn on the radio to listen to my favorite jocks. This day their serious tone tells me something huge and heinous is happening. We've been attacked, and thousands of innocents are about to die, on our own home soil.

Recruit training goes on, per usual, on our base. Though I hate what happened on 9/11, the world doesn't change as much for me and fellow Marines as it does for others. We have faced terrorism overseas and known its consequences for decades. Then, however, as the days go on and our enemy gets a face and name and home base, I know America will fight, and Marines, as always, will go in the first wave. Since we're going to the Middle East, I know tanks will be part of the tactical plan.

Time to get out of here and back on an M1A1.

I go through my chain of command, requesting transfer back to the Fleet. Looks okay at first, but then suddenly, for no discernible reason, "You're good to go," changes to "Negative. You're staying put." For a guy just six months short of the end of his tour, this doesn't make sense.

Wanting my answer straight from the top, I go to the regimental commander, another tanker, who tells me in so many words, "Tough Shit" and that I'm wrong for not taking "no" in the first place. I walk away feeling like I got kicked in the nuts.

The feeling lingers.

I actually get new orders specifying that I serve out every single day of my tour on the depot. With my old units training for a fight, this drives me wild. Let me go back to the Fleet, where I belong, where they need me!

Finally, on April 1, 2002, they turn me loose. On April 2, I report to Bravo Company, First Tank Battalion, at Twentynine Palms. I get command of the tank designated Bravo 2-4, aka White 4 because our platoons go by color names and Bravo Company's second platoon is White. I also become White's platoon sergeant and the demanding slave driver I need to be to get us ready for war.

54

Rightness

There is only one way to get ready to leave home for a combat deployment:

Get right with your God.

Get right with those closest to you.

Say every "I love you" that you feel in your heart, embarrassing or not.

Say everything that needs to be said.

If you're pissed-off, guilty, messed-up about something with somebody, get it out and set it straight. Every single thing you would have put in one of those stupid Hollywood "in case I die" letters, take care of it now.

Put your personal affairs in order. Fix things so un-done business won't pile up while you're gone and make problems. Make sure those you leave behind know what they have to do.

Then say goodbye with no home worries and a clear head and conscience and your soul unburdened and pure.

As General James N. Mattis, the great leader of Marines says, "Fight with a happy heart."

55

One Day in Iraq

In March 2003, when we cross the border in Operation Iraqi Freedom, I don't especially like the Iraqi people. Why would I, given that my only prior contact involved fighting their nation's troops in Kuwait, a country they invaded and pillaged. Now that we're fighting again, I don't especially want to like them.

A funny thing happens, though, as we pass through town after town and pretty much swim in the local citizens and those on the move to escape bombing and battles to come up ahead. I see a lot to admire and develop a genuine fondness for these people.

For all they've gone through, the oppression under Saddam and now a foreign invader decimating their military and rolling over their territory in huge numbers, Iraqis remain amazingly calm and upbeat. Dads come out and play with their kids fifty feet from my tank, like the whole point of our advance is to give guys time off work to enjoy their families. Being next to my tank puts a guy in the FEBA—Forward Edge of the Battle Area—so if fighting breaks out it happens right here. Even with no fight, my arrival means their world just turned upside down—for good or bad, people don't know yet. But nothing screws up the day. Absent immediate fear or grief, people smile almost constantly and make jokes with each other. So lighthearted in serious situations, they remind me of Marines.

I also appreciate their courtesy and regard for each other. Our route of advance northward follows major roads, with refugees walking south on the roadsides. Those in houses put out big cooking pans full of water with ladles for the thirsty. Friendly visits often follow the stops for refreshment. Giving a damn about your fellow humans—I like it.

When I need help directing locals, like telling them to stay off the road ahead when our advance halts, I just ask for an English speaker, who invariably appears and cooperates whole-heartedly. Some really dig playing traffic cop. You can't help but notice that Iraqi males like to tell others what to do.

In these human contacts you get what you give. I make a point to come down off my tank and speak with respect, man to man. After all, I'm asking for a favor. I'll find out later that dismounting to talk to people instead of shouting down from the cupola has a very positive impact. In the Arab culture, when a man occupies a position of power, like commanding a 68-ton tank with a cannon and three machine guns, but deals as if the power doesn't matter he shows himself to be very honorable and therefore trustworthy. Later I'll also learn to seek out the oldest man present, because people here equate age with wisdom and leadership. I'll find out, too, that people don't get offended if we make accidental gaffes. Iraqis consider America a very young country with a young culture, so we seem to them like kids who don't know how to be polite yet.

While the grownups generally hang back and keep their cool, kids go nuts when we pass, giving us the peace sign and thumbs up and little written signs that say "Bush Good" and such. From television exposure, I guess, they seem to equate Americans with entertainment and big fun. Dismounted, I go around like the Pied Piper. Though I keep telling the mobs of kids that it's dangerous to stand so close because somebody might shoot at me, they stick around anyway, and I love it.

I never forget that being up front, I'm usually the first American people meet and first impressions last. It drives me nuts to think how much damage is done by undisciplined turds and idiots who entertain themselves teaching children obscene words and gestures, showing them Playboy, or bullying people around just because they can, thus confirming anti-West, anti-American propaganda. How can such assholes not get that they're helping the enemy? They might as well open recruiting offices for the insurgents or pick up weapons and shoot at their fellow Americans. Fortunately, as a staff NCO, I can enforce discipline and help set the right command climate. Every abuse you ever heard of could have been stopped by quality leadership. I'm proud to say no

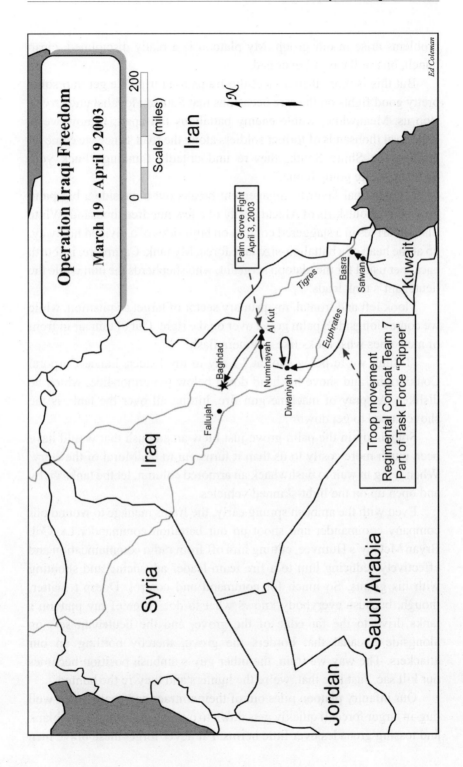

Operation Iraqi Freedom
March 19 - April 9 2003

Scale (miles)
0   200

Ed Coleman

Iran

Tigres

Palm Grove Fight
April 3, 2003

Al Kut

Baghdad

Numinayah

Euphrates

Diwaniyah

Basra

Safwan

Kuwait

Fallujah

Iraq

Troop movement
Regimental Combat Team 7
Part of Task Force "Ripper"

Syria

Saudi Arabia

Jordan

problems arise in our group. My platoon is a really disciplined, clean bunch, one of the best I ever had.

But this is more than a meet-the-Iraqis road trip. We get into some pretty good fights on the rare occasions that Saddam loyalist units try to stop us. Meanwhile, whole enemy battalions fall apart. I know we're looking at thousands of former soldiers along the road. Since we come up through the Shiite South, they're undoubtedly thinking "Fuck you, Saddam, we're going home."

My personal favorite engagement breaks out alongside a big palm grove on the outskirts of Al Kut, a city of a few hundred thousand. White Platoon drives in a staggered column on both sides of a divided highway, up at the head of a battalion-size task force. My tank, Carnivore, is fourth back, per usual for the platoon sergeant, who shepherds the unit while the lieutenant's tank leads.

I look left and frontal, my primary sector of target acquisition, while we come alongside a palm grove over on the right. Out of thin air in front of me comes what looks like a camera flash.

"I think we're being shot at," I say to my loader, Lance Corporal Conkwright, and shove his head down below the armor-line, which he dislikes. A spray of machine gun fire, hitting all over the tank, is the shove I need to get down.

Somebody in the palm grove just blew an ambush that would have been much more costly to us than it turns out to be. Moral of the story: When lying in wait to bushwhack an armored column, let the tanks go by and open up on the light-skinned vehicles.

Even with the ambush sprung early, the Iraqis manage to wound our company commander and shoot up our battalion commander Lt. Col. Bryan McCoy's Humvee, cutting him off from radio communication and effectively reducing him to a fire team leader advancing and shooting with his grunts. So much for command and control. Doesn't matter, though, because everybody knows what to do. Three of my platoon's tanks drive to the far edge of the grove, and the lieutenant sets up alongside a canal that borders the grove, thereby bottling up our attackers. The way we train, the other guy's ambush position becomes our kill sac. Just like that, we're the hunters and they're the hunted.

Our infantry platoon piles out of their amtracs and charges at a well dug-in larger force. It quickly gets down to our guys shooting point blank and tossing grenades over little berms. I'll never forget these brave men and what they do. They might look like kids, but they're Marines, hard as nails and happy today because they've got somebody to fight and kill. This is really a treat for them, because infantry platoons attached to a tank company spend too much time riding in our tracks and hearing about the good stuff on the radio. Not today. Their turn to shine. Also to pay the price. They take casualties, including one dead.

Alongside the infantry, I plunge Carnivore into the grove. First off, we gun smoke three camouflaged armored personnel carriers hidden in the trees and brush. My caliber-50 would do, but I use the main gun just to add some additional terror and psychological damage to the already screwed-over Iraqis. Nothing left to do for those guys, except to die. I put Cpl. Schroeder, the gunner, to work with his machine gun, tearing up bunkers and sundry targets, so thick and close-in that I pull out my pistol and start popping guys from the cupola. Fish in a barrel from ten feet up. Our driver, Lance Cpl. Hagewood, needs only minimal commands and maneuvers Carnivore with surprising finesse. Great crewmen, all three.

Not only do we wear out the enemy we see, we help the infantry herd the bad guys toward certain death trying to swim across the canal covered by our platoon commander Lieutenant MacLaughlin's tank. He comes over the net and says, "Whatever you're doing in there, keep doing it" and fills the canal with bodies.

My company XO, commanding a tank designated Black-5 and acting as my wingman, spots a target he can't ID. I make out a tiny bit of metal amongst the trees, about 200 meters away. Could be any sort of vehicle, a truck or another personnel carrier, maybe. It takes a good bit of maneuvering to line up a clear shot through all the palm trunks. We have a round with armor defeating capabilities in the tube so that's what we shoot. Lucky for us, too, because it's a tank! This we know because the lieutenant radios that we just hit a T-62, which he didn't see before it explodes because it's in a revetment with dirt built up around it on three sides.

I might owe my life to the XO's eyes and my gunner's good shooting and sheer luck. A little later that T-62 would have had a clean shot at my flank with his 115 mm cannon, capable of penetrating my armor.

Icing on the cake, that tank. I love this particular engagement because we win with personal initiative in the absence of orders. The infantry's fearlessness and ferocity carries the day, too. We win because we're

Marines. And the other guys, who have everything we have, lose because they are not.

We stay on the move toward Al Kut, do a little more shooting on the outskirts, then back out to open ground to consolidate, reorganize, refuel, and re-arm. The White Platoon tanks take up a battle position on the city side to serve as a blocking force and protect the battalion while it resupplies, a very vulnerable position. Parked on the highway and static, we have time for post-action recap and appreciation of the big ass-kicking in the palm grove. Lots of talk, while the crews take care of the tanks, always with somebody in the cupolas manning the weapons:

"Those assholes thought that was going to work?"

"Next time, they'll have a better escape plan."

"Can't believe that was a T-62. Thought it was a damn truck."

Nobody gets all high-five and goofy, but we feel really good. After the fact I always get much more amped-up than during actual shooting. As always, I replay the whole thing and trouble-shoot every decision I made and the entire platoon's performance. What could we do better? Today I can't come up with a single thing I would change or any deficiencies in White Platoon's performance. A-plus, guys, with extra credit for doing it on the fly with no orders from higher-ups. I give myself good marks for taking Carnivore into those trees, violating traditional wisdom to stay out of tight spots, where infantry rules, and then using every one of our weapons from the main gun down to a Beretta 9mm pistol. No hand-to-hand, but close. I like to think my actions saved some of our infantry's lives and kept bad guys from getting away. And killing a tank, even when you think it's a truck, always makes my day.

Normally I'd jump off the tank for a walkaround inspection. Today, though, I stay up in the cupola and watch all my guys, glowing like Dad at the head of the table on Thanksgiving Day. Great, just great.

"Everybody got that truck?" somebody hollers.

He means a white truck in the distance, the first vehicle coming our way. Looking through the three-power sight on the commander's caliber-50, I see a big commercial dump truck with a high cab like a semi, flying bedsheet-size white flags on each side. It must be coming 45 miles per hour straight at us.

Closing, closing, closing. How can they not see four tanks blocking their path?

Civilians and no threat, I'm almost sure, but nevertheless prep my .50 and arm its electrical trigger. Meanwhile, Lt. Mac stands up on his fender and makes big arm signals to halt. He then shoulders his rifle and aims, usually all it takes to stop people in their tracks. But the truck, closing on 100 meters away, keeps coming. The lieutenant shoots right in front of the truck. Still no effect, so he fires into the cab, trying to hit somebody.

Still, the thing keeps coming, and I put my eye to the sight in the commander's weapon station and put my thumb on the trigger. I give the people one more second, wondering as I have all along what is wrong with them. I get mad at them for making me do what I do not want to do.

No choice now. I put a short burst into the truck bom-bom-bom, and it finally skids to a stop maybe 15 meters from the muzzle of Carnivore's cannon.

You probably wonder what's wrong with us that we don't obliterate the truck much prior, as anybody would today. But remember, then is not now. So early in the war the use of vehicle bombs, a weapon of choice for insurgents for years now, is a freak occurrence. Tactically, my war stories are ancient history. As a good friend says, if you were in Iraq six months ago, you might as well have been in Vietnam.

Oh God, I don't want to hear this. A woman wails, long and high, out of grief for some horrible happening.

"Schroeder, man the cupola," I say and grab my rifle, hit the deck, and run toward the truck. The woman keeps wailing while I hope against hope that this is not what I know it is.

I open the passenger-side door and pull out a lady in a bhurka and two guys, handing the people off to Sgt. Ariaga, commander of White 2, and Marines from other tanks. No bleeding or obvious wounds in sight, but the wailing goes on and on. Now I know it comes from the truck bed.

My worst nightmare. Blood everywhere and a dozen people lying flat. Men, women, kids. Tiny kids, toddlers. And all this blood.

"Call for a medevac!" I yell back to Schroeder.

The people have chickens and goats, too. But above the animal odor I pick up something horrible. A smell that I know, combining BO and a metallic element, like a penny in your mouth except it's in your nose. Blood and a body's insides on the outside, that's what I smell. Bad, bad, bad.

The people lie there and look. Slinging my rifle cross-body behind me tells them, I hope, that I mean no harm. It also frees my hands to go to work. Fast as I can I start picking up kids, the smallest first, looking them over and handing them down to Ariaga, who hands them on to other Marines, who set up like a bucket brigade for handling civilians.

I don't do it out loud, but each unhurt kid gets a big "Thank God" in my head and silent sigh of relief. Not a scratch on one of them. Thank God, thank God, thank God. I handle women with all possible respect while looking into their faces for signs of pain and shock and inspecting their garments for tears and blood. I must do all right in terms of showing courtesy and giving reassurance because the wailer finally goes quiet. Not a scratch on any women, either.

My first male casualty, a teenager with a small wound in his forearm, frets and whimpers to the point that I get a little annoyed. Come on kid, man up, you're going to be just fine, and both of us ought to be thankful. I'm not proud of these feelings, but there they are.

The last guy I look over turns out to be our one and only casualty with a life-threatening wound. He's about thirty, a little more healthy and prosperous-looking than your average Iraqi, with a face that reminds me of somebody I knew back at Terre Haute North High School. He lies there, calm as can be, like he's just waiting for his turn to get looked over. Now with the others gone, I see his pants are shredded, showing an open upper thigh wound, and a big pool of blood under him.

I yell for Ariaga to get up and give me a hand. After we lower our casualty to the deck, we set up to apply pressure and stop the bleeding, which will kill him if we don't, because he's missing a fist-size chunk of meat were the left thigh meets the ass-cheek. Digging in and pressing hard will hurt like hell, and I get out my phrase book and point to "doctor" as a shortcut way to tell him we're rendering First Aid.

About the time we finish dressing the wound, Doc Rose, our company medical corpsman, arrives and says we have a medevac inbound.

"Good job stopping the bleeding," Doc says to me. Looking back, I think he might be applying some psychological first aid, knowing that I need to hear something positive in this horrible situation.

When I get up to leave, the wounded Iraqi grabs me with both arms and kisses me on the cheek, which I don't mind. An Arab thing, not a gay thing, he's just trying to say thanks for helping him out.

"As Salaam Alaikum," I say, "Peace be with you," and he responds in kind.

At no time am I tempted to communicate that I'm the guy who shot him. No way. After the medevac, Doc Rose will assure me that he made it fine.

We have one last surprise casualty. The driver of the truck caught a 5.56 mm projectile, Lt. Mac's single M-16 shot at the cab. His actions now seem even more bizarre. A bullet didn't make the son-of-a-bitch stop. Iraqis score a perfect ten on the bull-headedness scale.

The driver wouldn't have said anything at all, except the woman from the front seat, who speaks very good English, tells me he's hit, after which he pulls up his shirt and shows me where the round sits just under the skin and on top of a rib.

With the woman translating, I say, "We have a medevac coming for the other man. Go with him, and our doctors will take care of you."

He rejects the offer, so I up the ante. "They'll do a really good job so you heal up nicely and don't get an infection. You'll get some money for your trouble, too."

He refuses at length, acting like it's funny that I make a big deal out of the bullet in his side. "In Iraq under Saddam, it is not uncommon, getting shot. I'll go home and pluck it out with a pocket knife," the woman translates.

This pair, the woman and the driver, make quite a contrast. She wears the full-on female Muslim rig, with her face below the eyes covered, and she's obviously well educated. The driver is strictly blue collar, wearing a white wife beater and Dickey's-type work pants. He'd fit in at a truck stop back home.

Though I've got nothing left to do, I stay on the deck by the truck, which still has the chickens and goats in it. I believe the blood splattered all around the back must have come from wounded animals. Nothing else can explain the volume.

My God, I just shot people I'm here to help. Nobody dies, and I'd do the same thing all over in the same situation. Right calls sometimes lead to bad outcomes, and you can't do one damn thing. I know it and still feel miserable and wish it didn't happen. I wish the people were all fine and headed somewhere safe and better than wherever they came from.

Capt. Lewis, the company commander, comes up and asks, "What's going on, Pop?"

"I did this." I say. Not an answer to his question, but it comes out. I need to confess, even knowing I didn't do anything wrong.

"Okay," the Captain says, "What I need you to do now is get the fuck back on your tank and get back to work. "

The perfect thing to say. He means this is over and done with. This ship has sailed. And the guilt I feel turns to shame that my CO has to tell me to get back in the game.

Four years later and change, it still bothers me to remember all this. Nobody even dies here, but it bugs me more than any other battlefield event. Looking into the back of the truck at what I believe at first is a massacre of innocents is the only thing that ever scares me in combat. And it scares me all to hell. This is the one and only time I fail to make the warrior's disconnect between me and those in my gunsights and allow myself to feel human emotion. Nobody else knows how rattled I am at the time except the CO who brings me back without saying a thing about it. Thanks, Black Six, otherwise known as Capt. Lewis.

That night we advance toward the Diyala River, where in two days we meet the last organized resistance between us and Baghdad.

56

"The Cigar Marine"

April 8, 2003
Central Baghdad

A wide boulevard with landscaped islands in the middle, lined with nice urban-type mid-rises in surprisingly fine shape. A very attractive and peaceful-seeming city, especially compared to the suburbs we just went through, where looting of government buildings has already broken out—it's like a combo carnival and open-air Walmart where everything is free.

But here, deep in Baghdad, we don't see a soul.

I keep thinking of the old Charlton Heston sci-fi flick Omega Man, where the last non-zombie human male on earth speeds up and down the streets of a major metropolis in his car. I'm part of a column comprising two tank platoons and our infantry platoon in three amtracs, but still the silence and sense of isolation closes in. Very eerie.

In the distance, straight up our boulevard, stands an enormous statue that can't be anybody but Saddam Hussein. His likeness is everywhere, to the point that guys make up funny names for some of the images—in a white suit and hat he's Fantasy Island Saddam.

The statue, flanked by shorter commemorative columns, stands in a round mini-park within a traffic circle where our boulevard ends. The big open area is nothing but round, but for some reason they call it Firdos Square. The tallest building on the square is the Palestine Hotel, in front of which we see a growing crowd. Westerners one and all, it turns out, most of them media types loaded down with journalistic weaponry. As our tanks pull in, the crowd crosses toward us like iron filings drawn to magnets. We follow the circle and take up positions at points where streets lead away from the square. It turns out to be a perfect set-up for a defensive perimeter. I park my tank next to the Palestine Hotel, orienting down a street that stops at the banks of the Tigris River just a block away.

People now pour out of the hotel, mostly really happy to see us and shooting bazillions of pictures. But then—can you believe it?—the first person to talk to me is a truly repulsive British woman belonging to a small flock of anti-war protestors. They call themselves Human Shields and carry a big banner that reads, "Go Home U.S. Wankers."

Great, I'm thinking, I get the assholes. The battleaxe, who seems to be trying to bring back the Sixties, stands next to the tank and shouts up abuse like "You fucking murderer!" while I crack up, which drives her more wild. With the banner in front of my tank, facing away, her group obviously wants international photo and video coverage, heroes in front of heavy armor like in Tiananmen Square. Of course my tank ain't moving, much less shooting, and nobody buys their bullshit. The reporters totally ignore these clowns.

I lean down and say to my new girlfriend, "This is just grandstanding. If you really want to be a Human Shield, you should go across the river. They're bombing over there right now. Listen, you can hear it."

"Fuck you," she says.

Great comeback. After a little more total indifference from the press, the group, disheartened, wanders away.

About this time, Capt. Lewis, puffing on a stogie, comes by and asks to use my radios. As he takes the handset he gives me the cigar.

I look at it a few seconds.

Why not?

I take a few puffs. Can't call myself a connoisseur, but it tastes damn fine to me.

While I am puffing on the captain's cigar, a French journalist takes a still shot of me. Little do I know it, but my smiling mug, with Saddam's statue in the background, will run on front pages all over the world. It's Black Six's cigar and only a loaner, but I become known as The Cigar Marine.

All the while, Iraqis arrive. At first they come by ones and twos, acting very cautious. After nothing bad happens, word gets out and people pour into the square until we've got a happy mob, an anti-Saddam Woodstock. Locals love abusing the statue, gesturing and throwing stuff. Many pitch shoes, which shows particular disrespect because to them the bottom of the foot is lower than low. Every good hit on the statue gets wild cheers.

I give passing thought to the security implications of the mob scene. Could be die-hard Baathists all around, guys checking out our defensive positions and firepower. Who cares? We can take all comers and attack in any direction at battalion strength. And who could deny the people their party? Until the loyalists hauled ass this morning, nobody would have dared to flip off Saddam's image. A banged-up Portugese reporter shows us video footage taken by a friend. In it one of Hussein's henchmen clubs the reporter repeatedly with the butt of an AK-47. That happened right here, just yesterday. The guy's a mess but deliriously happy to see us.

The joy and gratitude of the Iraqis beats all, though. People shout out their thanks and try to hand up flowers and other gifts. I can't help but get caught up in the celebration and what it means, both to them and to me. Three weeks back, I thought about nothing but defeating the enemy's military and knocking off their regime. Now that defeat looks like a victory beyond anything I imagined. This is what I fought for. It's why I put heart and soul into the Marine Corps way back when. A pure, one hundred percent Marine mission, setting people free from a tyrant they couldn't get rid of on their own. Forty years, they knuckled under to this murderous son of a bitch because they had no choice. Now, with our help, he's on the run and they're dancing in the streets, literally, because he will oppress them no more.

The crowd goes especially wild when a big, burly Iraqi whales away at the statue's pedestal with a sledge hammer. This guy is huge, like a circus strong man, and he attacks the statue's base so it will fall over. Not such a bad idea if he had a jackhammer, but it'll take forever with his hand tool.

I don't know who should get credit, but the Marines come to the strong man's aid. People go beyond wild hearing the V-12 diesel on our M88, our maintenance vehicle, fire up and then seeing its long boom swing up and out in front like an arm. Here's our statue killer. It's a miracle nobody gets run over or hurt climbing on the vehicle's deck while it creeps through the crowd toward the statue.

Now all eyes are on the M88 guys. After the driver, Lance Corporal Riley, positions the machine, a mechanic, Corporal Chin, climbs up to throw a loop around Saddam's neck and hook it up to the winch cables that run out the boom. Our corpsman, Doc Rose, also rides the M88, the reasoning being that broken tanks will likely have broken Marines on board. He assists Chin. Pictures of Chin and Doc Rose will go out all over the world, great for them because they usually labor in obscurity. After one good pull on a heavy rope loop around Saddam's neck breaks the rope, the guys rig a towing chain.

Later rehashes by unfriendly press aside, nobody in the square takes the least bit of offense when an American flag goes over Saddam Hussein's head. The Iraqis cheer like crazy. The flag doesn't mean we conquered anybody—just "Saddam, you're through." Obviously, though, it doesn't play so well politically, because an order comes down from on high to remove the Stars and Stripes. So an Iraqi flag goes up, and people cheer for that, too. The McDonald's flag would do the trick, or a giant bedspread. I like both flags fine and dig the image of Saddam with his head covered by cloth and a noose around his neck, like he's about to be hanged.

The M88 commander, Gunnery Sergeant Lambert, a famously methodical and fastidious individual, makes a major production out of pulling the statue down. He does it by inches, backing up and winching out cable bit by bit, retrograding to where the statue won't fall on his vehicle. Come on, Gunny, yank that fucker down already, you're killing us. Though we expect the statue to topple over, it does something cooler, buckling and breaking at the shins so two feet still stand. Not only is the guy down, we can see inside his statue. He's hollow.

My crewmen ask if they can dismount and mingle. Sure guys, you earned it. They come back looking starry-eyed, and then it's my turn to get down and be amongst the crowd, one happy moe among many. One man and I actually show each other our kids' pictures. The more I get to know the locals, the more I see they're just like me, and the more I want them to have a shot at a life as good as mine. Glad to help, more than glad, and proud.

Inadvertently, I'm a huge help to that Frenchman who took the cigar picture. A couple hours after he took the picture, he finds me in the crowd, shakes my hand and says, "You have made me a lot of money, my friend." As I understand, his shot got picked up by the Associated Press and made a big hit worldwide.

After some back and forth, I say to him, "Since I did this for you, I want to ask you to do me a favor."

"It will be my pleasure," he says.

"I will write down my home phone number. Could you please call it and tell the woman who answers to watch what's happening here on TV? I want her to see this."

"Call her yourself, my friend," he says and flips me a satt phone.

After April picks up, I tell her to turn on the news, and she laughs and says she and other wives have been watching together and taping everything, having their own Firdos Square in Twentynine Palms.

"We haven't missed a thing," she says, "We're so proud of our guys."

Can it get any better than this?

Well, yes, it can. We were married twelve years ago today.

"Happy Anniversary, Beautiful Woman," I say.

*   *   *

Firdos Square was an incredible moment, as anybody lucky enough to have been there will tell you. I was fortunate to spend a few more weeks mopping up and keeping the peace on the streets of Baghdad. When I think of that city during those times, I think of people I liked, kids, smiling faces, laughs, and happiness. The promise of freedom was pure and real.

However the situation in Iraq comes out, I'm proud that I fought to give those people a shot at a better life.

57

Back to the Fight

Marines who laughed at some of the touchy-feely stuff I already put down are going to piss themselves now because I'm quoting Shakespeare:

> For he to-day that sheds his blood with me
> Shall be my brother; be he ne'er so vile,
> This day shall gentle his condition;
> And gentlemen in England now-a-bed
> Shall think themselves accurs'd they were not here,
> And hold their manhoods cheap whiles any speaks
> That fought with us . . .

— St. Crispen's Day Speech, Henry V

Oorah.

Gives me chills every time.

This is the king firing up his men before a fight that a lot of them won't survive. Translated into Marine-ese, he says that those who get into the fight will be better men for it. And those who stay home will feel like half-men forever, especially when the vets are around.

Maybe, at my age, I should be immune to the call to arms. After all, what the hell do I have left to prove? But Shakespeare sums up my feelings to this day. It's me, it's us, it's the Marines. And it explains what I do back at Two Nine.

After two months at home, I hear that one tank company out of the battalion will be attached to the First Marine Division, now about to redeploy to Iraq, this time up in the Sunni Triangle. We thought we were done over there for good, job complete, but there's a new crowd of bad guys to beat, and the nation calls on the Marines—who else?—to go back.

The day word gets out and I hear that Charlie Company, not Bravo, will go, I beeline down to battalion CP.

"I want in that company," I say.

I get a Marine answer, "Yeah, well, people in hell want ice water," and absolutely no strokes for volunteering. But I don't worry because Charlie needs guys like me. Sure enough, I get my orders in a few days and join the company as platoon sergeant of First Platoon, designated Red, made up mostly of volunteers in a hurry to get back into the fight.

So why don't I tell the whole story to April? Why do I omit the fact that I volunteer to go to Charlie instead of getting picked by command? Good questions, and I don't have good answers, except people do dumb things. And you try telling your family, "I really love you, but I feel the need to leave you for another seven months, and maybe not come home at all."

Maybe I'm not really lying, anyway, because I probably would get picked to transfer and redeploy whether I want to or not. In fact, I'm pretty sure of this. But the half-truth, which April sees right through, adds a little bit of weird background noise at home. Nothing wrong, really, but not quite right.

Meanwhile, Pop rides again and loves it. We train our asses off, and since we're the only company going to fight now, we get priority for whatever assets we want—parts, weaponry, ammo, personal gear, use of training areas with no down time. You name it, we get it. Throw in my all-volunteer platoon, and this is a dream come true for me. Then, at the beginning of January, 2004, just a few weeks before deployment, I get promoted from staff sergeant to gunnery sergeant, not a huge deal in terms of what I do day to day but a sign that the Corps recognizes my contributions. And "Gunny" adds a certain additional prestige and pride in my rank.

Happy New Year.

Still, though, there's this funny little vibe on the personal front. Preparing myself to go, mentally and spiritually, I hit a couple rough spots. Before I get right with the Almighty, I get sideways, having a brief crisis of faith.

Is there a God?

Are my beliefs valid?

Am I part of a plan?

I don't like this because I never doubted before and my faith is my core. Then, thank God, it's over before I get on the plane.

Of course I also ship out in violation of my say-it-all-before-you-go rule by never mentioning volunteering.

No biggies, though. As soon as my boots hit the deck in Kuwait, jump-off to Iraq, I feel right about everything. I did the right thing, and this is exactly where I belong, where I am meant to be.

Good to go.

58

Who I Fight For

Late March, 2004
Fallujah, Iraq
Eastern Outskirts
The Cloverleaf

If you want to know why I believe in this mission, check the guy who gets out of a car that pulls up in front of Bonecrusher. His driver, also apparently his bodyguard, gets out packing a pistol in an old-school leather holster. I dismount and greet the unarmed man in Arabic. He returns the greeting and says, "I am the Mayor of Fallujah, and I need to speak to your battalion commander."

He hands me an American military-issue ID card, which I look over because he presents it, not because I don't believe him. Nobody would claim to be the guy supposedly in charge of this fucked-over, lawless city unless it was true. What a rotten job, trying to bring a semblance of justice and good government to Iraq's Dodge City, famous for its bloodthirsty maniacs and now a magnet for the most hard-core insurgents and fanatical foreign fighters.

For months the bad guys have been gathering and terrorizing the populace and talking shit. If it's a fight they want, they'll get it. On the other hand, if they wise up and get on board with guys like the mayor, we'll build a school or whatever people need. Like our Division Commander, Major General Mattis, keeps saying about the Marines, No better friend, no worse enemy. The choice is theirs.

I tell the mayor I'll make a call, climb up, and use the radio to pass on his request to see our Battalion Six. This takes some doing, because the message has to be relayed back to the firm base.

Eventually headquarters comes back, "Battalion Six en route. Stand by," and I get down to tell the mayor he'll have to wait here for a while before his meeting.

I stay down on the deck with him.

"How long will this take?" he keeps asking.

"A little while," I say. Vague, but still better than the standard Iraqi response of "God willing," which could mean next week or never.

He acts more and more jumpy, pacing around and looking back toward the buildings closest to us at the edge of town. This neighborhood happens to be a notorious shit-hole. Nobody messes with the tanks in there, but the infantry get in firefights all the time.

Finally, the mayor says to me, "Look, if I stay here any longer somebody's going to try to kill me."

I tell him to stand on the far side of the tank, which gives good cover. And something hits me. Pretty cool. This isn't just a couple guys waiting to meet the boss on a sales call. No, they're facing death trying to make life better for the people of their city. Just by dealing with Americans they put their lives and the lives of their families in jeopardy, because our opponents massacre people, particularly officials, for any kind of cooperation with us.

How noble, I think. The mayor's a patriot leader who chooses to face death every day, every minute, for the future of his people and nation. He takes greater risks than I do, no question about it, with no sanctuary, no firm base, to go back to at the end of the patrol. His bodyguard is a marked man, too, along with his family. To me, he might be even more noble, because he does his job out of pure belief. Why else would a regular moe do something so dangerous?

Real-deal standup men. Am I proud and privileged to stand with them? Damn straight.

Just ask yourself, would your mayor put his ass on the line, knowing he probably won't live out his term but trying to do right by his people anyway? Would you have the balls to strap on a weapon and make a stand in broad daylight, like the bodyguard, putting yourself and your loved ones square in the sights of murderers lurking in the shadows of your neighborhood?

For me the bodyguard represents the entire country, where anonymous everyday people take unbelievable risks and pay horrible prices for trying to make things better. Guys die by the hundreds and thousands at police and military recruiting stations, where more guys line up after the bombings. Men and women will vote in the face of intimidation and death threats, in bigger percentages than back home in America. Every minute, the enemy terrorizes and kills good, brave people. All those people want is a better life for their kids. The way things are now, grownups might not live to see it.

If you know Iraq in person and out on the street, instead of from TV reports from the Green Zone, and really try to understand things as people here do, it gets to you, inspires you.

Thank you, Iraqis. I'm honored to know you and fight for you and with you.

59

Culmination

Tuesday, April 6, 2004
1100 Local
Jolan District, Fallujah, Iraq

W hoa, what's this?

Sounds of sustained gunfire instead of the usual couple quick bursts and silence. No shoot and scoot. The enemy stands and fights. 'Bout fucking time.

The fight breaks out only about 200 meters to my front but out of sight because it's behind the first row of buildings at the edge of town. Just this morning my tank section—Bonecrusher and my wingman's tank commanded by Sgt. Escamilla—hooked up with Fox Company 2/1, aka Pale Rider. These 150 or so Marine infantry maintain a defensive position at a railroad overpass at the city's northwest outskirts. Last night a Marine got killed here by small-arms fire, which is why Pale Rider has us today. Battalion uses tanks as mobile reinforcements and hard spots.

When the fight breaks out, I'm parked behind a dirt berm at the center of the Marines' line. Two things surprise me: Shooting starts only about ten minutes after a security patrol leaves our position. The bad guys are closer than we thought. And, the shooting hasn't stopped yet.

In the ten seconds before we fire up the tank turbine and I put on my noise suppressing helmet, the sound tells me a lot. The volume of AK and RPG shots says the enemy group is at least fire-team size, probably bigger. And the numerous bursts from an RPK machine gun tells a whole new story from anything I've heard in Fallujah so far. You don't use those things on the run, which means they're fighting stationary and trying to hold ground instead of attempting to paper-cut us to death per usual. Big news.

Also good news, from my point of view. To this point, Fallujah has been a lot of nothing for tanks. I get what we're doing completely, cordoning off the city and shaping the battlefield for an upcoming assault at regimental strength. But, especially since the bad guys desecrated the bodies of four American contractors in the city last week and amped up their trash-talking about how this will be a graveyard for Americans, I've been itching to go in and shut them up for good. Clean house and be done. This is what I and every other Marine are chomping at the bit to do.

I get on the net and ask the Fox Company Commander, Pale Rider Six, if he wants tanks to support the ambushed squad.

He comes back, "Roger, Red Four. Roll tanks, roll tanks!" Music to my ears.

I radio Escamilla, "Red Three, this is Red Four. Follow my move. Out." Now don't let me break track or bury the gun tube taking Bonecrusher up and over the berm. We slam down hard but undamaged and charge ahead.

Seeing a Marine with a face wound and a corpsman tending him, I know I'm at the ambush sight. Then I make out the rest of the squad. Deaf to everybody else's shooting in the tank, I get all my cues about the enemy's disposition from the Marines' cover positions and where they point their weapons.

Keeping my head just high enough above the cupola ring to give my eyeballs free rein, like a crocodile hanging at waterline, I look every which way—rooftops, manholes, side alleys, windows, doorways, behind garden walls, trash drums, cars, everywhere. I owe the Marines on the deck my first target acquisition. I align the gun tube with their weapons, put an eye in my 10-power sight and pick up a fighter about 75 meters straight down the street. He fires in kneeling position from a low-walled terrace on top of a building's first story, using the wall for cover and moving between bursts.

"Gunner, Coax, troops. Fire and adjust," I bark out, telling the Gunner Cpl. Chambers to cut loose with his coaxially mounted 7.62 mm machine gun, which lines up with the main gun and uses the same fire-control system, the most advanced in the world. Chambers shoots with perfect precision from a 68-ton platform, rock-solid, with no movement from recoil. No walking on target, either, because of the dead-on aiming, so the first burst is a killing burst. Chambers also shoots from a 2,800-round bin. No worries about sparing ammo, like for the infantry, who probably wouldn't even shoot a machine gun at a single target. Chambers shoots until the wall's gone and we know, no question, that the target is dead.

New rules, with us in the fight:

You can't shoot from concealment, because if you can see me, I can see you, and a hell of a lot better with the tank's optics. Deep in shadows, six blocks away, you might as well be shaking my hand. With thermal sights, night's as good as day—better, actually.

Cover doesn't save you. Anywhere in this town I can reach out and touch you. If the Coax won't do it, my caliber-.50 will, and the main gun doesn't just make big holes in walls, it shoots shaped charges that punch through and fill the space behind with high explosive.

While Chambers shreds his first target, I acquire mine, a guy who pops out and takes a shot with an RPG that flies who knows where. He then ducks back into the doorway, and my .50 follows him inside and kills him like there's no wall between him and me. Gotta love this weapon.

We move forward about a block to acquire some new real estate and make it safer for the Marines to medevac their casualties. This gets Escamilla into play and provides a breech point into the city for a new platoon of Fox Company infantry, Pale Rider 2. While the ambushed patrol egresses, the new guys work their way up to my position on both sides of the street. This takes about an hour, and all the while the enemy attacks Bonecrusher by ones and twos and threes.

Nonstop shooting with no rhyme or reason to theirs. Even when they hit the tank, which is very rarely, their weapons have no effect. Rifle shots, which they take left and right, are completely idiotic. It's conceivable that an RPG could hit a track and cause me mobility problems, but the shooters don't even take aim at the tracks. And pulling the trigger seals a guy's doom, because the RPG backblast makes a cloud of trash and dust behind him so he stands out in silhouette. Might as well hold up a great big "Shoot Me!" sign.

At first, their growing respect for our weapons makes the exercise even more self-defeating, because they potshot without really looking, so we're even more safe. They, on the other hand, still give us targets. Basically, we're in a shooting gallery, and they're the ducks popping up. We don't hit them all, but we rack up at least a dozen good kills in about an hour, more than we've had in a month.

With the infantry abreast we move deeper into Fallujah, where streets get more narrow and densely packed with two- and three-story structures. At this point the infantry platoon surges ahead, darting from cover to cover. According to doctrine they belong out in front of the tank in city combat, but this takes me out of the fight. With both Marines and enemies out in front, doing pretty much the same thing—shooting and seeking cover—it's hard to tell who's who. I can see the infantry becomes confused, too. We need to get organized and methodical.

With this in mind I radio the platoon leader, "Pale Rider 2, this is Red Four. I can't tell the friendlies from the targets. I need for you to reel your guys in behind my POS so I can put the tank back in the fight."

Pale Rider 2, a lieutenant, could tell me to pack sand because he outranks me, but he sees the problem my way.

"Roger, Red Four, sounds good to me," he radios. "Gimme a couple minutes."

He must be a good lieutenant with good NCOs, because their guys go firm, account for everybody, and pull back in a cool and professional manner.

Once they're behind, I dismount, leaving Chambers in the cupola and in command and walk to the lieutenant's position in the front room of an abandoned dwelling. I take my time, which is sort of a risk but also a signal to whoever's watching.

Our street now.

The new sheriff is walking over to the new marshal's office.

And they ain't scared of you.

The lieutenant wants to come out and meet me, except a junior Marine cuts him off at the door. The lieutenant allows himself to be herded like he doesn't even notice. What's this about? Later the platoon sergeant, a big tall monster also in the room, will explain that he assigned the lance corporal to keep the boss alive. "He takes care of the lieutenant when he's too busy taking care of us," the platoon sergeant says.

I can't say much about the platoon commander's appearance. Not tall, not short, with hair a little grown out for a Marine—field hair, I call it. Can't tell you the lieutenant's actual name, either. He's "Pale Rider 2" on the net and "Sir" in person. Nevertheless, he's already well up there in my book because of the quality and fighting spirit of his platoon. And he's willing to listen to a Gunny he has never met before and adapt.

"This time when we advance, let's lead with my tank, Sir," I say, "Put it out ahead about half a block."

"That makes you vulnerable to AT," he says.

"Not here. They have no anti-tank weapons, just RPG, and that can't hurt me. And the wingman watches my six. Anybody behind is red mist."

That fast, the lieutenant gets on board and even out ahead, telling me, "Sounds good, Gunny. I can get my Marines on the rooftops to give you eyes forward and conduct counter-sniper operations."

"How soon before you're ready to move, Sir?" I ask.

He looks at his man mountain sergeant, who nods, and says, "Time now. Let's go kill some bad guys."

This is great! We put our heads together and in one minute write a new page in the How To Fight In Fallujah book—restructuring our task organization to meet the tactical situation, is how I'd put it if I were trying to sound important. Very simply, we go ahead and clear for them instead of them leading and clearing for us. The old way made sense because in a city, against enemy infantry with good training and AT assets, a tank is your coffin unless your own infantry takes care of the other guys. Here the enemy can't hurt anybody but infantry, while I can kill the hell out of them and protect our guys.

In the first block, we know we have an unbeatable combo, no missing pieces, everybody in straight killing mode, taking ground and putting them down. Two plus two equals five, maybe ten. We do much more than the sum-total of separate operations.

With 40 more eyeballs, left, right, and up at roof-level, I get multiple targets for every one of the tank's weapons. Besides the gunner's Coax and my .50, the loader, Lance Cpl. Hernandez, comes up and uses his swivel-mounted M240 machine gun. And with the infantry spotting, we have a lot more main gun targets. All the while, too, we're giving the infantry more targets. The tank out front forces the enemy to commit, either to attack or haul ass. Either way, he exposes himself. The riflemen up high kill a lot of guys trying to duck out side doors and alleys that I can't see. And the tank keeps pulling them in. We're the forward element of something they want more and more to stop. The farther we go, the more they get riled up and want into the fight.

As we push ahead, the bad guys sometimes ease up, but all it takes to pull them out is to retrograde. I back up, they jump out to take one more shot, like they're trying to get in the last word. I think we discover this by accident, just adjusting position. After that they fall for it over and over.

Fight you die. Run you die. Try to hide you die. Hey, works for me. There aren't all that many of them, and they're helping us make a big dent in a hurry. The only way out for the enemy is put their guns down and blend into the civilian population, but today they're not in the mood.

And the company commander, thank God, is in the mood to let us roll and see what happens. It doesn't hurt that we report success after success.

"Engaged and destroyed four enemy."

"Engaged and destroyed six enemy."

Every block, more dead insurgents go down in front of the tank's guns. My three-man crew and I do more damage than entire companies. And the infantry racks up its own tally. Why even think about stopping? My plan is to push through Fallujah and out the other side.

Then, though, the enemy finally gets in the way. Up ahead, where our street opens into a courtyard, they've rigged a sort of net with lines strung between telephone poles. Training and experience says to stop way short of it, because obstacles are meant not to catch you but to stop you in a kill sac covered by fire. Give these guys a D-minus, because they put their bunkers behind the wire obstacle on the open ground and in plain view to me, thus providing us with more easy pickings. Who the hell could have thought this was a good idea?

After about five minutes, they're down to one strong point, a three-story building on the far side of the courtyard with a sand-bagged wall protecting the entrance. A command post or logistics point, undoubtedly. We make a mess out of the front with main gun and suppress movement in and out, but it remains active and will, because I don't have the ammo to bring the building down.

With ammo getting to be an issue, I back up closer to Sgt. Escamilla's tank and the Pale Rider 2 guys to hump a dozen main gun rounds from the wingman's tank to mine and to cross-deck numerous belts of machine gun. The fact that Escamilla shoots less doesn't mean he does less. My life and all our lives and tactical success depend on him doing his job, covering my tank's and the infantry's rear. It's a credit to the guy that I don't think much about where he is and what he's doing, because I know he's right where he belongs.

Okay, enough sitting still. We don't totally lack for productive activity, because we have the CP to suppress with machine gun and the enemy makes more futile and suicidal attacks. But I hate giving them the initiative even when they don't know what the hell to do with it. Weird things happen, too, like little old ladies with canes tap-tap-tapping across the street between us and the CP. Penguin, is our designation, and we don't shoot penguins. Putting them out in front suppresses my fire, but the real point, I think, is to trick us into killing noncombatants and feeding the big fanatical anti-America bullshit machine. Same thing for the kids they send across the street.

No dice, because we have the optics to keep it clean, and armor protection lets us err on the side of caution—a luxury infantry does not have. They can die for mistaking a rocket for a shovel in someone's hands. For us, it's only a missed kill. In my book, a tank is the best possible forward weapons system for urban fighting in a counter-insurgency, where you can't win unless you can kill very selectively.

Though we've won big already, and the other guy hasn't even scratched us since the initial ambush on the security patrol, in my mind he starts to win when he stops us. I hate it, and I'm dying to get into the courtyard and clear that strong point. Looking for a bypass around the wire obstacle, I pull up closer and scan down a street running right. There, maybe fifteen meters in, sits a fuel trailer big enough to roast us if it blows at close quarters. Not so dumb, they've set up what we call a turning obstacle.

Frying pan into the fire. No thanks. I back up and start thinking about breaching the wire. Minus assets to blow this rat's nest down, I could crash through it, which involves a very good possibility of being wrapped up so I can't traverse the turret or even move because wire gets wound around the sprockets and track. On top of that, the courtyard undoubtedly has unseen enemy positions.

Does a great big fish voluntarily jump in the net, with fishermen waiting with spears? Well, maybe, if he's a Marine fish getting pissed off and impatient and he can open a breach for other fish also itching to fight.

By low-sun time, crashing through seems like a pretty good idea or at least better than parking here and letting the enemy work on his own plans. Even bozos like these might cook up trouble if we give them enough time. I call a radio huddle with the lieutenant and Escamilla, telling them to tighten up to me so they can assault through behind me after I breech. While we work out the details, the company commander comes on the net.

"Red Four, this is Pale Rider Six. I can get air on-station to breech your obstacle."

"Roger that. Sounds great," I answer, and don't even mind when he says we have to wait until after dark for our air, a C-130 Specter gunship that flies too low and slow for daylight operations.

Next problem: My map doesn't have the required detail for an accurate grid so the gunship can hit the right target. A street-width net, from a thousand feet up, is tiny and near-invisible. Relaying messages through Pale Rider's fire support coordinator, we come up with Plan B, to mark the target with an IR chem stick, a little thing that shows up bright and clear on the aircraft's infrared sighting systems. To put it on-target, I roll up and toss it.

Immediately I hear, "Specter has a tally on the target. Let me know when you're 125 meters back."

Thinking this is probably over-caution, I make the call at about 100 meters. Too close for comfort, it turns out. In two seconds, it's the Fourth of July, like somebody planted tons of ground-level pyrotechnics. You don't see the ordinance coming down, but the impact and detonation make intense light, like bright-white lava fountains. It is very intoxicating to be the one calling down this rain of fire.

After the gunship obliterates the obstacle, I call in shifts to the fuel truck, which blossoms in flame and keeps burning—they really could have cooked us—and then the CP strong point that was bugging me. End of story there, too. Down to rubble in minutes, with who knows how many dead.

Should we stop here? Negative. I call in the BDA, Battle Damage Assessment, and say the road's open and I'm ready to go.

"Roger," I hear, "Air will remain on station and support your attack."

The infantry goes firm so my tanks can speed up and go on the hunt with our partner in the sky.

Another brand-new beautiful friendship is born.

Nobody comes out to play for the first couple blocks. Either they died hunkered down in the CP or they're holed up in the fetal position. I cannot imagine the psychological effect of what just happened to them.

Relayed from the Specter gunship, we get this: "Up ahead of you, around the corner to your east, vehicle in the road with seven dismounts."

Air doesn't shoot because they can't tell if those are targets or civilians with a broken-down car. But we can break the corner at speed, gun tube already oriented, ready to shoot the instant Chambers gets a look through his thermal sight and confirms they're armed. Coming in blind on our own, we'd go slow because we don't know what's around the corner and give the enemy time to get away. Tonight, though, we put down seven gun-totin' bad guys before they can move.

We, in turn, designate targets for air. Say the bad guys flee into a certain building, we can put a machine gun on it so the Specter knows their exact location and can take it down from directly above, without touching anything else.

An odd partnership, sort of like a rhino running around with a pterodactyl, but my God does it work. Everything about it works. Just the roar of rotor-wash from above makes it easier for the tank to catch guys in the open because they can't hear us coming. The enemy has absolutely no clue how well we see them, either, from both the tank and the air. I keep finding them out in the street making easy targets. Looking back, I think they normally wait for night to come out and move around in safety, so this turkey shoot really throws them off-balance.

I wouldn't be surprised if our combined tally of kills actually exceeds that of my tanks and infantry during the day. With no infantry with us, we never own any ground, but when we give it back it's piled up with insurgents' bodies. We're here to attrit, and that's what we do.

By 0400 on April 7 we're black on ammo and getting low on fuel. Running out of darkness, too. Time to go back to where Pale Rider 2 went firm. We shut down in defensive positions, with a tighter interval between the tanks and closer in to the infantry.

Though you wouldn't be reading this without the event that opens the entire story, now just hours away—me getting hit—I would much rather be known for what I did on April 6 and the few hours after midnight. These are the crowning achievements of my life as a trigger-puller and leader of Marines. I like to think my initiative and leadership in this engagement, which was devastating to the enemy, outlasts my time in the combat zone. The new ways of shuffling the deck that we came up with—tanks leading infantry in urban terrain, tanks and gunships patrolling together at night—became common practice after this.

For my actions I was awarded the Silver Star, which I prize because it means that the Corps, too, recognizes that I made a significant difference in the First Battle of Fallujah in spring 2004.

But I never forget that none of it would have happened if I didn't go into Fallujah with like-minded men who exemplify all that makes Marines winners; that great infantry platoon and its leaders, the men in the airship, and the command that took a shot and turned us loose.

If I have to go out on a gunfight, and it looks like I do, this is the one.

60

Bang

Wednesday, April 7, 2004
Jolan District, Fallujah, Iraq

It's still full dark when I hear three quick cracks of rifle fire followed by a burst of Marine SAW, Squad Automatic Weapon. The fire comes from close and toward me, and then stops in silence so total I hear the brass from the machine gun ringing down on the deck loud and clear. I scan frontal, to the side. What the fuck? Who are we fighting? Where are they? I gotta see so I can shoot.

I hear snickering from three stories above. I shout, "What's going on up there?"

"Three of them trying to infiltrate you, Gunny," a Marine calls down and says, like it's a laugh line, "You'll see 'em when the sun comes up."

Indeed I do, three dead insurgents not much more than 10 feet from Bonecrusher's right rear fender. Obviously getting into position to try to pop me or maybe Escamilla.

Thanks, Marines.

And thanks to the Fox Company guys who bring in ammo on foot after first daylight, two guys hauling each heavy-ass crate of machine gun ammo, crate in one hand, rifle in the other. This blows me away, because even though I asked for resupply, I didn't think I had prayer of getting it. But here they come running, looking like leathernecks from some old Guadalcanal combat footage.

Semper Fi, Marines. Thanks for the home delivery.

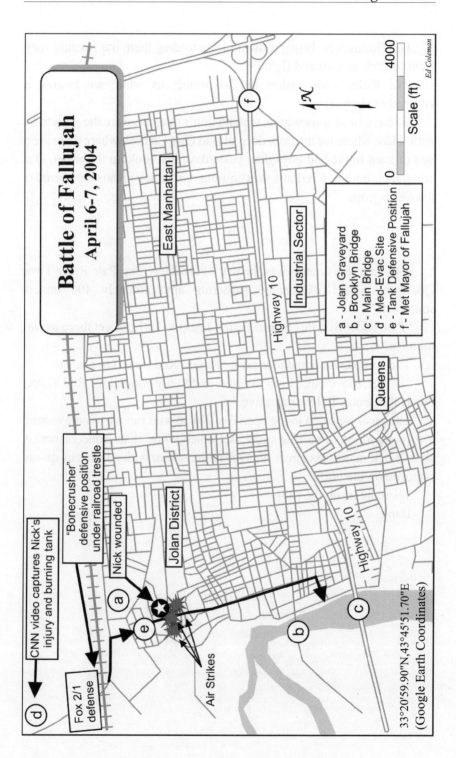

Battle of Fallujah
April 6-7, 2004

East Manhattan

Industrial Sector

Highway 10

Queens

Highway 10

Jolan District

Nick wounded

"Bonecrusher" defensive position under railroad trestle

Fox 2/1 defense

CNN video captures Nick's injury and burning tank

Air Strikes

a - Jolan Graveyard
b - Brooklyn Bridge
c - Main Bridge
d - Med-Evac Site
e - Tank Defensive Position
f - Met Mayor of Fallujah

33°20'59.90"N, 43°45'51.70"E
(Google Earth Coordinates)

0   4000
Scale (ft)

Ed Coleman

The Gunny who brought them in has to drag them out because they want to stick around and fight.

Pale Rider Two pushes out to protect us while we re-arm, a vulnerable position.

If I have to sit somewhere, which I don't like, these are the guys to sit with. I like where we are, too, deep in Bad Guy Central, where there are a hell of a lot fewer bad guys than yesterday. Just look up the street. Our brass, their bodies. Civilians start coming out, which means the enemy is losing his grip.

*   *   *

Mid-day, this comes over the net: "Pale Rider Six, Pale Rider Two. Observing squad-size enemy gathering approximately 400 meters southeast."

"Pale Rider Six, this is Red Four," I respond. "I can get there in two minutes."

The company commander says, "Roger, Red Four. Go get 'em."

"Driver, move out," I say to Frias, and to my wingman, "Red Three, this is Red Four, follow my move."

The guys we catch in the open die. Those who run we pursue around a corner and into a narrow street, not much wider than Bonecrusher. A short block in, a cross street runs off to the south, with a little cul-de-sac opposite on the north.

There he is, on the roof.

Bang.

— Epilogue —

The Tip of the Spear

I was already living in the civilian world when the Marine Corps awarded me the Silver Star for what I did at Fallujah on April 6, 2004—the day before I got shot.

I'm still proud beyond words, but I keep perspective. Medals go to guys who happen to do something great when officers are paying attention. In Iraq I saw dozens and dozens of Marines, including my own tank crew, perform medal-worthy deeds that went unseen and unrecognized except by the guys who fought beside them. For us, though, that is enough.

Proud as I am of the medal, I'm prouder when Marines come up, all excited, and say, "I was in Fallujah that day, too, Gunny. I was there with you!" They know what I know, that a medal like mine shines glory on many people. We were all there, at the tip of the spear, doing great things.

I want to go back to the tip of the spear. And I fully intend to. Not as a Marine, of course, but in this new life that is still strange to me. I want to put my highest ideals and beliefs into action, do everything in my power to do some good, to make a difference, particularly for young Americans as I once did as a leader of Marines.

When I decided to go back to college and study to be a teacher, I knew this career would suit me. It wasn't a calling, though. Frankly, after all the years of serving my country and the world in such exciting and challenging ways, I felt lukewarm about it.

This changed only recently, after Marine General Michael Lehnert asked me what my plans had been before I had to take my medical retirement. I said I never even thought about anything but staying in the Corps and, I hoped, becoming a Sergeant Major.

And then General Lehnert said something to me I will never forget: "You know, Gunny, you'll impact more lives as an educator than you ever would have as a Sergeant Major."

Then and there I had yet another man wearing our proud uniform to say thanks to, for my new calling and new mission worthy of a Marine.

Semper Fidelis.

INDEX